THE TAMING OF
THE NATIONS

*A Study of the Cultural Bases
of International Policy*

Ox Bow Press books by F. S. C. Northrop

The Prolegomena to a 1985 Philosophiae Naturalis
Principia Mathematica
The Logic of the Sciences and the Humanities
The Meeting of East and West
Science and First Principles
The Taming of the Nations

FOREWORD

The reprinting of *The Taming of the Nations* provides a timely opportunity for reexamining the practical foreign policy implications of a major reconstruction of philosophy and the relationship between natural and cultural science. This reconstruction represents the lifetime labors of Filmer Stuart Cuckow Northrop, Sterling Professor Emeritus of Philosophy and Law at Yale University.

Professor Northrop's prolific and profound philosophical investigations touch the premises of the major fields of knowledge. The most recent statement of those premises can be found in *The Prolegomena to a 1985 Philosophiae Naturalis Principia Mathematica* published in 1985 by Ox Bow Press. The simple style and the choice of political topics which is characteristic of *The Taming of the Nations* should not be mistaken for armchair philosophy. Professor Northrop's disciplined work in philosophy of science and law is intimately and logically related to his seemingly practical comments in *The Taming of the Nations*.

Taming, originally published in 1952, pointed out that the end of World War II, with the rise of atomic power and the shift of events from the traditional political stage of Europe to Asia and other parts of the globe, had given rise to an entirely different global perspective. Decades later, we are still far from harnessing major weapons to rule of law and comprehending that Western Europe is no longer the major stage for international politics. Theories of power politics, where the units of analysis are nation states and their military and economic variables, still dominate both political science and practical foreign policy-making. When values are analyzed, most frequently the opinions of the reigning elites are taken to be the substance of reality.

In contrast to most theories of international politics, *Taming* provided, in 1952 and again now, the challenge of creating a science of international politics more in the manner of fundamental chemistry than of a game of chess. As in chemistry, analysis of mass is not enough. One needs an understanding of the substance of the major entities by specifying the constituent relations. The contemporary resurgance of many forms of nationalism shows that the analysis of national entities is not an easy matter. It is this task that is the challenge undertaken by Professor Northrop.

In addition to the clarification of key principles *The Taming of the Nations* is full of substantial and intriguing insights on specific political cultures and their internal and external relations. The careful reader will note that the first printing of the book was in 1952. Many "empirical" events have occurred since the appearance of the book, yet the possibility of a chemistry of politics continues to be suggested by the enduring relevance of most of the generalizations made decades ago.

With respect to Indo-China, Northrop pointed out that while it is difficult to organize the collective use of force in a Buddhist ethical system, it is occasionally necessary in order to deal with violations of law. However, the force of power politics is not enough to preserve the community if the political elite cannot identify with the "living law" of the society. Additionally, if the primary obligations of the elite are to familial piety and the demands of extended families, the work of nation and community building is even more difficult. To follow the parallel of the French actions on a purely power political basis will, he warned, hand the masses in Indo-China and elsewhere "to the communists upon a silver platter made of the shiny dollars of the United States taxpayer's money."

The rise and fall of Diem, the Catholic elite in a Buddhist land, the succession of generals, the pouring of American resources and blood, the limits of power politics and the ability of Ho Chi Minh to appeal to the living law are instructive confirmation of Northrop's insights. Similar lessons may well be waiting for us elsewhere if we depend on heavy hardware but do not understand the nature of the political entities that are involved.

Marxists, of course, do not want perpetuation of the living law. They too are interested in the transformation of societies. However, they are more analytical and careful than is the U.S. about the nature of the "opium" of religion and belief which from a Marxist standpoint contemporaneously enslaves the masses. Mao's ability to relate to key symbols held by the Chinese masses as contrasted with Chiang Kai Shek's blend of piety and force are additional examples of the importance of the living law.

Some of the comments on Communist China may now seem strained, particularly in the appearance of insufficient distinctions between the Russian and Chinese Marxism. Much has happened in Sino-Soviet relations since the book was written. But the main point remains: Chinese Marxism is a careful Western grafting on an old society. While force is used in the bonding, there is also careful manipulation of mass symbols.

A prophetic title of one chapter is "The Resurgence of Islam." Decades later, and in some cases too late, have Western policy makers begun to be sensitive to the nature of Islamic entities: the vital religious passions that define seemingly minute and mundane actions, the fusion of church and state, the close ties between the military and religious functions, and the firm commitment to a Koranic "absolute truth." While Iran is not at the heart of the discussion, readers may well add to their own insight on the Iranian revolution. As in the case of China, the comments on Islam should not seem as deterministic prophecies but as analysis of the main elements of the entities of politics. After all, even Islamic leaders can be insensitive to the living law, as was the case in the foundation of Bangladesh.

Northrop's comments on India continue to have major significance for the understanding of Indian political culture. In principle, the cultural and linguistic roots give India an initial advantage for development over China. However, there are several barriers not the least of which is the need for the educated political elite to be able to relate to the masses, as Gandhi repeatedly pointed out. Northrop, however, points out that the deep rooted Gandhian aversion to force is not sufficient for dealing with all aspects of domestic relations or for foreign relations. About nine years after Northrop's comments on the roots of Indian neutralism and Nehru's foreign policy came the end of Indian innocence with the Chinese excursion into India after years of suave diplomacy by Chou En Lai.

Still relevant is Northrop's critique of the tendencies toward a

monistic state in India. The appearance of federalism notwithstanding, the Nehrus of India have been overly committed to a
Western monism or national unity with the attendant deep distrust
of a loose knit pluralism. Given the diversity of South Asia, monism
will *not* work. The forces that led to the creation of Pakistan and
the more current problems in Hindu-Sikh relations point to the
importance of a middle road between an unlikely and unachievable
monism and an uncooperative disintegration.

In addition to Northrop's comments on China, Indo-China and
South Asia, there are some important comments on Japan as well.
Northrop's analysis of the Shinto factor in Japanese culture, the
Japanese management structure, and the linguistic advantage of
Japanese over Chinese in dealing with scientific abstractions pro-
vides a set of principles with which to understand the rise of con-
temporary industrial Japan.

In much of the discussion of the living law of other societies,
Northrop appears to be critical of a right-of-center heavy hardware
approach to foreign policy. However, the book is hardly a soft,
liberal manifesto. In the discussion on the foundations of Communism, the contempt that communists have for liberals is touched
upon. The Marxist analysis after all sees any state as the embodiment of force. Consequently any approach to world order involving
communists must include the willingness to use relevant force on
behalf of international law, provided the appropriate level of support exists in the international community. Force alone is not
enough. The book vividly reminds us that post-Hiroshima mankind
has the imminent capacity to destroy itself.

International law is not positive law based on pronouncements of
states. The pluralism of the living law is the most reliable basis for
creating world law according to Northrop. It involves not only treaties and contracts but a Bill of Rights where the major right holders
are the persistent and vital cultural living law entities of the world.

An international Bill of "National" Rights, with resulting contracts supported by the legitimate use of controlled power and a
healthy dose of intuition and compassion, is Northrop's major
guidepost toward world order. While his journey into practical pol-

itics is occasionally sketchy and even perplexing, careful reading
will illuminate the depth of the principles involved and the prophetic quality of the insights. After several decades of theories of
power politics, the reprinting of *The Taming of the Nations* points
toward an alternative foundation for a theoretical and practical
chemistry of international politics and a cosmopolitan and richly
intercultural world order.

Joyotpaul Chaudhuri

Arizona State University
Tempe, Arizona
December, 1986

PREFACE

The aim of this book is indicated in its title and subtitle. The method to be pursued is outlined in Chapter I. Results achieved appear not merely in the concluding chapters of the book, but also along the way. In fact in so far as the book throws light on specific problems of foreign policy in the contemporary world, as well as upon general principles, the prescriptions will be found in the middle sections of the book where the specific nations and problems are considered.

Throughout, the aim has been to keep close to concrete fact by means of a consideration of recent events in the international field while at the same time pursuing the analysis of the cultural background, basic beliefs and principles necessary to understand these events and to make correct decisions of policy with respect to them. The world situation, or any specific nation or culture, is even more complicated than this inquiry indicates. Of necessity one cannot consider everything. Selection of the most relevant factors has been inevitable. The character of contemporary events and issues has in every instance determined the cultural factors which have been selected for analysis.

In the case of India, the complexity of its recent behavior has necessitated a more systematic and complex analysis of its culture than the traditional literature has provided. If Indian and other scholars of India's pre-Western culture are not to misunderstand the final conclusions at which we arrive, it is essential to keep two things in mind. First, the conflict between

Gandhi's way to settle the disputes of men or nations and that of the equally popular Subhas Bose, the contemporary Maharajas and the Aryan Hindu law books, is a fact which demands a cultural explanation, since both forms of behavior appeal to the ancient Hindu classics for their moral justification. Second, this explanation is found within these classics in the distinction between that portion of them and of Hindu culture which seems to have been there before the coming of the Aryans and that portion which was brought in from the West by the ancient Aryan conquerors in the second millennium B.C. Reasons are given for finding the explanation of the aforementioned conflict in the difference between the purely Asian or non-Aryan component of Hinduism and the component with quite different ways and values imposed by the Aryan conquerors. Traditional Hindu India in its full content is, as has been generally recognized, as much Aryan as it is indigenously pre-Aryan and purely Asian. What this amounts to is the realization that one of the first meetings of East and West occurred in the second millennium B.C. in Aryan Hindu India. Gandhi's program of nonviolence arises when the ancient Aryan contribution to this synthesis is rejected, and only the purely Asian component common to Hinduism, Buddhism, Tavism and Confucianism is retained.

This analysis is important for another reason. It suggests that, quite apart from Muslim and British influences, the Indians are better prepared, through their ancient Hindu Aryan culture, to combine modern Western ways with Asian ways than are any other Asian people with the possible exception of the Japanese.

The writer is indebted to the Editors of *Life* for permission to reprint under a different title in a very much expanded form an article entitled, "The Mind of Asia," which appeared in that publication in its issue of December 31, 1951. This article appears in the present book as part of the chapter entitled, "The Contemporary Mind of Islam and of Asia." The reason for this change of title is that in this book the term Asia is restricted

to the Confucian, Taoist, Buddhist and Hindu cultures of the
Far East. Islam, even when present in the Far East, is treated as
one of the three Semitic religious and Greek scientific cultures.
The reason for the latter assignment is obvious since Islam regards itself as a fulfillment of the Hebrew-Christian tradition
and has a culture which has absorbed Greek scientific and
philosophical thought. Clearly Confucianism, Taoism, Buddhism and even Aryan Hinduism derive from quite different
cultural roots. This basic difference in derivation puts Islam,
therefore, more with the cultures of the Middle East and West
than with those of the Far East.

Even so, Hindu India, as we have noted above, has a Western
component in it due to the ancient Aryan factor. This component entered Hindu Indian culture, however, antecedent to
the Muslim conquest of India and even to the coming to India
of Alexander the Great. Nonetheless there is an essential bond
with the West due to the fact that Sanskrit, like the languages of
Greece, Rome and modern Western Europe, derives from a
common Western Aryan linguistic root. There are reasons,
however, for believing, as the sequel will show, that the ultimate
value in Hinduism became the indigenous Asian one, and that
the ancient Aryan contribution was made secondary thereto.
This in fact is the source of Gandhi's hold upon the masses.
These complexities must be kept continuously in mind if what
is said about India is not to be misunderstood.

This book would have been quite impossible without grants
from the Viking Fund, now the Wenner-Gren Foundation for
Anthropological Research. Over the past five years these grants
provided not merely for the release of time to investigate this
complex field, but also for a field trip to South Asia in 1950 and
1951. The writer expresses herewith his sincere gratitude not
merely for the grant, but especially for the personal encouragement of the Foundation's Director, Paul Fejos, its President,
Richard C. Hunt, and its founder, Axel Wenner-Gren. To
them this book is dedicated. Always throughout the research,
field trip and writing there have been the aid and companion-

ship of my wife. Without this also, what appears here would not be.

The author is very much indebted to Helen H. Livingston. The entire preparation of the manuscript and the index is hers. Her unstinted attention, care and concern have made possible the completion of this book while its author's memory of so many of the persons, places and events of which it treats is still warm. To his friends, Samuel Robbins, David Driscoll and Lilian Closson Manley, the writer is most grateful for aid in reading the proof and for many valuable suggestions.

All the footnote references are by chapters at the end of the volume. The author expresses his indebtedness to each of the publishers for quotations from their publications made in the text, as indicated by the reference number accompanying each quotation. He is especially grateful to the Cornell University Press, The Macmillan Company, W. W. Norton and Co., the Public Affairs Press and the Yale University Press for permission to quote from their publications; also to Professor A. J. Arberry for permission to quote from his translation of Iqbal's *The Tulip of Sinai*. It has been a pleasure to be associated again with Susan Prink and Charles E. Cuningham of The Macmillan Company. They make the labor of publication a pleasant experience.

F. S. C. Northrop

The Yale Law School
New Haven, Connecticut
July 24, 1952

CONTENTS

THE TAMING OF
THE NATIONS

*A Study of the Cultural Bases
of International Policy*

1

THE NATURE OF THE PROBLEM

If open diplomacy openly arrived at is to succeed, the people, without whom the statesmen cannot be effective, must be informed. It is with the provision of this information that this book is concerned.

The problem is much more complex than even most statesmen have assumed. All too often issues of domestic politics have been regarded as decisive and sufficient for the determination of foreign policy. Others have regarded national self-interest as the ruling factor. Still others put its basis in the idealism of one's own country or in an undefined ideal of all.

In an imperialistic age, an international policy based on national self-interest has some chance of succeeding, since the imperialist is able to determine in major part what happens. But the contemporary world is not congenial to imperialism. Everywhere it is on the wane. The masses of men are against it. Every sign indicates that its day is done. This means also that the days of foreign policy based on national self-interest are over.

Even if this were not the case, national self-interest will not work in foreign affairs. There are at least two major powers in the world today. Moreover, one of these powers, as the sequel will show, is dominated by an ideology that commits it and its allies to revolutionary world conquest by resort to force. Already this power has put this program into effect throughout

1

the whole of eastern Europe and in Asian Korea. No nation in the world today, not even the United States, is able alone to defend itself and its different ideological and cultural values against this major power. Thus even national self-interest is forced to generate its opposite. Nations must learn how to cooperate or else they perish. Also, there is the atomic bomb. It is not likely that any nation can survive an atomic world war. Again the choice is between collaboration and suicide.

Collaboration requires that nations and their statesmen must learn new ways. We have both to act and to go to school in order to learn how to act. The statesman must also be a scholar. But if statesmen are to be scholars, international relations must become more than a speculative program or an art. It must also be a science, for when death is the fruit of error, one can ill afford to err.

But can there be a science of international relations? In this field are we not in the presence of imponderables? Yes. Imponderables are involved. In fact imponderables are crucial. But this need cause no dismay. For, as the sequel will show, imponderables can be specified. Moreover, when specified they become prodigious sources of strength.

The specification of imponderables calls, however, for new methods of inquiry. The old techniques of the traditional students of international relations and the accepted institutes of foreign affairs will not do. For their ways of approach to the subject matter of the meeting of the nations cannot specify the imponderables; they cannot locate the decisive, causal factors which can determine the pathways from war the nations not only may take but actually are taking.

The problem of a science of international affairs is not unlike that of the science of chemistry. No one would suppose that he had created a science of the chemical elements if he approached the subject from the standpoint of the properties of merely one of the chemical elements. An objective, sympathetic description and understanding of all the different kinds of chemical materials in the universe is obviously necessary for a

chemical science. The same is true for any science of international relations which can pretend to be adequate. Before any
theory of the way to relate the nations can be even attempted,
the character of at least the major individual nations must be
determined.

Like the chemical elements these national elements are not
identical. Their properties and respective reactions vary from
nation to nation. To suppose, therefore, that a trustworthy
theory for relating nations can be grounded upon a mere balancing of them as power factors is like treating the ninety-odd chemical elements with their radically diverse reactions in different
combinations as if they were identical physical entities determined as to their behavior by one physical property only, namely
their respective masses. Once this obvious characteristic of nations as of chemical elements is noted much of the mysticism of
the imponderables evaporates. Just as the unexpectedness of the
reactions of chemical materials becomes expressible in scientific terms when the individual properties of the ninety-odd
chemical elements are specified, so the imponderables in the
actions of the eighty-odd nations become amenable to scientific
treatment when the differing specific properties of these nations
receive the attention which is their due.

The method for determining the properties of the elements
of chemistry is well known. What is the corresponding method
for specifying the properties of the elements of international
relations? Fortunately recent investigations in the sciences of
cultural sociology, cultural anthropology and the philosophy
of culture give us the answer to this question.

A nation is a society responding as a unit. What is it that
gives a society this national unity? The answer is common
norms. Except as the people of a society agree upon at least some
common norms that society cannot respond as a national unit.
The key, therefore, to the understanding of any nation and to
the specification of those of its properties which will determine
its international reactions is to be found when the major
common norms of its people are determined. For unless the

people of a nation have a dominant ideology there is no consistent dominant response.

In fact without this dominant common ideology there is no domestic, to say nothing about an international, policy. The present weakness of international law causes us to overlook the fact that there has not always or everywhere been domestic law. Force and war have ruled within nations as well as between them. This reminds us that the science of international affairs is of a piece with the science of domestic relations. In ancient Greece and Rome, as in much of Asia today, law was restricted to the patriarchal joint family; between families, apart from the mediation of the village elders, there was often no law.

These historical reflections are important for another reason. They indicate that the way to peace in international affairs is not to apply between nations the power politics balancing which failed between patriarchal families and between city-states but to extend from nations to the world the rule of law after the manner in which the rule of law was successfully extended from the patriarchal joint families and the warring city-states to the nation. Precisely how this is to be done will concern us in the sequel.

The method to be used, however, can be made clear now. It is the method for gaining effective law anywhere. This method has been specified within this century by the distinguished Austro-Hungarian sociologist of law, Eugen Ehrlich.[1] He investigated what it was that distinguished law in his own society which was effective from law which was ineffective. He noted first that one never has law in any community without norms. He noted secondly that these norms are never given by any particular facts in any society such as the economic ones, the political ones, the ethnology or the climate. The norms are determined instead not by any particular facts given inductively by observation but by what he termed "the inner order" of all the facts. This means that there is never a legal, political or economic society except when all the facts of that society are ordered by certain common normative or, in other words, ideological principles. Law and its political institutions, and one may add also economics and its business institutions, are effective only as they correspond to and express this ideological or normative inner order. Hence, there can be no science of any nation or of the relation of all the nations without a specification first of the normative inner order of each particular nation and then of the relations between the many national inner orders.

The sociologist Sorokin in the case of many cultures and the anthropologist Kluckhohn for the society of the Navaho Indians have shown how the scientific determination of the normative inner order of any specific society is to be achieved.[2] It consists in specifying the meanings or philosophy held in common by the leaders and majority of the people of a given society. In fact, the philosophy of any society is but the name for the basic concepts and assumptions agreed upon by its people for organizing the data of their experience and ordering their relation to nature and to one another.

Once the normative inner order of each nation is specified, then the relations between the different nations can be given with similar objectivity. Thus, there is no more need for speculation about the *de facto* relationship between the eighty-odd nations of the world than there is for speculation concerning the normative inner order of the society of a given nation. Both can be determined providing one will examine ideological normative factors with scientific objectivity. In fact, the science of international relations may be defined as that subject which specifies the normative inner order of each nation and the relation between these national normative inner orders.

Ehrlich called this normative inner order of any society or nation its living law. The order specified by the constitution and rules on the statute books of a given society he called its positive law. What he found was that positive law is only effective when it corresponds to the underlying living law of the society to which it refers. Law is effective in any society when the norms which it introduces correspond to the underlying normative inner order habits of the living law of the people to whom it is applied. Law is ineffective, and to law may be added foreign policy and foreign economic aid, when the norms for ordering the relations between people which it prescribes contradict or depart too far from the norms and ideals built into the beliefs and bodies of the people as given in the inner order of their total behavior which is, to use Ehrlich's language, their living law.

To achieve, therefore, a trustworthy guide for international policy in the contemporary world we shall have to do three things. First, the normative inner order of beliefs and habits which is the living law of each national or cultural group in the world must be specified. Second, the relation between the normative ideology of each nation or cultural group and that of all other nations and cultural groups must be determined. In certain cases this relationship will be found to be one of compatibility. In other cases it will be found to be that of logical incompatibility and contradiction. This means that no single theory of the way to relate nations can be specified as a universal policy or panacea applicable to all nations. Nor should this surprise us. For if nations differ from one another with respect to their properties, just as do chemical elements, certain combinations of nations will produce a peaceful response whereas certain other combinations of nations, if pressed, will issue in an explosion. We shall find, for example, that Gandhiji's rejection of any use of force in relating men and nations is a correct program for any group of individuals or nations who hold the norms for the inner order of their society from which Gandhiji's pacifism issues. To apply this method, however, to nations whose normative inner order is the antithesis of this is to produce war rather than peace. Just as to put one chemical together with a second chemical may produce a healthful food and to combine the first chemical together with a third chemical will create dynamite or an atomic bomb, so to put Gandhi's inner order for society with that of Confucius will issue in peace whereas to combine it with that of Premier Stalin will result in something quite different. Programs of peace abstracted from the individual ideological living law properties of the nations are not merely vacuous; they are positively dangerous.

Having specified the normative living law of each individual nation or cultural group and having specified also the respective relations between these diverse national normative inner orders, the third task will be that of framing foreign policy and international law in the light of these international living law findings. Providing this is done, Ehrlich's criterion assures us that the results will be effective.

Throughout this inquiry it is essential that normative principles be kept continuously in contact with concrete facts. To this end it is important that we begin with the world of our recent and immediate experience.

2

PEARL HARBOR, HIROSHIMA AND KOREA

The place is Oahu. It is a Sunday morning, as peaceful and beautiful as only that Pearl of the Pacific can be. Everyone is sleeping, secure. Diamond Head, fair and innocent like a virgin mountain on Mars, stands on guard bristling with guns within, the Gibraltar of the Pacific, protecting the bay behind and the mainland beyond; and in between is the Fleet of the greatest power in the world.

To be sure, to the West, Asian imperialists have defied the League of Nations and the Kellogg Pact to hold Korea, Manchuria and North China, and to the East in Europe a tyrant offering peace to the world with his one more last demand already has a France which loved peace more than principle in his clutches, a rebellious Norway, Holland, Poland and Czechoslovakia underfoot, and Great Britain at the very edge of mortal death. But this does not apply to Americans in their God-given isolation on the mainland or to those similarly here who are luxuriating in bed until the surf will waft them peacefully into a second nap on the sands of Waikiki.

After all, why should these affairs in Europe and Asia be looked at from the standpoint of international public order or moral principle? Have not our historians of World War I and our professors of international relations assured us that foreign policy is nothing but power politics and national self-interest and that to act from the standpoint of a communal legal order or to moralize is to behave like naive children in fairyland, doing more harm than good? Let these foreigners give up their medieval imperialism and become dynamic, neutral, peace-loving people like us minding our own business. In any event, we are secure. Isolationism backed by overpowering defensive military might with its great saving in taxes is paying off.

Suddenly there is a sputtering in the sky. Some exceptional airman must have omitted the usual round of weekend parties last evening to be practicing so early on Sunday morning. Then the truth comes home. It is we—the neutral isolationists and power politicians—who are living in fairyland.

And what a fairyland it is. Instead of our heaven being graced with countless angels singing, "Hallelujah, God bless our strong peace-loving land," it is penetrated with but a few wasps shouting "Banzai."

The pay-off also is a bit more precipitous and far-reaching than the "expert" historians with their carefully chosen World War I documents and the geopolitical professors of international relations with their "realism" and sabotage of the League of Nations had suggested. Those noisy little wasps are spitting dynamite and hitting their marks of polished steel and Pearl.

Fair Diamond Head, the Gibraltar of the Pacific, still stands unmolested and unmolesting, as peaceful and innocent as ever. But the heart of the Pacific fleet of the "greatest" navy in the world lies in mud at the bottom of an inland fishing pond. The Pearl has gone out of pearl harbor. Truly, power politics and isolationism are paying off.

To call this the pay-off, however, is not quite accurate. It is merely the first down payment—a mere token of much more to come. Monday has now arrived after yesterday's Sunday. Even with Pearl Harbor's warning, another General at Manila watches the Far Eastern Fleet of giant bombers of the hardest hitting air force in the world go up in flames as he vacillates between one decision and another about what to do with them. The second down payment on an isolationist foreign policy based on a trust in the military is now here. The cost, moreover, is so great and embarrassing that the press is hardly permitted to mention it. And for some peculiar reason yet to be investigated and explained, this General at Manila with his ample warning was never cashiered as were his far less guilty colleagues caught without warning at Honolulu.

Nor is the saving in taxes quite as great as the experts had suggested. These powerful battleships and bombers which were to take the place of a hearty support of a legal world order under the League of Nations are not worth very much as rusty plates and twisted rods and sheeting in the junk yards of the world to which they must now go. Instead of contributing to an effective League of Nations, the second world war of this century and its aftermath must now be financed. And the end is not yet. Truly a foreign policy based on dynamic isolationism, power politics, national self-interest and the military alone is paying off with a vengeance.

One is reminded of the farmer who, after praying for rain, found himself in the midst of cloudbursts and floods: "Dear God, I did pray for rain, but this answer to my prayers is becoming ridiculous."

Even so the greater taxes and public debt were forthcoming. The Pacific Fleet and the Far Eastern Air Force more than recovered. In truly fairy-like fashion the story has a happy ending. Even the General at Manila survived, not merely to lead the military forces of his people to victory in the Pacific but also to become the Commander in Chief of the police force of a new legally constituted world community called the United Nations in which his country assumed even more than its share of the cost and the responsibility.

One thing, however, did not recover from the sinking at Pearl Harbor. On December 7, 1941, defensive power politics, self-interest and isolationism went down to stay down for all who have the capacity to remember. Eight years later the former Republican isolationist, Senator Arthur H. Vandenberg, sent a letter to Charles M. Rowan of New York in which he wrote:

In my own mind, my convictions regarding international coopera-tion and collective security for peace took firm form on the after-noon of the Pearl Harbor attack. That day ended isolationism for any realist.[1]

Hiroshima is the final response of the United States and her allies of World War II, Great Britain, China and the Soviet Union, to Pearl Harbor. Besides being, like Pearl Harbor, an event in the past, it is also an eternal object in each successive moment of the present. It hangs over men everywhere as an ever present threat—the threat of world war in an atomic age.

Hiroshima tells us that unless we can find effective, lawful means of meeting the economic needs of men, settling the dis-putes of nations and bringing to expression the spiritual re-sources and aspirations of mankind, there may very quickly be nothing to hold or cherish since there will be no one to do the cherishing. A little mathematical calculation applied to scien-tific data available for anyone to read makes it likely that the number of atomic bombs sufficient, because of the accumulated radiation, to destroy all human beings on this planet, if dropped within a brief space of time, is well within the range of present possibilities. If Pearl Harbor tells us that to turn back to power politics balancing and isolationism is folly, Hiroshima teaches that to move forward to an effective legal world order is the child of necessity.

There is also Korea. Between Hiroshima and Korea the United Nations was created at San Francisco. This place of its birth expresses the responsible role which the United States has played in this second attempt to solve the problems of nations by legally constituted means. Korea represents the first major challenge to this new legal world order. The results to be sure have not been all that one might wish. Minority domestic critics in the United States and majority critics in Asia exist aplenty. In this criticism the real source of weakness exhibited in the

United Nations' action in Korea on the one hand and the exceedingly important achievements on the other hand have been overlooked.

The real weakness and the provisions required for its removal will concern us later. For the moment, let us look at the very important achievements.

First, the legally constituted world community demonstrated in a way which any prospective aggressor will not forget that the legally self-organized world community does not propose, after the manner of the League of Nations before the aggression of Japan in Manchuria and Mussolini in Abyssinia, to be an institution of mere peace-affirming oratory and dead-letter words. Second, Korea made it equally evident that this peace-loving legally constituted world community does not propose to create a second Munich and its inevitable world war in Asia. The old habit of passively in the name of "peace" acquiescing in a present blatant aggression only to be blackmailed immediately by one more last demand is not to be repeated, nor has it been repeated, in Asia. The Briands of Asia who talk peace while they act war by acquiescing in aggression and praising only the aggressor have not undermined and destroyed the United Nations after the manner in which silver-tongued orators of "peace" made a farce of the League of Nations. For all the criticism from minority isolationists in the United States and from pacifistic isolationists in Asia, Korea is something of which the United Nations and the United States can be proud. The first test to decide whether the United Nations' professions of peace were to be purely verbal and forthwith a dead letter was met in Korea and passed with more than a good grade. Whatever Korea has not been, at least it is not the Abyssinia of World War III.

Nor has the lesson been lost on Communist China's Mao or Soviet Russia's Stalin. In December, 1950, this writer was in Thailand and in the Cambodian province of Indo-China. In Bangkok he met a Thai who had returned the previous day from an interview with President Chiang Kai-shek on Formosa. This old and very realistic Thai reported the Generalissimo as saying that the United Nations' action in Korea had disrupted the entire Communist timetable for Asia. It was the Generalissimo's considered opinion, based on firsthand reports from mainland China, that if this initial aggression had not been nipped in the bud and prevented from succeeding, the whole of Indo-China and also of Burma as well as Tibet would have been in Chinese Communist hands in December of 1950.

If this had occurred, Thai and foreign observers agree, the position of Thailand without United Nations support would be untenable since this country, loyal to the United Nations, would be flanked by aggressive Communist, militarily dominated countries on both sides. The independence of the Malay States would be equally untenable as would that of Indonesia with its active militant Communist minority.

To suppose that India, with all Asia to her North, East and Southeast in Communist hands, could then preserve her independence is to go back again into fairyland. To suppose moreover that before events had been allowed to go as far as this, World War III in Asia, rather than merely a defensive police action in Korea, would not now be history is to pick the side of the improbable.

Chiang Kai-shek supported this judgment of the importance of the United Nations' police action with the following considerations: Before the aggression in Korea there were large Communist armies on the borders of Indo-China and in South China. Apparently the aim of Communist China was not little South Korea but Indo-China and South Asia. The move in Korea was merely a preliminary protection of one's northeast flank before jumping off in Indo-China, after the manner in which Hitler grabbed Norway before launching the attack which was his main purpose. The quick action in Korea by the United Nations supported by the United States took the Communists by surprise. In any event, they moved their armies in South China north. Thereby Indo-China and probably South Asia were saved from Communist conquest in the fall of 1950.

Some may say that this is the report of a Nationalist Chinese leader who is prejudiced and that hence it is not to be taken seriously. This is a peculiar assertion to be made, however, by the minority of isolationists in the United States for whom Chiang Kai-shek is an Asian god and the key to a "wise" power politics handling of Asian problems. It is an erroneous answer also for Asian neutral isolationists. None of these Asian professors of peace believe their professions so far as the behavior of Communists in their own Asian countries is concerned. Prime Minister Nehru's government has thrown habeas corpus and the Bill of Rights into the wastebasket so far as domestic India is concerned to a degree which would shock even Senator McCarthy in the United States. At home these Asian orators of neutral isolationism and the peaceful purposes of Communist nations in foreign affairs have to deal with facts, they cannot indulge in mere words and still persist as the heads of a constitutionally established law-abiding domestic community. Moreover, at home they believe that law requires policemen to bring physical force to bear if necessary to nip in the bud the first violations of law. In no city of India did this visitor ever find law being enforced merely by orators, posing as statesmen, preaching its peaceful ways; there also were always policemen. Furthermore the Congress Ministers of State of both West Bengal and Bombay, Dr. B. C. Roy and Shri Morarji R. Desai, were explicit in saying that the key to peace and the prevention of Hindu-Muslim riots in both Calcutta and Bombay depended upon a leadership in defense of the law which gave every member of the community the knowledge that if any fighting started, the clubs of the policemen would come down instantly upon the heads of the disturbers of the peace regardless of whose heads they were.

This is what happened in Korea. The law of the world community was shown to be something more than oratorical speeches about "peace" throwing a smoke screen over a dead letter. San Francisco is not a second Geneva. First, the aggressor in question was prevented from succeeding. This eliminated the possibility of further blackmail. Second, the aggressor and all other nations contemplating aggression were given pause. They were made to realize that for the first time in history they were living in a new world—a world that proposed to be run neither by power politics self-interest nor by verbal pacificism, but by law with the police power behind the law necessary to make it effective.

Nor were the lessons missed by the national leaders in Peking and in the Kremlin. Notwithstanding the aforementioned movement of Communist Chinese armies from the border of Indo-China to North Korea, it was the opinion of French military leaders in Indo-China at the time, and of American newspaper observers who had been watching the situation at first hand over a period of months, that sufficient Chinese forces still remained to capture Indo-China had the leaders in Peking ordered them to move. Evidently the police action by the United Nations in Korea had the proper effect upon Peking and Moscow. By nipping in the bud the first aggression in Korea, a second aggression farther south in Asia was prevented. Thus the chain reaction from an Asian Munich to a third world war was prevented by backing the legal principles of peace with the deeds of policemen south of the 38th Parallel.

No amount of oratory or propaganda about peace from abroad or criticism by minority isolationists at home can ever cover up the importance of this achievement. Korea stands for the fact that a legally organized world community is not going to have its principles and provisions for the settling of international disputes by legal means turned, for the second time in this century, into a dead letter because of the failure of its majority members to act. In Korea the United Nations has said to every prospective aggressor that he cannot flout with impunity the legal principles defining proper international behavior. Korea tells us that this world is through with a spurious, verbal peace purchased at the cost of successive aggressive imperialistic wars.

If the isolationist minority in the United States and the majority in Asia have not yet learned this lesson, the majority vote and the subsequent police action of the United Nations shows that the rest of the world has. Yes, there is an isolationist majority in parts of Asia as well as the archaic minority in the United States. When for example Prime Minister Nehru of India, after the majority vote and action of the United Nations with respect to Korea, reserves to India the right of complete independence and freedom of action, he is indulging in an outmoded nationalistic isolationism as blatant as that of the United States before Pearl Harbor when it sabotaged the League of Nations to pursue an independent line of action of its own. During the debate on United Nations policy, independence of action and opinion for each individual nation, Yes! but after free debate and the majority vote, No! For independence of action against the legally constituted application of the principles of the world community means isolationism; it means the insistence in international policy of the superiority of one's own isolationist law to world law.

Fortunately, the wisdom of the majority in the United Nations, including Asian Thailand, has triumphed over the peace-professing words and isolationist acts of certain members of the United Nations. Otherwise the United Nations would at the present moment be the same dead letter which the League of Nations became when Japan marched its military forces into Shanghai and Manchuria and Mussolini marched his into Abyssinia. Not only would the third world war be inevitable now, as the second world war was inevitable then, but the probabilities are that the third world war would already have been a matter of history, started at the invitation most likely of India in the Spring of 1951 after a Moscow sympathetic Communist Chinese military machine had invaded and captured the whole of Asia to the north, east and southeast of the Indian peninsula.

Those Asians who believe there can be law without policemen internationally, even though they never suppose there can be law without policemen domestically, will undoubtedly say at this point that this account of what would have happened, had the United Nations not acted as it did in Korea, is mere fantasy based on reports of Chinese intentions conveyed by observers antithetical to the Communist Chinese. But what is Prime Minister Nehru's claim to the greater correctness of his intelligence over that of the United Nations' military commander and the Pentagon concerning Communist Chinese troop movements but independent testimony to the fact that Chiang Kai-shek's report of Communist military troops is correct?

Fortunately, however, it is not necessary to depend merely upon Chiang Kai-shek's or Western newspaper observers on the spot in Indo-China for our sole evidence concerning Communist Chinese intentions. Within India in October and November of 1950 there was unequivocal proof known to everybody that the Chinese Communists have no regard for a peaceful, traditionally Asian mediational way of settling foreign policy disputes, but insist instead on the recourse to military invasion and force. The issue has to do with China and Tibet. Prime Minister Nehru had offered the good services of his government and his country as a place and instrument for the peaceful settlement of this dispute by the traditional Asian method of mediation. In September and October of 1950, representatives of Communist China and of Tibet were actually in session in New Delhi pursuing this process of mediation with a sympathetic Asian government of India ready at hand to provide its services should any difficulty arise. Of a sudden, however, Peking issued orders to the Tibetan government in Lhasa and its delegation in New Delhi that the latter delegation must proceed immediately to Peking for the settlement of the Chinese Tibetan dispute. Apparently the good offices of an Asian government with its foreign policy of dynamic neutrality did not quite coincide with the background thought to be proper by mainland Chinese leaders.

But even this non-neutral Pekinese background for a mediation between China and Tibet was not sufficient to satisfy the Chinese leaders. Before the Tibetan delegation could get out of India, Communist China marched her army into Tibet.

The more important lesson, however, to learn from the Tibetan affair in its bearing on Korea is the demonstration within New Delhi's India which it gave in October of 1950 that Chinese Communists are not Confucian Chinese Asians but Moscow Communist Asians. The non-Aryan Asian method of settling disputes is mediation. Confucius teaches that the wise man will avoid litigation and resort always to the peaceful settling of disputes by mediation. In Confucian China the military is at the bottom of the social hierarchy, not at the top. As the later chapter on the theory and practice of Communism will show, its theory of dispute settling is the very antithesis of this. It is moreover the theory which President Mao's army followed in Tibet.

There was other evidence in India in 1950 showing the aggressive militaristic intentions of China's mainland leaders. One of India's most expert Asian newspaper reporters published articles in India's newspapers based upon months of observation at Peking before and during the North Korean aggression in South Korea. What makes his report all the more telling is that this Indian newspaper man went to Peking with the conception of China's mainland government held by Prime Minister Nehru and so many other of his Indian countrymen, dominated as they are by the Asian theory of mediation as the proper method for handling any dispute. This Indian newspaper man, like his own Prime Minister, believed initially that the Chinese leaders in Peking were primarily fellow Asians and only secondarily, if at all, Moscow revolutionary militant Communist international imperialists. What he saw led him, however, to a complete change of mind. He found every phase of personal and social experience being pressed into the Moscow mold. More than this, months before Korea he saw military preparations and troop movements on a scale such that they could be justified only for offensive and not for defensive purposes. Firsthand Indian information as well as the analogy of Korea to Munich enforces the conclusion that the United Nations' police action in the middle of 1950 prevented the chain reaction whose terminus would have been World War III.

Notwithstanding this achievement, of which the United Nations and the United States as a responsible participant therein can be proud, Korea exhibits basic weaknesses in this world organization. It also exhibits other weaknesses in the foreign policy of the United States.

These weaknesses show in the neutral isolationistic and in the negative critical reactions of so many Asians to Korea. To this negative reaction we must turn directly. The specifications for its removal will come later.

The negative Asian reaction to Korea has its basis, however, in a wider, deeper factor. This factor and its crucial relevance for both the United Nations and United States foreign policy become evident when we consider Pearl Harbor, Hiroshima and Korea together.

All three events bespeak the rise and challenge of Asia to the West and the necessity of a response. This means that the days not merely of an isolationist power politics but also of a merely European focused foreign policy are over. Henceforth any nation, if its foreign relations are to be on a realistic and sound basis, must first understand and then relate itself in the light of this understanding to the Asian as well as to the European, Middle Eastern and American areas of this world.

And of the major portions of the world, Pearl Harbor, Hiroshima and Korea tell us that the Asian sector is the most important one. Pearl Harbor speaks for the fact that it was an attack from Asia, not the previously initiated war in Europe, which brought the United States into the second major war of this century. Her declaration of war upon Hitler's Germany followed the declaration with respect to Japan.

Korea teaches the same lesson. Trying as recent events at Prague, Berlin and Vienna have been, they have not led to United Nations police action or to the loss of American lives in a United Nations police force. The Asian events have. Moreover in Korea the United States has had to carry the major share of the load.

The contribution of the United States is equally necessary for the preservation of constitutional processes in Europe. But it is necessary more as a backlog to instill the confidence in the Europeans necessary for them to use and coordinate their own cultural and physical resources. There are no such available allies for the defense of world law in the Pacific area and Asia. Australia and New Zealand are small in man-power and industrial capacity compared with the free nations of Western Europe. Thus inevitably a breach of the peace in Asia will entail a larger percentage of the burden being borne by the United States than is the case anywhere else. To suppose, therefore, as some suggest, that a sound foreign policy for this or any other country can center merely on Europe and Pan America and the preservation of the values of Western civilization is to fail to face the most obvious realities of the situation or to learn the most elementary lessons which Pearl Harbor, Hiroshima and Korea have to teach us.

But the Asian and European portions of our problem are not disconnected. The attack by Asians at Honolulu brought the United States immediately into a European as well as an Asian war. This will always be the case. Every Asian government is combining Western political forms and instruments with Oriental ways and values, and, as a consequence, inevitably has Western allies. At Pearl Harbor Japan's ally was Germany. More than this, Japan and Germany had peacetime modern social and legal values in common. The Japanese constitution was modeled most heavily upon that of Germany. Most of its foreign advisers in every walk of life, educational as well as military, came from Germany.

Korea illustrates this inevitable connection between Asia and Europe in an even more dramatic way. In this case there was no attack upon the United States or any other Western nation. A North Korean Asian people and government hurled itself suddenly against a South Korean Asian people and government. Why should such an apparently purely Asian affair disturb the people of the United States and the officials of the United Nations?

Yet disturb everyone it did and with a unanimity of response from every political party, including even Henry Wallace and his Progressives, and from every rank of life, which is rare in American or European history. The newspapers of mid 1950 show that the press and public response to President Truman's sudden decision to appeal immediately to the United Nations and to dispatch troops under General MacArthur to South Korea was practically unanimous.

But why did everyone believe that an Asian Munich confronted both the United Nations and the people of the world, which, if accepted passively, would make a dead letter of the United Nations Charter and set off a chain of events ending in World War III? Again the answer is that each Asian party in the Korean affair had Western allies and that a European and American as well as an Asian Korean issue was being raised.

But the United States had no treaty binding it to come to the defense of South Korea. It had completely withdrawn from South Korea. Also many proponents of the power politics theory of international relations had emphasized that from a power politics standpoint Korea was more of a liability than an asset. Thus the power politics theory of international relations does not explain the unanimous response of the people of the United States at the time.

It would be equally hard to prove that President Mao's China or Premier Stalin's European Russia were bound by treaty to support the North Koreans in their patent aggression. Why, then, were the people of the United States and the majority in the United Nations so sure at the time that a world war would ensue upon a failure to act?

There is but one answer to this question. It is the ideological answer.

Every American, European and Asian knew that however North Korea, mainland China and Russia may or may not have been bound to common action by treaty, they were so bound by an even more important thing—the tie of a common ideology. Beside the bond of common ideals and aspirations, the tie of a mere political instrument such as a treaty is a comparatively fragile thing.

Nor was anyone in error with respect to the fact of this ideological bond between North Korea, Peking and Moscow. In December, 1951, President Mao's China invited fifteen carefully selected, influential Indians to visit Peking.[2] Upon their return to India these Indians published what they found there. Impressed by Chinese assurances that mainland China is a Chinese China, not a Stalinist Moscow China, the Indian scholars have so reported. Unfortunately for their own astuteness these Indian scholars have also published beside their own reports an address delivered to them in Peking by the well known Chinese philosopher Fung Yu-Lan. This address by the present Peking professor is most interesting.

The test of the presence of ideological ties with Moscow is a very simple one. The philosophical ideology of Premier Stalin's Moscow-centered Soviet Union is contained in a small booklet by the Premier himself entitled, *Dialectical and Historical Materialism*. The philosophical ideology of Peking's China, as described to his Indian visitors by Professor Fung Yu-Lan in his official address of welcome and as published by them in India, is dialectical and historical materialism. More than this, Professor Fung shows in detail that this is the ideology of mainland China not merely in theory but also in concrete practice. Thus not merely initially but even in December of 1951 the theory and practice of President Mao's Communist China was identical with that of Premier Stalin's Russia.

One rather amusing warning appears at the beginning of Professor Fung's lecture of welcome to his visiting scholarly colleagues from India. He tells his visitors that they must not think of him as the author of the philosophical books which have given him his world-wide reputation. These books, he adds, no longer represent his philosophical position. Apparently Professor Fung is talking not merely to the Indians in his audience but also to the official censors who he knows will read what he has said. He hastens, therefore, to add that now he believes in a new philosophy—the philosophy of the New China. This new philosophy of the New China turns out, however, as he proceeds, to be the very old Marxist dialectical materialism of an equally old nineteenth century Europe now gone beyond recall.

Everyone knew also when the North Korean aggression occurred that European issues were raised in other ways than by the ideological bond between North Korea, Peking and Moscow. South Korea had its ideological ties to the West and especially to the United States.

Its more general ties to the West arose from the fact that in a very special sense South Korea is a child of the United Nations. All too many nations in the United Nations who bestow more sympathy on the North Koreans and the Chinese Communists because they are not members of the United Nations than they bestow on the South Koreans, forget too easily the fact that long before the North Korean aggression the United Nations voted the bringing into being of a united Korea with a single government determined by free elections supervised by a United Nations commission. The South Koreans accepted this United Nations decision; the North Koreans did not. By deeds, therefore, the North Koreans and their Chinese supporters showed that they did not want to become responsible members of the United Nations. Hence, the Korean affair was more than a test of whether the United Nations would prevent an aggressive defiance of its legal principles from succeeding. It was also an attack of a government which had set itself up in defiance of United Nations decisions and fair free elections under the supervision of the United Nations upon a government which had accepted the United Nations recommendations and supervision. In a very specific sense, therefore, the attack of the North Koreans upon South Korea was an attack upon the United Nations itself.

Similarly everybody knew that the ideology used by the South

Koreans in building the Westernized portion of their political and social institutions, as accepted by the South Koreans themselves in free elections supervised by the United Nations, was the ideology of the free democratic West as introduced under the tutelage of the United States before the United States withdrew from Korea. Consequently the North Korean attack was in its ideological meaning an attack upon the United States itself.

It followed, therefore, if the United Nations did not act that it was saying to the world that any nation which peacefully follows the vote and advice of the United Nations can expect nothing but empty words about peace when it is attacked by a nation that flouts the decisions and advice of the United Nations. Similarly it is the two ideological factors in the Korean aggression which made the people of the United States realize instantly that for the United Nations and the United States to let the matter go unchallenged would be tantamount to telling the Communists in Peking and Moscow, with their prodigious land armies and air force, the largest in Europe and Asia, that they can carry on the forceful, aggressive, imperialistic imposition of their ideological dictatorship on the rest of the world with no fear of police action, and that peoples anywhere who choose to build their institutions upon any other principles can expect no effective protection against imperialistic aggression from either the United Nations or those nations in the United Nations which are alone able through that body to protect them.

Pearl Harbor, Hiroshima and Korea stand, therefore, as eternal reminders of several very important things. Pearl Harbor demonstrates the political and financial folly of neutrality and its isolationism and of both defensive and offensive power politics as a basis for the foreign policy of the United States or any other nation. It reminds the world also that there are Asian imperialists. Hiroshima tells us that we are in an atomic age, and thereby makes the establishment of an effective, legally constituted world community the child of necessity. Pearl Harbor, Hiroshima and Korea together tell us that important as Europe is, Asia is more important so far as the foreign policy of the United States at least is concerned. Korea itself tells us, for all its shortcomings and long drawn out consequences, that the second attempt in this century to create a legally constituted world community for the prevention of the success of aggression has established itself as something more than verbal oratory obscuring a dead letter and has in all probability already prevented the world from being in a third world war. Of Korea, therefore, the United Nations and the United States, as a hearty assumer of its full share of the responsibilities of the United Nations, can be proud. To have set up for the first time in history the sobering precedent that any prospective aggressor must think twice before he sets off, through an initial easy success, the chain reaction that terminates in a world war is by no means a small achievement however much minority isolationists and power politicians at home and Asian orators of verbal peace abroad may deprecate what has been done in Korea by the United Nations and the United States as a member thereof.

This does not mean, however, that when an aggression occurs a member of the police force or of the United Nations has the right to turn that police action into a war against a country which is the neighbor of the one in which the aggression occurs, even when the ideology of the aggressor nation and of the neighboring nation is identical. The business of a legally constituted police action is to stop the aggressor—not to change his ideology or that of his neighbors. The ideology of a given people is their business, not that of anyone else, including even the United Nations. When policemen police only those who hold their particular political or social philosophy, all law and order break down. Upon this point our Asian friends were correct, as was the President of the United States when he called home the Commanding General of the United Nations who wanted to turn a police action of the legally constituted world community into a war against a country which was a neighbor of the aggressor.

The issue here is, to be sure, a subtle one. For the neighbor was in part the aggressor since he supported the aggressor morally and by encouraging "volunteers" from his own people and country. But the point of police action is to nip initial aggression in the bud and to keep it from spreading. It is not the function of law or of its policemen to pass from the defensive to the offensive by turning a police action against an aggression into an attack upon the aggressor's neighbor.

The United Nations police action protected the principles for which it stands and achieved its purpose when it prevented the initial ingression from succeeding and thereby setting off a chain reaction leading to a third world war. It is not the business of policemen nor of law to tell what the individuals under the law shall believe. This is something sacred to them. No legal world community can or should determine it. The business of law and of police action under law is to protect this right and negatively to stop any interference from outside with it. This the police action in the United Nations has accomplished.

But, it may be said, the action still goes on. There is no peace. This is true, but such is the nature of society under law. Police action against an individual murderer does not instantly end all murdering so that the policeman can go home and the police force can be dismissed. It is of the essence of the peaceful settling of disputes anywhere by means of law that the policeman must be perpetually present. Consequently the United Nations police force can withdraw from Korea only when the precedent established by its presence there is established in a manner which the North Koreans and the Chinese Communists accept in deed. Already this action has prevented the Communists from carrying through their obviously arranged plans to invade Indo-China. When they realize that come what will, however long it may take, the world community and the people of the United States as a responsible part of that community have made up their minds to prevent Communist aggression from succeeding in Korea, the folly of continued pressure on South Korea will become evident even to them. Then and only then, truce or no truce, will police action by the legally constituted world community in South Korea be unnecessary. The legislator, the judge and the policeman cannot decide when the police may return to the police station. Only the law breaker or the potential law breaker can make this decision. To suppose, therefore, that in a defensive police action to prevent aggression from succeeding one can, by an all-out blow, solve the problem of policing for all time is to fail to learn anything from what we know about law. It is as if one supposed that the local police in one's own city by clubbing a present fighting thug with sufficient force would forever after make the need for police action unnecessary.

Korea also has a negative lesson. It reveals that the United Nations contains a serious flaw. This flaw shows in the response of India to Korea.

CHAPTER 3

INDIA'S RESPONSE TO KOREA

In 1945 at San Francisco the Government of India, through her official representative, affixed her signature to the Charter of the United Nations. However ambiguous its terms are, and this will concern us later, this Charter was clearly understood by all to be dedicated to the task of preserving peace in the world, not by Gandhi's method of non-attachment and non-cooperation, but by recourse to law backed with police power. The existence of its Security Council testified to the latter fact. Furthermore, by no stretching of the imagination could its directors be regarded as puppets of Wall Street capitalists or instruments of military brass hats in the Department of Defense of the United States of America. Its first General Secretary having the loyal support of Soviet Russia and supported also by the United States was and remained through the Korea affair a Norwegian Socialist, Trygve Lie.

Behind this second attempt in this century of the world community of nations to put the relations between nations under the rule of law backed with police power rather than under the rule of force uncontrolled by law was the memory of the failure of the first attempt initiated at Versailles and of the three errors which produced this failure. These three errors, clearly recognized by all, were the permission by the League of Nations of the Japanese military invasion of Manchuria, Mussolini's military invasion of Abyssinia with nothing more than a verbal reprimand and Hitler's military invasion of Czechoslovakia. These events had demonstrated supposedly to all that the world law of the League of Nations, notwithstanding all the speeches about peace which continued to be made in its name at Geneva, was mere words and a dead letter. Every responsible government at San Francisco knew, and still knows, that Manchuria and Abyssinia led straight through blackmail acquiesced in at Munich to World War II. This was not to happen again.

On October 13, 1949, Prime Minister Nehru addressed the Congress of the United States. In this address after saying that "in drafting the Constitution of the Republic of India we have been greatly influenced by your Constitution," he added: "We have placed in the forefront of our Constitution those funda- mental human rights to which all men who love liberty, equality and progress aspire—the freedom of the individual, the equality of men and the rule of law."

In the next sentence he added that: "We enter, therefore, the community of free nations with the roots of democracy deeply embedded in our institutions and in the thoughts of our people." [1] Apparently by this he meant that India entered the United Nations with the clear understanding that entry entails settling international disputes by the legally authorized deci- sions of that body. His statements on foreign policy make it ex- plicit that this is what India's membership in the United Na- tions means. For to the Congress of the United States he con- tinued:

The objectives of our foreign policy are the preservation of world peace and the enlargement of human freedom. . . . We have to achieve freedom and to defend it. We have to meet aggression and to resist it and the force employed must be adequate for the pur- pose. . . . Where freedom is endangered, or justice threatened, or where aggression takes place, we cannot be and shall not be neutral. [2]

However, a year was not to elapse before the following things happened: The North Koreans, without warning and with no antecedent suggestion that there was a pressing dispute between them and the South Koreans, invaded South Korea in military force. A United Nations Commission on the spot reported the North Korean action to be aggressive. The Security Council of the United Nations with the Assembly and India in the first vote concurring, branded the North Korean behavior an aggression and ordered the police action authorized under the Charter. Nevertheless, Prime Minister Nehru, with the overwhelming support of Indian public opinion, not merely announced a policy of neutrality but, as the following quotations from India's press and leaders demonstrate, suggested often, and explicitly affirmed frequently, that the majority of the United Nations and especially the United States who participated in the police action were warmongers and war-makers rather than protectors of the peace, not merely misguided in practice but also immoral in principle, far more guilty even than the North Korean aggressors and those who befriended them.

A more unequivocal betrayal of Prime Minister Nehru's word to the Congress of the United States and of his own statement there of what India's membership in the United Nations means can hardly be imagined. Such is the judgment which seems to follow. In part such is the judgment that must follow if the principle upon which the United Nations rests of preventing war by law backed with police power is not to be betrayed today in Korea as it was betrayed yesterday in Manchuria, Abyssinia and at Munich.

Yet to make such a judgment as if it were the whole truth in the contemporary world situation is as unfair to Prime Minister Nehru and to the Indian people as his and their judgment has been unfair to the majority in the United Nations and to the United States. For as the sequel will show there was another factor in Prime Minister Nehru's speech to the Congress of the United States as there is another concept of the way to settle disputes in the indigenous Asian mind. This additional factor in India's response to Korea must be understood and incorporated into any foreign policy for the United States and any program for the United Nations which is to be informed and realistic.

The process will be painful for American readers. Nevertheless, the best way to understand the response of Prime Minister Nehru and India to Korea is to face the following comments made by Indians in 1950 about Korea without passing moral judgment upon them. Judgment, if it is to be fully informed, must be left to the end of this chapter at least and preferably to the concluding chapter of our entire inquiry when all the major factors in the contemporary world situation are before us. In return it is perhaps not too much to ask our Indian readers before they pass judgment on the United States and the majority in the United Nations to do the same, paying attention to every major factor in the world situation and not merely to the single Indian and traditionally Asian element in the situation which the remainder of this chapter and the next will attempt to exhibit.

On October 14, 1950, the Delhi edition of *The Times of India,* which has the largest circulation of any paper in Asia, carried the following two-column headline: "U.N.'s Condescending Attitude to Asia," followed by:

The Indian delegates [at the Pacific Relations Conference at Lucknow] protested against the condescending attitude towards the Asian countries of the U.N. which, they said, was virtually controlled by the Anglo-American Bloc. Whatever representation these countries had had in the U.N. bodies was not because of the recognition of their importance but as a mark of courtesy.

The Hindustan Times of Delhi added that the "majority of the Indian delegates . . . pointed out that the U.N. had not struck deep roots in Asia. . . . The U.N. had not shown sufficient concern over Asia." Another page carried the headlines, "Russia's Peace Call to U.S.A.," followed by, "The Soviet Minister, M. Vyshinsky, today appealed to the U.S.A. to return to its war time policy of cooperation." *The Times of India* confirmed with, "Russia Urges U.S. to Co-operate."

The next day *The Sunday Times of India* had the following from the address of Mr. Sampurnand, Minister of Education in the United Provinces:

Let me not be misunderstood. We in India have always been friends of the Soviet Union. Great experiments in development carried out in that great country have had magnetic attraction for us. . . . We are grateful for offers of material help and technology from the West but this is not enough by itself. Asia's self-respect must be restored to the full and this will not be possible so long as she feels that imperialism and colonialism have not been buried for ever. What may appear to Western nations as justifiable maintenance of status is likely to appear to the people of Asia as an attempt to perpetuate political and economic stranglehold on Asian soil.

On October 19, 1950, the main editorial of *The Times of India* bore the title, "U.S. and Asia." It said:

President Truman, fresh from his conference with General Mac-Arthur, has called on the Asian people to join the U.S.A. in "the partnership of peace." The invitation would have been more meaningful if he had tried to dispel some of the doubts which U.S. policy in Asia had fostered in the minds not only of Asia's peoples but also of those throughout the world who were intelligent enough to grasp the basic fact that the key to Asia's problems lay not in building situations of military strength but in creating situations of political freedom, economic development and social justice. There was nothing that the people of Asia would have liked more than lending their support to any policy or programme designed to preserve peace. But they had learnt by bitter experience to judge policies and programmes not by the labels they carried but by their contents or, better still, their likely results.

The Hindustan Times, edited by Mohandas Gandhi, son of the Mahatma, had a similar main editorial entitled, "Partnership of Peace." It affirmed that "American policy at present does not have Asian support" and concluded that the "policy of strength on which President Truman places reliance is not for other nations which must find it difficult to maintain their standard of living, let alone better it." On another page appears the two-column headline, "U.S.A. Determines to Oppose Strength with Strength."

The next day the main editorial of *The Times of India* entitled, "Remnants of Colonialism," added:

White colonialism, whether uncovered or masked, has been an ardent ally of indigenous reactionaryism in Asia. Is this phenomenon not vividly illustrated by foreign endeavours to strengthen the last stronghold of Chinese reactionaryism in Formosa? Even to a superficial observer, if he is not wearing the almost opaque glasses of partisanship, . . . what has happened in China is essentially a reaction against white colonialism. So is the upheaval in Korea. The Rhee regime in its southern part was never regarded by Asian leaders as based on the will of the people. To say that a fossil was dug up by the hidden hands of white colonialism and on it some sort of a representative Government was built up might be tantamount to making an uncharitable assertion. But there is no doubt that the Rhee regime has been looked upon by the Koreans with distrust, for it is likely to be soft to white colonialism to which it owes much. . . . Is not French colonialism trying to strangle resurgent nationalism in Viet Nam openly? The unabashed manner in which some white Powers are trying to help it militarily and financially only goes to prove that the homage which they pay to democracy on ceremonial occasions is not sincere.

On October 24, 1950, *The Hindustan Times* under the two-column headline, "Future of World Depends on Fate of United Nations," quoted Prime Minister Nehru as saying:

The United Nations came into existence to give expression to the world-wide desire for peace and co-operation between nations. . . . Today the United Nations faces a severe crisis. . . . We should try our best to get over the present crisis and stop this drift to war. . . . India is devoted to peace and because of this it is supporting the United Nations and will continue to support it.

The same issue carried the following interview with Pandit Nehru by Marquis Childs:

Prime Minister Nehru . . . expounded the philosophy behind India's foreign policy. . . . The reasons why the Nehru Government was working incessantly . . . to avoid seeming to align itself against Peiping emerge. . . .
First is its belief that World War III would mean reversion to barbarism over large areas of the earth. . . .
. . . second . . . is the belief that "in the long run China can never become a satellite of Russia or a Communist State in the Russian pattern."

The third reason for Indian policy is the profound influence of the Gandhi philosophy on Nehru and most members of the Government. . . . Nehru makes plain in almost everything he says the influence on him of Gandhi, who was like a father and brother to him. Gandhi's non-violence, which deeply swayed the Indian masses, lives on in the hearts and minds of those who are trying to establish democratic self-government in this land torn by religious strife and burdened by ancient traditions.

This Gandhism partly explains the revulsion here for mass killing and destruction in Korea, even though India joined the U.S.A. in the U.N. stand against the aggressor. The remark Gen. MacArthur made, which was widely printed here, saying the sight of dead North Koreans was good for his old eyes caused a highly unfavourable reaction.

This also is related to the suspicion that the West considers Asians expendable and that the desire of Europe, and perhaps of America, is to fight the war against Communism in Asia where weapons of mass destruction, such as the atom bomb, can be used.

. . . fourth . . . is fear of American imperialism. . . . He says what Asians fear is not old-fashioned imperialism but "economic imperialism."

Under the four-column headline, "The United Nations and Its Future," the *Indian News Chronicle* of October 25, 1950, carried the following by B. B. Saksena:

The Korean War put the U.N. to a severe test. Though Russia had walked out of the U.N. yet it had to walk in again. That shows the tremendous power U.N. wields today. . . .

Pandit Nehru explained at a recent Press Conference that he was opposed to the creation of U.N. forces in each country. This would, according to him, convert the U.N. into an organisation for war, not peace. . . . He also emphasised that the Far East crisis might not have arisen had the New China been admitted to the United Nations at the proper time. As a matter of fact if the U.S.A. succeeds in checking the entry of New China into the United Nations, resurgent Asia would lose all faith in the impartiality and fairness of the U.N. and would consider it to be a "pocket-borough" of the U.S.A. Moreover the indiscreet manner in which the U.S.A. has been carrying on many objectionable activities under the label of the U.N. during the Korean war is sure to lower the prestige of this great Organisation.

On October 25, 1950, *The Hindustan Times* had an article from its special correspondent in Hong Kong, under the heavy type headlines, "Communist China Has No Aggressive Designs. Alarmist Reports Unjustified." Another page carried ·the headlines: "Nehru Reaffirms U.N. Ideals—India's Policy of Peace—War Preparations Condemned."

On the same morning *The Statesman* carried a brief editorial entitled, "Tibetans Leave for Peking Today," in which it said: "Members of the Tibetan delegation . . . will carry with them the good wishes of the Government of India for a peaceful solution of the Sino-Tibetan problem."

The next morning Delhi's *Times of India* had the following headline across the top of its front page: "Chinese Communists Invade Tibet." Immediately beneath were the two-column headlines off center to the left of the page: "Announcement of Peking Gov't.—Three Million People to Be Liberated." Focused directly in the top center of the page was a cartoon no one could miss. It portrayed an American jeep containing two sour-looking military brass hats in its front seat with guns on their shoulders, and a third military brass hat in the back seat beside whom was sitting General MacArthur from whose mouth came the words printed above his military cap, "Rather embarrassing is it not?" These words referred to the rider and his wooden horse on wheels which were attached to the jeep and being drawn by it across a line marked "38th Parallel." The horse bore on its chest the words, "Rhee's Regime." Beneath the cartoon was its title, "Dr. Rhee said that he would bring North Korea under his own regime." Beneath this title were the two-column headlines, "U.N. Troops Ordered to Reach Manchurian Border."

The Hindustan Times of the same date also attempted to give the impression that this United Nations police action in Korea, undertaken only after full debate in the United Nations, was worse than the Chinese invasion of Tibet. Its front page carried a four-column headline entitled, "U.N. Troops to Complete N. Korea Occupation—Drive to Manchurian Border Ordered."

Only two columns on the right in similar type were devoted to
the headline, "China to Invade Tibet—Official Announcement
in Peking." The top middle of the page carried a picture of the
Tibetan delegation's departure. Under the picture was the
statement, "Members of the Tibetan delegation yesterday left
Delhi by train for Kalimpong 'en route' to Calcutta. They are
on way to Peking 'via' Hong Kong for talks with China Government on Tibetan affairs."

Its editorial entitled, "The U.N. Day," said:

M. Vyshinsky, speaking for Russia, has asked for sabre-rattling to
end and has offered to meet the West "half way," . . .

We think the proposal for five-Power consultations for settlement
of outstanding differences offers the best opportunity for utilizing
the present atmosphere for a peaceful settlement. On their part,
Russian leaders should realize that Communism must be contained
within its present limits and that no attempt should be made to
extend it through subversion or civil war. The people of the West
consider the Communist doctrine a threat to human values while
Eastern peoples think that it threatens all spiritual values. If M.
Stalin really believes that the two systems can co-exist he has not
yet shown it by his actions.

Only the British owned *Statesman* made the Chinese invasion
of Tibet the main feature on its front page on October 26, 1950.

On the next day *The Hindustan Times* had the following editorial headed, "Invasion of Tibet":

The news that the People's Government of China have ordered
an invasion of Tibet at the very moment when, after weary months
of waiting a Tibetan delegation is on its way to Peking to negotiate
with the Chinese Government seems almost incredible. . . .

In India, especially, the news, again assuming that the report is
true, will be received with amazed concern. . . . That the Chinese
case for admission in the U.N. would be prejudiced by invasion and
China will, in addition, alienate the sympathies of her friends are
additional reasons for Peking not embarking on an enterprise in
which military success may elude her but political complications
are certain to arise.

The next day on the editorial page of this same newspaper a
remarkable innovation occurred. A three-column headline in

very large type read as follows: "How Roosevelt Pressed for India's Freedom—Churchill Tells the Story." Forthwith followed three columns of quotations from Mr. Churchill's *War Memoirs* prefaced by the following introductory comment from its New York correspondent:

While it is no news to the people of the U.S.A. that India was Mr. Churchill's blind spot, they have felt thrilled by the confirmation through the *War Memoirs* of Mr. Churchill published in the *New York Times* of the part President Roosevelt played in pressing on the British war leader India's claim for freedom.

A more effective way of changing India's image of America from that of a sabre-rattling militaristic imperialist to that of a friend of India and a friend of Asia can hardly be imagined.

Forthwith *The Statesman* constantly portrayed the role of the United States and the United Nations in Korea as it is envisaged in American eyes. On December 19, 1950, for example, letters to the editor of the following character were typical of what occurred regularly in this newspaper.

Sir,—I congratulate you on your frank stock-taking of a difficult situation in your Editorial of Dec. 11–12. The prospect is really grim and the time short if Mr. Mao decides to exploit the demoralization rampant in the camp of democracy. . . .
The challenge of Communism is not moral and spiritual but brute and physical, in the face of which democracy should arise unashamed because it has achieved a lot and given time would achieve a lot more. The strongest bulwarks of democracy in S-E Asia are indigenous nationalisms. These appear passive and distorted because leaders of democracy have not cared to inform them about the fate of the common man behind the Iron Curtain, while Moscow continues to feed them on myths of a socialist paradise. . . . Yours, etc., Sita Ram Goel

Sir,—At no period in human history has mankind been confronted with a situation so difficult and decisive as today. . . . The only way to preserve peace is to threaten the aggressor with war and convince him that you have the will to wage it. . . . There is no peace by concessions; surely we realize that by now. All that the world needs today is a leader who must be a defender of peace and civilization.—Yours, etc., Moni Bagchee

Unfortunately, however, only *The Statesman* continued this portrayal of the nature of United Nations police action and its way to preserve peace. Even *The Hindustan Times* reverted to its pre-Tibetan version. Other papers did even worse. In its main editorial on December 21, 1950, the *Hindustan Standard* opened as follows:

> With the appointment of General Eisenhower as Supreme Commander in Europe, military preparations in the West reach a new high level in the cold twilight between war and peace.

Then followed:

> In due course a European MacArthur may well find in Berlin or divided Germany a cause to launch action against aggression in the Korean model. The Brussels decisions of the Atlantic Pact Council settle almost irrevocably the future course of events. The Powers are not drifting towards war; on the contrary, they are inviting it and preparing for it as being inevitable. . . . The proponents of the Atlantic Pact might object to designating it as a jungle law. But a most cursory analysis reveals the thinness of the veneer of civilisation covering it. . . . There is just the faintest hope that war might still be averted by the pressure of neutral opinion in Europe as well as in Asia. That is not much but still the only hope against the triumph of the jungle principle on a scale too dreadful even to contemplate.

In an editorial entitled, "The Choice for China," the *Amrita Bazar Patrika,* the newspaper of the Hindu Right, affirmed the following on December 22, 1950:

> The departure of the Communist Chinese delegation from Lake Success for Peking is calculated to damp the ardour even of the most robust optimist who hoped that after all peace would come and the world would not be thrown into the whirlpool of another global war. . . . He [Mr. Wu] is also understood to have told Sri Rau that perfect understanding between India and the new China should continue. . . . India has the advantage of all the attributes of a mediator. The leaders of the hostile camps have always India's services at their disposal. It is difficult to predict anything about the real intentions of Russia. But we adhere to our belief that if the cards are played well, a closer understanding will be easier to reach

with China than with Russia. The efforts of the 13 Asian nations should be immediately directed to this end.

On December 24, 1950, *The Sunday Hindustan Standard* carried a two-column article on its editorial page by J. K. Banerji entitled, "What Next in Korea?" Its main point was:

. . . The essence of this Far Eastern problem is the challenge of New China to the claim of the U.S. that the entire Pacific Ocean stretching right up to the shores of China is the security zone of the U.S.

On December 26, 1950, the Allahabad edition of *Amrita Bazar Patrika* concluded its main editorial as follows:

There is nothing to be unnerved at if India is at times misunderstood by any of the armed camps. National interest and national self-respect alike demand that India should not align herself with any of the armed blocs sacrificing her brain and judgment.

In a neighboring column, Dr. Mookerji, the leader of the Jana Sangh party, reported that:

. . . despite differences in political outlook of their respective Governments, India and China had to maintain their friendly relations.

He said great political revolutions had taken place which changed the character of the Chinese Government. Similarly, another revolution had taken place in India whereby the people of India had won independence after 200 years of foreign domination. If there was close understanding between the peoples of these two countries, if both worked in unison and were determined to maintain peace in the world, it would undoubtedly become the most powerful factor in world politics, . . .

On December 28th, *The Statesman* carried a picture in the middle of the top of its front page of a state banquet that had been held the night before in Government House in honor of Mr. R. G. Menzies, the Australian Prime Minister, with the following description of the five people facing the camera:

. . . Seated from left to right are Mrs. Novikov, wife of the Russian Ambassador, Mr. Menzies, Mrs. Indira Gandhi, the Prince de Ligne, the Belgian Ambassador and Lady Nye, wife of the U.K. High Commissioner.

Beneath this description appeared two headlines, the first in heavy type: "Friendly Relations with Australia—Nehru's Address at State Banquet for Menzies." Because this banquet brought new factors into the situation, it is important to quote this newspaper's report of Prime Minister Nehru's address and Mr. Menzies' reply in some detail.

The countries of the Commonwealth are meeting soon in conference in London. . . . But since this conference has been called, other developments are taking place in the world. . . .

A heavy burden rests upon the Prime Minister of Australia, as on me, as well as on others at this juncture. We go to London for many reasons. . . . But I take it primarily the purpose of our going to London is to find the way to peace. . . .

There is a lot of talk of peace and there are plenty of people who pay . . . lip-service to that idea, till the very word itself becomes somewhat debased and one does not know what it means. Nevertheless, there is something called peace, which we all know, and there is such a thing as a peaceful approach to a problem. But talk of peace in the warlike way is not peace. . . .

You have come, Sir, from a country which might be called a new country. I belong to a country and to a people which have their roots in the immemorial past, going back to the origin of history, and yet in another way we are rather new and very new. Generally we are a mixture of the old and new and sometimes these mixtures produce certain complications. . . .

There is not very much in common outwardly between India and Australia, but, of course, there are tremendous problems we have in common, not only the fact that, being in the Commonwealth, we meet together and discuss common problems, but another fact which must necessarily bring us together closely, and that is the fact that Australia derives its past and present inspiration from the West, but finds today inevitably that geography and other things point towards Asia.

. . . It may be that when you are too close to each other, conflicts also arise. Anyhow, the closeness remains, whether it is one of conflict or otherwise.

Mr. Menzies replied:

When the Prime Minister said just now that it might seem that India and Australia did not have a great deal in common, I knew that he did not intend to convey quite what those words would indicate, because the longer I live, the more I believe that countries all over the world have found more in common than they are disposed to admit at any given moment.

India and Australia, in fact, have great things in common. I shall always believe that they have in common a tradition of Government, a tradition of the sovereignty of the law, a tradition of the equality of people before the law which is, in essence, the tradition of Australia, the tradition of Great Britain and the tradition of a score of countries we might name in this world. . . .

I have had in the last 24 hours the experience of coming out of the clouds of newsprint into ordinary flesh and blood and hearing the voice of two or three of the greatest men of the world and the experience of meeting them, and I was going to say talking to them, but I would prefer to say of being talked to by them. This is one of the best experiences that I ever had. . . .

India has set out, with all her ancient history and her great traditions, only recently to practice for herself complete self-government, and I do not need to say to your distinguished Prime Minister that the business of self-government is just about the most difficult thing in the world, because it requires from so high a percentage of the people a capacity for self-government and aptitude for it.

Nobody who has had as long an experience as I have had in this business of self-government can fail to have the warmest understanding and sympathy with the tasks that you have undertaken. . . . [Also] I should like to be able to say—if it were not an impertinence—to every citizen of India—and you count them like the sands on the seashore—"You cannot leave the business of self-government to one man or 10 men or to a 100 or 500 men."

This state banquet in honor of Prime Minister Menzies is important for several reasons. Prime Minister Nehru's address suggests that "talk of peace" by recourse to world law backed with police power is to "talk of peace in a warlike way" and that this "is not peace." His address suggests also that, notwithstanding the fact that India and Australia are fellow members of the British Commonwealth, there are basic differences in outlook which generate problems. There is the suggestion also that the age-old ties of India with traditional Asia may be even stronger than the liberal, democratic, constitutional ties to Australia and the Anglo-American world and the other free nations of the

West. Most important of all is the fact that all this was said in the presence of the Soviet ambassador with his wife in the position of honor upon Mr. Menzies' right. This takes us to the heart of India's foreign policy and Prime Minister Nehru's conception of his role as a peace-maker in the Korean affair. This role is not that of the world law of the United Nations supported with the police action necessary to make it effective. Instead it is that of a mediator between Australia and other supporters of the United Nations' legally constituted police action and the Soviet Union which sympathizes and supports the North Korean aggressor. This conception of the way to peace as that of the mediator has its roots in something basic in Asian mentality and culture. In fact it is precisely this which is behind Prime Minister Nehru's suggestion that ties to Asia may turn out to be stronger than ties to Australia and the liberal, democratic West. We shall find this faith in mediation rather than in law supported by police action to be more and more important as we go deeper into Indian and Asian mentality and practice.

On January 2, 1951, *The Times of India* carried the four following articles:

(1) "Separate Asian Bloc Advocated—Averting Disaster of War."

Mr. Jayaprakash Narayan, the Socialist leader, addressing a New Year Day meeting in Bombay on Monday, advocated the formation of a third international bloc of peace-loving Asian nations which would effectively check the Russo-American drift towards war. . . .

(2) "U.K. & Action on Korea—Public Feeling in Canada"

The Manchester Guardian and The Times of India Service Ottawa, January 1:

Following the departure of Mr. St. Laurent, the Prime Minister, for London, there is throughout Canada a widespread feeling that if the British Government had enjoyed a decisive voice about policy in regard to Korea wiser courses than those adopted by the Truman Administration would have been followed. . . .

There is little sympathy in Canada, apart from extreme French-Canadian isolationists, for Mr. Herbert Hoover's proposal to abandon Europe and make North America a self-contained fortress of democratic freedom and Mr. St. Laurent . . . has become acutely

conscious of the value of the Commonwealth as the best available
link with Asia.

He is just as averse as Mr. Attlee to seeing the Western democracies committed to a full-scale war with Communist China. . . .
But Canada is today so much at the mercy of the United States
economically that its Government, while they want to avoid the
charge that they are subservient to Washington, cannot afford to
oppose outright the policies favoured by the Truman Administration.

(3) "U.K.—Ceylon Defence Talks"

London, January 1: The Prime Minister of Ceylon, Mr. D. S.
Senanayke, began defence talks here today with the British Defence
Minister, Mr. Emmanuel Shinwell.

The talks deal with problems arising out of existing Anglo-
Ceylonese defence arrangements.—P.T.I.-Reuter.

(4) " 'Chinese Intervention in Korea Result of Fear'—Effect of U.N.
Action: Mrs. Pandit's Views"

Washington, January 1, "India does not believe that Communist
China has aggressive designs in Asia but thinks she has been fright-
ened by the U.N. military action in Korea," said Mrs. Vijayalakshmi
Pandit, India's Ambassador in the U.S., in an interview . . . on
Sunday.

"We believe that Chinese domination is something not nearly as
threatening as the Western world thinks it is," she added.

"We do not believe she has any aggressive designs, unless she is
provoked by actions around her. . . . We feel that war is a greater
threat to us than Communism in Asia," Mrs. Pandit said.

. . . Regarding relations between South-East Asia and the West,
she said: "I believe that East and West must co-operate and I believe that a strong and democratic India can be America's strongest
ally In Asia to interpret you to other countries there."

Asked why Indians regard the U.S. with fear as an "imperialist"
country, Mrs. Pandit explained: "It is partly because you do not
interpret yourself properly to India and partly because the U.S.
approach is usually through the dollar and that alarms people. But
India is not as afraid of encroachments of the West as she is of wars
which the West might land her into."

Mrs. Pandit observed later that America needed a much better
"public relations man," and said that she would like to have the
job.—U.P.A. & P.T.I.-Reuter.

On the same day *The Times of India* carried the following main editorial headed "Commonwealth Defence":

It would not be surprising if certain aspects of defence, as London reports suggest, were to bulk large in discussions of the Commonwealth Prime Ministers' Conference in London. Mr. Menzies's recent statement at Karachi that he favoured the setting up of a Permanent Commonwealth Defence Secretariat emphasises this possibility. . . .

Mr. Menzies, while propagating his idea of a Permanent Commonwealth Defence Secretariat, wryly confessed that the project attracted little support. Ceylon's Prime Minister, Mr. D. S. Senanayke, is reported to have expressed himself against it and India is unlikely to commit herself to any joint defence scheme. . . .

In the right-hand corner of the foregoing editorial page appeared the following two-column headline in heavy type: "India's Role in Conflict Between World Ideologies—Triumph of Self-Govt. Idea in Half Century."

London, January 1. In a survey of the half century that has ended, the "News Chronicle" today said that "India may be the decisive factor in the conflict between the two world faiths of Communism and Social democracy—which is a spiritual one far more than it is a material one."

The next day, January 3, 1951, the Bombay edition of *The Times of India* under the caption, "Current Affairs—Failures in Foreign Policy," carried a two-column article by Vivek prefaced by the editor's comment that "The views expressed by 'Vivek' do not necessarily reflect the official policy of *The Times of India*." In this article, Vivek said that:

. . . the Government of India can scarcely do better than resolve that in all spheres of policy and action they will attempt to see things as they are, have a clear objective based on knowledge, and move towards it in realistic fashion. While many of the difficulties of this country have been due to causes outside its control, many are vividly attributable to failure to follow one or more of these three cardinal points.

Our chief set-back in foreign policy during the last year has been the occupation of Tibet by the Chinese in spite of our many representations. Clearly we did not see things as they were. The Government of India seems not to have been aware both of the real militarist nature of the Chinese regime, and of the real opinion of that regime about the Indian Government. From Peking's use of it as a medium of communication with other Governments, it deduced much more goodwill than really existed.

In a short editorial in the same issue entitled, "Less Talk," *The Times of India* also raised the question whether it is

. . . necessary for the Government of India's representative [in the United States] to continue stressing Peking's non-aggressive intentions in Korea. . . . Such differences as exist between the American and Indian foreign policies are not likely to yield to unilateral moralising or preaching.

On January 8, 1951, the *National Standard* of Bombay carried the following article with its headline in large type: "Millions Put Peace Hopes in Nehru":

Singapore, Jan. 7. Describing Mr. Jawaharlal Nehru as "a man of destiny" Singapore's British-owned 'Straits Times" today editorially quoted an unidentified British newspaper which said that millions of people were behind Mr. Nehru in his efforts to save peace in Asia.

Eight days after its brief editorial on Madame Pandit, *The Times of India* published a lengthy leading editorial entitled, "Alarums and Excursions." This editorial opened as follows:

Like Narcissus who saw his image in a pool and mistook it for a nymph's, America looks into the storm-tossed world of today and mistakes every passing shadow for a Red phantom. No sane man denies that we face a perilous situation. But peril calls for faith, not fear, for calm, steadfast thinking and strong nerves. As the leader of the democratic world, America carries heavy burdens and responsibilities. She has rebuilt and rearmed many shattered countries, more particularly in Europe, and Marshall Aid in its magnitude and method represents a gesture unique in its generosity even if cynics persist in describing it as "philanthropy and 10 per cent." To think in terms of superlatives and speak in expletives may be a habit of the New World. But it disconcerts her friends while delighting her enemies. The cry of "wolf" can be overdone. It is in any case not normal to put out a conflagration by piling faggots on the fire.

This is what the United States now appears to be doing. Even while the three-men U.N. Cease Fire Commission was meeting during the week-end to draft a last-minute plan to stop the war in Korea, the U.S. delegation at Lake Success served notice on thirty other countries that it intended pressing for drastic action against Communist China if the cease-fire attempt failed. America wants these nations to brand China as the aggressor in Korea and to impose political and economic sanctions against her. Not many weeks ago, even while General Wu and his colleagues were on their way to Lake Success, General MacArthur ordered the U.N. forces to sweep towards the Manchurian border in a "Home by Christmas" offensive. The timing was, to say the least, not tactful and as events have proved, the action was unfortunate. Where is the sense in truculence without power to enforce your will? As matters stand, American prestige, battered badly by the initial North Korean offensive, has suffered grievous damage from the Chinese. The remedy is not another dose of mistimed truculence but a renewed effort to liquidate the war in Korea by a "cease fire" and to contain Peking's offensive by removing the root causes of Chinese resentment. Communist China, indignant at her exclusion from the United Nations, can only regard further efforts to ostracise her economically as adding insult to injury. Peking's rightful claim to a seat in the United Nations must be conceded. This is not appeasement but common sense.

We do not agree with many in India who regard Mao Tsetung as a potential Tito and Communist China as a land hungering for democratic affiliations. Peking has chosen to cast her lot with Moscow, and unless one deems war with Russia as inevitable and desirable, that is entirely Peking's business. The political alignments which a country chooses to make are her own concern provided they do not impinge on or interfere with the corresponding rights of others. We believe that given an earnest and mutual desire for peace, the Communist and democratic systems of government can subsist side by side. American actions suggest that the basic U.S. thesis is otherwise. Hence the political palpitations of the New World which threaten to reduce the entire globe to a state of perpetual jitters. War then becomes an inevitable safety valve. It is not a civilised solution. The pity is that the politicians who talk the world into wars are relatively immune from harm when the guns begin to go.

Having sampled the press and editorial opinion of the three main northern centers, New Delhi, Calcutta and Bombay, let us shift to South India. The *Indian Express* of Madras, under date of January 17, 1951, carried a leading editorial entitled, "Record Spending," from which the following three excerpts are taken:

Progress in modern times can be certainly measured by public expenditure. In the year 1946, the U.S.A. spent over 63.7 billion dollars. In the year 1951–52 the President proposes to spend over 71.5 billion dollars. His economic report, dwelling on the resources and productive capacity of the U.S.A. in peace, certainly suggested that expenditure would go up sharply. He had certainly hinted at taxing till it hurt, . . .

. . . Mr. Truman's message suggests that the Truman Doctrine is now global: it is no longer limited to the Mediterranean.

The most encouraging feature of the President's budget message is the reference to foreign aid. "Our total programme of assistance to the non-European areas of the Free World must place proportionately more emphasis on building security through helping the people and the Governments of these areas to solve pressing economic problems." . . . There need not be much alarm hereafter in Europe over the military might of Russia. The Budget message, coming only a week after the review of the U.S.A.'s tasks and responsibilities, underlines the whole purpose of rearmament. There is no weakening of purpose despite the attacks on Mr. Acheson. There is no indication of retreat into the New World. . . .

. . . The mass of figures is a matter for experts: for the plain man they are reassuring proof of the goodwill and strength of the U.S.A.

The same page of this newspaper carried a two-column headline in very heavy type: "Victory Soon for Nehru in Battle for Peace."

Let us look also at the Communists' weekly *Blitz*. It has the format of the *New York Daily Mirror* and is to be found at the main newsstands of any city of India. Its Bombay issue of November 11, 1950, carries the following front page headlines: "Dalai Lama, De-Robed! Peking's Charges Against 'Evil Men' Who Plotted to Sell Tibet to U.S.A." Then follows:

Fifteen months ago . . . Anglo-American agents began their treacherous conspiracy in Tibet . . . Lowell Thomas: U.S. Secret Agent . . . Dalai Lama Teen-age stooge of "evil men."

Beside this is a jet black square broken by the words: "Nehru . . . God That Failed? Page 9 to 15." On the top of page 9 above a picture of Prime Minister Nehru are the heavy type headlines: "A Common Man Writes to Nehru . . . Are You Really the God That Failed?" Then follows:

My dear Panditji

Happy Birthday to you and many Happy Returns of the Day! . . . Allow me to ask you a question that rises like a thunder all over the country from a million angry throats: What Is Freedom and Where Is It? . . . May I put the question in a slightly different manner? *What has been the record of the Congress rule in the country? What is India like today?*

Then comes the Communists' answer:

A servile state, with its splendid strength caged up, hardly daring to breathe freely; her people poor beyond compare, . . . incapable of resisting disease and epidemics; illiteracy rampant; vast areas devoid of all sanitary and medical provision; unemployment of a prodigious scale, both among the middle classes and the masses; Socialism, Communism are, we are told, the slogans of impractical idealists, doctrinaires and knaves; the test must be one of the well-being of the people as a whole. That is indeed a vital test, and by that test India makes a terribly poor show today.

The middle of the paper carries the two-page headline, "Ten Families Control Our Destiny," followed by, "Instead of confiscating foreign capital, you went all the way to America to invite some more. . . ." The next page has the heavy type headlines: "Rape of Korea: Our Shame! War, or Peace? What Do We Stand For?" Then follows:

As far as the public opinion in our country is concerned, the responsibility for the rape of Korea is on the Americans. . . . How did our active neutrality act in the Korean rape? Did we not vote for the rubber-stamping of the Yankee aggression in the Security Council and that too as it would please MacArthur? . . . True, we did not agree to the crossing of the 38th parallel. But even at that late stage, when there were hardly any illusions about the motive of the Americans, did we boldly dissociate ourselves from that criminal invasion?

Clearly from the Indian Communist standpoint Prime Minister Nehru is on the side of the United States.

The Bombay January 6, 1951, issue of *Blitz* carries the heavy front page headlines: "Nehru . . . Beware! 'Help Us—Or We'll Starve You!' . . . Commonwealth Demands Bases in India in Exchange for Food Shipments. . . ." Page two carries the heavy headlines, "Indo-U.S. Food Talks Fail. . . . Government Refuses to Walk into American War-Trap." Then follows:

Washington: America's so-called offer to sell at a "concessional" rate two million tons of foodgrains to India has turned out to be one of the biggest political swindles of high-pressure dollar diplomacy. . . .

Right from the beginning, political observers in the world capitals suspected some foul play when, all of a sudden, the American Government, which only 14 months ago insolently turned down Prime Minister Nehru's appeal for a loan of one million tons of foodgrains, became interested in India's food problem.

Nor do the leaders of India's Socialist Party fare any better than Prime Minister Nehru in Indian Communist opinion:

[Their] recent gang-up with the so-called World Free Trade Union Movement, which has gone hand-in-glove with the American murderers of Korean and Viet Namese people, would appear to suggest that Washington is fast becoming a Mecca of people and parties other than the imperialists and capitalists.

If this is the manner in which Socialists are going to lead their "New Socialist Era," they may as well abandon hope. The destinies of India are irretrievably linked up with those of New China and South-East Asia. Together this blessed region of Asia is marching and shall continue to march into the confident dawn not merely of a great new Socialist Era, but even more so of a great new Asian Century.

. . . If that is how our Socialists plan to bring about "The Birth of a New Socialist Era," the people of India would prefer the devil of Congress, bad as it is, to the abortion of a "Third Force" . . . the Socialists are labouring to bring into this part of the world, as the lesser of the two evils.

Then follows the two-page headline of an article by Devaki Pannikar, "People's China Marches Happily to a New Dawn

. . . ," followed in heavy type by, "Indian Ambassador's Daughter Gives the Lie to Western Slanderers of New China." The middle of the paper carries a two-page article by D. N. Pritt, "Famous British Barrister," with the heavy headlines, "Who Wants War America . . . or . . . Russia?" and "America Attacks Peace Movement." The article says:

> . . . America is indulging in an armament race and incidentally it is the most profitable business. . . . You have all heard the story of one of the American radios which puts out that "If anyone comes to your door and talks Peace, send for the police."
>
> . . . instead of indulging in an armaments race, the Soviet Union is not increasing her armament expenditure at all. . . . In the last two or three years, USA and Great Britain have increased their expenditure over and over again. . . .
>
> . . . So far from fearing the Stockholm petition weakening the will to resist, she [the U.S.S.R.] encourages her citizens to sign it. She does not actually want war at all. . . . Her adult population is about 115 millions. And in five weeks she got 115 million signatures to the Peace appeal.

The article concludes with the shouting words:

> If we rally our forces in this country and the world over, and build our Peace movement, we will be able to say "PEACE SHALL TRIUMPH OVER WAR."

That this Communist paper gets its readers is demonstrated by the fact that it is filled with advertisements by American, British and Indian firms. *Blitz* presents, therefore, the interesting phenomenon of a Communist newspaper financed in considerable part by the advertisements of capitalists. It reminds us also that the best friends the United Nations and the United States have in India are Prime Minister Nehru and the Socialists.

It is a relief to turn to the opinion of Sukhu and his village friends in Sam Sing on the slopes of the Himalayas deep in West Bengal. Merely to be there is to feel with Rousseau that the good is to be found in a return to the pristine freshness of nature. But Sukhu, proud of his family, and his village neigh-

bors have heard of Korea also. Moreover, friendly as he is to
America, he and they do not like it. With a roll of the shoulders as if sloughing off some pollution, he says, "We here in the
village do not like this war." The intonation is clearly such as to
mean, "Why are you doing it?"

Nor are the invading Chinese Communists far away. For on
the other side of the mountain, upon whose southern ridge
Sukhu lives, is Tibet, and at the very moment he spoke China's
invading army was there. Every Sunday Tibetans came over the
mountain from the north to trade in his local village. Clearly
Communism and the police action of the United Nations do not
mean for India's leaders and people what they mean for most
in the West.

A conversation in Calcutta with a Swami of the very influential Hindu Ramakrishna Mission made this explicit. Immediately he took it for granted that what the United Nations and
the United States were doing in Korea is evil. The following
suggestions of a different interpretation were ventured: "Can
you not see that from an imperialistic standpoint the United
States has little to gain in Korea and that, if what you suggest
is its purpose, Canada or Mexico would be the much more
obvious objects of its aggression? Why are you in Asia unable
to see that the Americans and others under the United Nations
in Korea are laying down their lives there in order that Asians
may have the right to build their institutions in their own way?"
The Swami's reply was: "If the drug which you administer to
me is to you good and to me a poison, do you accomplish your
purpose in administering it? No! There is a factor in human
nature which your President Truman when he acts thus in
Korea does not understand and has not taken into account."

These responses of this sincere Hindu Swami and of friendly
Sukhu make certain things clear. The reason for India's failure
to assume responsibility for United Nations police action in
Korea and for her criticism of both the United Nations and the
United States with respect to Korea go far deeper than the ques-
tion as to whether Prime Minister Nehru's military intelligence

or General MacArthur's was the more correct with respect to the expediency of crossing the 38th Parallel which many Westernized Indians give as the major reason. It is doubtful if Sukhu knew about the 38th Parallel or would have understood what it was if he had. My Swami friend never mentioned it. Moreover Indian opinion was against support of the police action even before the possibility of crossing the 38th Parallel arose. Sukhu's objection was a deep-seated, intuitively felt one; the Swami's condemnation was a philosophically moral and spiritual one; neither represented a mere difference of opinion with respect to instrumental expediency. What the Swami was saying was that we and our leader President Truman in our use of physical force in Korea were violating something fundamental in the Hindu Indian's, and one may add the Far Eastern Asian's, concepts of the true peace maker and the true moral man.

To move about India following Korea in the fall of 1950 and the early spring of 1951 was to meet on every hand from every walk of life and in every political party the feeling that however much they may disagree with Prime Minister Nehru on domestic policy, he was, in the overwhelming opinion of his people, bringing the deeper spiritual values and wiser way of India to bear for the first time in centuries upon world affairs. Nor was this feeling restricted to India. Something universally Asian as well as truly Indian was being expressed by him.

To be sure there were important Indians like Ministers Ambedkar and Munshi, parliamentary member Minoo Masani, and even the greatest Indian saint, Shri Aurobindo, who were for the United Nations police action and the part of the United States therein. But the overwhelming press opinion and public feeling were the other way. For example when Mr. Minoo Masani in the debate on foreign policy in India's parliament in December of 1950 urged the correctness of the policy of the United States and the importance of India making it her own, he was answered with sarcasm by India's Prime Minister and voted down by an overwhelming parliamentary majority.

The reason is not far to seek. It is to be found in an early paragraph in Prime Minister Nehru's address to the Congress of the United States. This paragraph is:

In India there came a man in our own generation who inspired us to great endeavour, ever reminding us that thought and action should never be divorced from moral principle, that the true path of man is truth and peace. Under his guidance we laboured for the freedom of our country, with ill-will to none, and achieved that freedom; we called him reverently and affectionately the Father of our Nation. Yet he was too great for the circumscribed borders of any one country, and the message he gave may well help us in considering the wider problems of the world.

Near the end of this address to Congress comes the following:

India may be new to world politics, and her military strength insignificant by comparison with that of the giants of our epoch. But India is old in thought and experience and has travelled through trackless centuries in the adventure of life. Throughout her long history she has stood for peace and every prayer that an Indian raises ends with an invocation to peace.

It was out of this ancient and yet young India that arose Mahatma Gandhi and he taught us a technique of action which was peaceful and yet it was effective and yielded results which led us not only to freedom but to friendship with those with whom we were till yesterday in conflict.

It is this new message and technique of Gandhiji that gave to Prime Minister Nehru and his people the feeling that India's way to peace by way of neutrality and the non-attached mediator was the right one and that the way to peace by law backed with police power of the United Nations majority of which the United States was a member is the way to war and evil. In other words, in Prime Minister Nehru's address to the Congress of the United States he affirmed his loyalty to both Gandhiji's way and the United Nations' way with "the force employed . . . adequate to the purpose," but in the emotional crisis of the Korean moment Gandhiji's way alone triumphed.

One is reminded of an explanation given in the 1920's by Yale coach T. A. D. Jones as to why his Yale team, in one particular year, pushed its opponents all over the middle of the field but so frequently failed to score when it came near the goal line. The answer was that the players came from different preparatory schools with different systems of play unconsciously established as habits and that when they were in the middle of the field with less pressure on them their conscious attention enabled each one to execute his part in the single coordinated form of play he had taught them. Here they used their power effectively. When, however, they neared the goal line the emotional strain from the increased pressure threw out the newly learned, conscious control and caused them unconsciously to revert to their respective diverse preparatory school habits, thereby losing their coordination as a team.

Similarly, Indians when they put their Westernized legal consciousness to work, believe in the way to peace by law backed by police action as much as does the United States or the other members of the majority in the United Nations. But, when under the tension of the Korean affair, the force appears which lawful police action requires, the emotional disturbance is such that they forget the conscious attachment to law made effective by police power to which they committed themselves when they entered the United Nations and revert to their older, more indigenously Indian and Asian habits which Gandhi embodied as the true basis of moral judgment.

If not merely Indian but also Asian behavior is to be understood, Gandhi's technique and message and its appeal to Asia's masses must be clearly grasped. This will not be easy; the roots are deep in the classics and culture of Buddhist and Hindu Asia. The effort will, however, be worthwhile.

Meanwhile, India's policy of neutrality with respect to Korea persists with a new and more consistent emphasis. The December, 1951, number of *The Modern Review* of Calcutta carries the following note:

Observers close to Pandit Nehru, indicate that a perceptible change has occurred in the last few months in our foreign policy, the sole architect of which is Nehru himself.

The hysterical rush towards Communism and its satellites has been stemmed; the hitherto unnecessarily aggressive attitude towards America and the Western Democracies has been halted. From an unreal neutrality which appeared to favour Soviet Russia and Red China on every vital issue, Pandit Nehru has plotted a new middle course: a real, balanced, defensive neutrality which while it does not hitch India to the American star, does not preclude a smooth, working arrangement with that power and the promotion of mutual respect between the two peoples.

This is perhaps the most important change that has occurred in India, and in Asia, since the Communist exploitation of Asian nationalist sentiments the effects of which are clearly seen in many Far Eastern countries.[3]

4

GANDHI'S WAY TO PEACE

At the beginning of his *Autobiography* Gandhi writes, "such power as I possess for working in the political field [has] derived [from] my experiments in the spiritual field." [1] Of the latter he adds that "truth is the sovereign principle," [2] and that the Hindu's Bhagavadgita is "the book *par excellence* for the knowledge of Truth." [3]

To be sure he knew and was influenced also by Christian, Muslim and other religious works. Always, however, the Gita was the touchstone of the truths which they contained.

He tells us also that initially he read the Buddhist *Light of Asia* "with even greater interest than . . . the *Bhagavadgita.*" [4] Actually it was a Bhagavadgita Hinduism made equivalent to Buddhism by the dropping of both caste and fighting that was Gandhi's final Gita. Such a Buddhist Hinduism is in fact a purely Asian Hinduism with the ancient Aryan contribution of castes, fighting and legal codes dropped. Similarly with respect to Christ, Gandhi accepted only the passages on pacifism and omitted entirely Christ's coming, not to reject the law as a method of achieving peace, but to fulfill the law. As we shall see later, the use of law to achieve peace is of the essence of the spiritual roots of the Western Greco-Roman Christian world. And of Christianity itself, Gandhi wrote that "the arguments in proof of Jesus being the only incarnation of God and the Mediator between God and man left me unmoved." [5]

What is the spiritual Truth of Gandhiji's Gita?

Its "cardinal teaching" he tells us is "the duty of a man of equipoise to act without desire for the fruit." [6] In the words of the Gita, it is to so identify oneself with Brahman that one lives "without attachment" to any determinate thing. As India's Ambassador to Thailand said to the writer in December of 1950, "The basic belief of India is non-attachment." One is reminded also of Mr. Munshi, former Minister of Food and Agriculture in Prime Minister Nehru's Government, and his analysis of India's persistence through the ages, while one after another of the nations of the Middle East and West has come and gone—Persia, Arabia, Assyria, Egypt, Greece and Rome. His explanation was the Bhagavadgita and its doctrine of non-attachment. Whereas other nations had their attachments to determinate forms and doctrines which had their day and passed, India's non-attachment to determinate codes and principles and her attachment instead only to the intuitively felt, all-embracing immediacy in its timelessness and formlessness which is Brahman, has enabled India to persist.

Practically this means, when a dispute arises, that one does not settle it by recourse to determinate legal principles, but pursues the Buddhist-Gita "middle way" between the determinate theses of the disputants, by fostering the all-embracing intuitively felt formlessness common to all men and things. Precisely what this all-embracing Brahman-self is will become clearer in subsequent chapters as we meet it under the same or other names in one Asian community and context after another. Not legal principles of a world or domestic community made effective by the force of police action, but inexpressible intuitive feeling is the way to peace. As Gandhiji wrote in his diary a few days before his assassination, "I dreamt the dream of communal unity of the heart." [7]

Nor is this Buddhist-Gita technique of peace peculiar to Gandhiji's India. We shall find in the sequel Chiang Monlin telling us that it is the way also of the pre-Western Confucian China of his youth. Buddhist Ceylon agrees also. On January

20, 1951, the *Ceylon Daily News* contained the following letter
to its editor:

> Your leader in Tuesday's issue on the Commonwealth's peace
> move, under the caption "The Middle Way" was quite apt and
> commendable. Many a realist thinker will, I hope, agree with me
> in believing that at last a way has been found to solve or at least to
> ease the present tension in international affairs, which has almost
> led to a Third World War. As you have stated this new move owes
> its initiative to the three Asian countries and especially to . . .
> Ceylon's Premier, Mr. Senanayke.
>
> . . . The Four Powers comprise the now opposing blocks—the
> Anglo-American and the Sino-Russian. So far we haven't a single
> instance where a meeting of this kind has succeeded. Both parties
> appeared unyielding and uncompromising. . . . You have quite
> correctly stated that "we are justified in suggesting that it would
> have a livelier prospect of success if Shri Jawaharlal Nehru were
> present at the discussions so that the new approach based on the
> philosophy of the 'middle way' may be kept continuously and effec-
> tively in view."

This illustrates not merely the new Gandhian technique for
peace of which Prime Minister Nehru spoke to the Congress of
the United States, but also, as the sequel will show, the spiritual
source of the unity of non-Aryan, non-Western Buddhist-Gita,
Taoist, Confucian Asia. As the very distinguished Japanese,
Kakasu Okakura, says in the first sentence of his book, *The
Ideals of the East*,[8] "Asia is one." The Hindu Swami Nevedita
of Calcutta echoes this judgment. Both the Japanese and the
Indian find this unity in an underlying identity of the basic
Hindu, Buddhist, Taoist, Confucian and Japanese Bushido doc-
trines of India, Tibet, Burma, Indo-China, China, Korea and
Japan.

To be sure there are differences also. As will become evident
later, there are Aryan contributions from the West in Hinduism
which do not occur in any other of these Far Eastern cultures.
Similarly there is a Shinto addition in Japanese Bushido not
present in Korea, China or any of the Buddhist, Hindu nations
to the south. Also the basic, intuitively known factor common
to all men and things, in which Gandhi found the religious

source of his politics and from which the Buddha's middle path and the Confucian distrust of law and litigation derives, may be pursued in different ways. When it is pursued in and for itself, the yoga practices of Hinduism, the retreats and monasteries of Buddhism, the non-action of Taoism and Gandhi's prayer meetings and calm, quiet early morning periods of devotion arise. When this factor is pursued with respect to its practical implications for the settling of disputes and the creation of warmheartedness between men, the mediational technique common to all these eastern nations and the man-to-manness of Confucianism, which is called *jen,* become emphasized. Thus the practical concern and worldliness of the Chinese, which so many point to as evidence for a radical difference between Confucianism and the other Oriental philosophies, is merely an evidence of a greater emphasis by the Chinese upon the practical implications of the common Asian doctrine.

In any event, India's leaders of every political party, and the masses also, feel, express and act upon the assumption that Asia is one.

On May 15, 1951, the inauguration of the Indo-China Friendship Association occurred in Bombay. Of the occasion *Blitz* wrote four days later:

The meeting swelled into a rally; the rally became a demonstration; the demonstration climaxed into a thousand-throated chorus thundering the song of India-China friendship. As the President put it, we were witness to the birth of a new power in the Orient. . . . The power of the people of India and China and the whole of Asia united, resurgent, invincible, almighty!

That the Communistic Chinese who were present held a philosophy which was the very antithesis of the spiritual roots of the unity of traditional Asia did not matter. The old Asian tie was stronger than contemporary ideological differences imported from the West.

To be sure, this is the Communists' *Blitz* speaking. The leaders of every Indian political party, however, echo this same Asian feeling. Two sensitive and observant young Americans who spent several months recently in intimate contact with Indians in the villages have written:

. . . the Asian half of the human race [is] . . . fundamentally anti-Western . . . in any world struggle Indian opinion will emotionally incline against the West. If that struggle pitted America and England against China, nearly every Indian would feel the pull of an almost irresistible racial [cultural would be the better word] loyalty.[9]

This emotional antipathy to the West presents an apparent paradox. For all its intuitive, open-hearted toleration and its "middle way," Gandhiji's and the traditional Asian's moral way to peace is not neutral. It takes a side; the intuitive Asian side.

Nor should this surprise us. For Buddhist-Gita-Taoist Confucianism is a particular philosophy of the spiritual roots of human nature. As we shall see when we examine the spiritual foundations of Western civilization, there is another philosophy and religion of the spiritual which prescribes as the essential and just method for settling disputes and achieving a peaceful social order the use of determinate laws before which all men are equal and by means of which all breakers of the peace are judged and with police power restrained and punished.

Prime Minister Nehru gave expression to the latter conception of the way to peace, rather than the Gandhian one, in his address to the Congress of the United States when he said, "We have to meet aggression and to resist it and the force employed must be adequate to the purpose." It is interesting to note that in his domestic policy the latter way to peace was used and that in his foreign policy Gandhiji's way has been followed, except with respect to the princely states and Pakistan. In Hyderabad, Kashmir and the other princely states, New Delhi moved in with its army. And with respect to Kashmir and Pakistan, Prime Minister Nehru insists absolutely on the letter of the law.

Gandhiji's opposition to the use of law implemented with police power is dramatically illustrated in his attitude toward both the West and Western law. Notwithstanding his training in England as a lawyer, he writes of his early period in South Africa as follows: "I . . . deplored . . . the civilization of

which the Natal whites were the fruit. . . . Western civilization . . . [is], unlike the Eastern, predominantly based on
force." [10] Speaking of his Christian friends there and of Christianity, he adds: "We knew the fundamental differences between us. Any amount of discussion could not efface them." [11]

On the next page of his *Autobiography,* in answer to the
question of how he would stand by his "principle of non-
violence" if the whites carried out their threats to attack him,
he wrote: "I hope God will give me the courage and the sense
to forgive them and to refrain from bringing them to law." [12]
At the beginning of his period in South Africa, Gandhi found
himself about to win his first major case for his client, Dada
Abdulla. Of the latter experience he writes as follows:

I saw that the facts of Dada Abdulla's case made it very strong indeed, and that the law was bound to be on his side. But I also saw
that the litigation, if it were persisted in, would ruin the plaintiff
and the defendant, who were relatives and both belonged to the
same city. . . . I became disgusted with the profession. As lawyers
the counsel on both sides were bound to rake up points of law in
support of their own clients. . . . This was more than I could
bear. I felt that my duty was to befriend both parties and bring
them together. I strained every nerve to bring about a compromise.
. . . An arbitrator was appointed, the case was argued before him,
and Dada Abdulla won.

But that did not satisfy me. If my client were to seek immediate
execution of the award, it would be impossible for Tyeb Sheth to
meet the whole of the awarded amount, . . . There was only one
way. Dada Abdulla should allow him to pay in moderate instalments. . . . It was more difficult for me to secure this concession of
payment by instalments than to get the parties to agree to arbitra-
tion. But both were happy over the result, and both rose in public
estimation. My joy was boundless. I had learnt the true practice of
law. I had learnt to find out the better side of human nature and
to enter men's hearts. I realized that the true function of a lawyer
was to unite parties riven asunder.[13]

Chiang Monlin and Francis S. Liu make it clear, as Chapter
VII will show, that this emphasis upon mediation rather than
legal codes and litigation is the way to settle disputes in pre-

Western Confucian China. In Buddhist Thailand even today the same attitude prevails notwithstanding the imposition from above of a French continental type of codified law.[14]

This does not mean that Buddhist-Gita India, Thailand and Confucian China do not have codes. They do. But the attitude toward them is entirely different from that of the West. The proper way is not to use codes, but mediation. The code is regarded as an evil to be used as a last resort for settling disputes between immoral men when the moral way to the settling of disputes by the intuitive feeling and mediation fails. It is to be emphasized that Aryan Hinduism is to be distinguished from Gandhiji's Buddhist-Gita Hinduism. The former has codes, castes and a foreign policy of power politics, as will be shown later.

But what, it may be asked, is the connection between Gandhiji's antipathy to law with its physical police action as a way to peace and his Buddhist-Gita religion from which he says it derives? Two statements by Gandhi will lead to the answer to this question.

If India takes up the doctrine of the sword, she may gain momentary victory. Then India will cease to be the pride of my heart. I am wedded to India because I owe my all to her. I believe absolutely that she has a mission for the world. . . . There are eternal principles which admit of no compromise, and one must be prepared to lay down one's life in the practice of them.[15]

I think it is wrong to expect certainties in this world, where all else but God that is Truth is an uncertainty. All that appears and happens about and around us is uncertain, transient.[16]

How is the certainty involved in the laying down of one's life for eternal principles of the first statement to be reconciled with the emphasis upon uncertainty and the transient nature of knowledge of his second conviction? The answer is to be found in the Gita and connects the religion of the latter with his antipathy to legal principles and codes.

He into whom all objects of desire enter, as waters enter the ocean, which, (though) replenished, (still) keeps its position unmoved,—

he only obtains tranquillity; . . . he who . . . lives free from attachments . . . obtains . . . the Brahmic state. . . .[17] [Such actions] defile . . . [one] not, [since the] acts of one who is devoid of attachment, who is free, . . . are all destroyed.[18]

This inexhaustible supreme self, being without beginning and without qualities, does not act, and is not tainted, . . . though stationed in the body.[19]

It is, moreover, "separated from . . . all qualities, neither this nor that, without form, without a name, it cannot be told." [20] In short, the absolute "principle" for which one will lay down one's life is not in the strict sense of the word a principle at all since it cannot be expressed in words or laws, being formless, without any qualities or predicates. Conversely, anything that can be said or expressed in terms of a definite code or law is uncertain, referring only to the qualities and things which are transient. Hence laws cannot be made the basis for settling disputes except as a last resort with men who are unreasonable. Trust must be put instead in the intuitively felt formlessness which is Brahman that is common to the transient rights and differences of the disputants. No code can express this common factor since it is formless. It can be found only by intuition and warmly felt communion of spirit. From this standpoint to appeal to law merely entrenches the disputants in an insistence upon their transitory, determinate rights and differences, thereby increasing discord and conflict rather than removing it.

But what is this inexpressible Brahman? "An ocean is that one seer, without any duality; this is the Brahma-world, O King." [21] Thus answers one of Gandhi's Hindu Upanishads. Put more concretely, what this means is that Brahman is the totality or ocean of immediacy embracing each particular thing or wave which comes and goes within it. To soften down, therefore, the transitory rights and differences which legal codes express and to bring into the foreground of warm feeling the common inexpressible universal formlessness, the same in each person, which is the Brahma-self, is Gandhi's way to peace.

Every villager of India who has absorbed the oral tradition

that has come down over the centuries to him through hymns and story tellers is immersed in this intuitively immediate, inexpressible formlessness out of which man comes as a transitory form at birth and into which he fades at death. The ordering of a theoretically directed world by means of legally drawn contracts, constitutions or charters is alien to the Asian of the villages. But this Buddhist-Gita intuition of the all-embracing formlessness which is Brahman or Nirvana, he knows. This is why the last thing Gandhi said to his country's leaders before he died was: "Go to the villages" [22] and identify yourselves with those whom you find there. The villagers knew by intuition the religion which was the source of Gandhi's politics. Moreover, they responded to his politics by the hundreds upon hundreds of millions, because, as the contemporary Indian Nirad C. Chaudhuri has recently shown, Gandhiji tapped the constant, indigenous Asian values which were there even before the coming of the ancient Aryan conquerors, and which have persisted through the ages unharmed by ancient Aryan, medieval Muslim, or modern British influences from the West. He writes:

. . . before politics could become capable of rousing the masses of India . . . it had to become identified with the intuitive, timeless, and humble morality of the masses, that morality which . . . [is] as irresistible and pervasive as the dust of the Indo-Gangetic plain. This was the thing which constituted the lowest and simplest and common factor between Indians of all classes. . . . Mahatma Gandhi brought about this simplification and transformation of the nationalism of his country and by so doing was able to convert it into a mass movement, [thereby giving it] . . . a backing of sheer numbers which it had never had before.[23]

Such are the indigenously Asian spiritual roots of Gandhi's way to peace. By means of it he held the masses in his hands politically during India's fight for independence. Truly his politics did derive from his religion. He also captured Pandit Nehru in part. It was the part which was captured that explains India's foreign policy with respect to Korea and the response of India's and Asia's masses to this foreign policy.

There is more, however, to the contemporary mind of Asia than Gandhiji's technique and message. There are non-Gandhian elements. There are also the facts in daily experience which lead to Gandhiji's philosophy and religion. These too we must understand.

5

THE CONTEMPORARY MIND
OF ISLAM AND OF ASIA

The previous chapters have shown the response of Asia to the
action in Korea to be disheartening. Notwithstanding the fact
that Americans and Western Europeans are laying down their
lives in Korea in order that Asians may have the right to build
their social institutions in their own way, the response of most
Asiatic and many Islamic nations has been neutral if not positively hostile.

This unfavorable result is undoubtedly due in part to Asian
and Middle Eastern wishful thinking concerning the real nature
of North Korean, Chinese and Russian Communism. But this
is certainly not the sole cause. Prime Minister Nehru gives us a
clue to the underlying reason when he suggests that Western
nations continue to make decisions affecting the lives of Asians
without taking the mind of Asia into account.

It is obvious that any policy in Asia and the Middle East
must command the support of at least a majority of the people
if it is to be successful. We must therefore face and answer these
complicated questions: What do Asia and Islam think? And
why?

We have already come upon their idea of Western imperialism. The presence of any Western troops upon Asiatic or
Islamic soil, however good may be the reasons for their being
there, is suspect. Nearly every Far Eastern and Middle Eastern

country has experienced the imperialistic rule of some Western power. In many instances the Western power justified the presence of its army and its political administration there on the ground that the people in question were being protected from a worse invader. So the Korean war is not the first time that Western troops have been put in Asiatic countries for the protection of Asians.

We must recognize that the Muslims' and Asians' concept of Western imperialism has three components: (1) political, (2) economic and (3) cultural.

The political component is now generally recognized. Most Europeans and Americans accept the fact that the old days of Western political imperialism in the Middle East and Asia are over.

It is not so well realized that the era of economic imperialism too has passed. Unless this point is grasped, their uneasiness about the acceptance of Point Four aid and the much-needed importation of American investment capital will not be understood. Informed Islamic and Asian leaders fear that to accept technological and financial aid is to place themselves under the direction of Westerners.

The cultural component in the fear of Western imperialism is the one least understood by Europeans or Americans. Witness General MacArthur's suggestion of the Christianization of Japan. Recall the frequent public demand for a "hard-hitting Voice of America" which will convert the rest of the world to the American way of life. All such suggestions strike the Asian as demonstrating that America and the West are withholding a political imperialism and slightly restraining an economic one merely to impose an even more dangerous cultural imperialism.

It is not that information about America is not wanted. What Asians object to is not so much the culture as the cultural pressure. When they take from the West, they want to choose what they take in their own good time, in their own way. Already Western and American ways of life and value have poured into Islam and Asia to a greater extent than either can digest. Additional proposals of loudspeaker pressure merely increase their difficulty and augment their negative and even hostile reaction.

But even more important is the fact that Muslims and Asians must also be themselves. They have civilizations and cultural values and ways of life of their own, thousands of years old. These native beliefs, values and habits they cannot throw off even if they would.

So far in this chapter we have spoken of Islam and Asia together. It now becomes necessary to separate the two. The mentality of Islam stems from the prophet Muhammad and embraces Arabian, Persian and Turkish components. This Islamic mentality holds sway from the northwest tip of Africa, opposite Gibraltar, eastward by way of Egypt through the entire Middle East, Pakistan and Indonesia to the Philippines.

The mentality of Asia proper rises out of Hinduism, Buddhism, Taoism and Confucianism. This Far Eastern mentality embraces present-day India (except for her remaining Muslim minority), Tibet, Burma, Thailand, Ceylon, Bali, Indo-China, China, Korea and Japan. The four Far Eastern religions and philosophies provide the basis of Santha Rama Rau's recent discovery in this area of what she aptly terms "the solidarity between Asians." [1] This solidarity is to be distinguished from the solidarity of Islam as well as from the influence of Western nationalism whether the latter be exerted by the free democracies or by Marxist Soviet Communism.

If we study recent developments in the Middle and Far Eastern areas we see that the Muslims and Asians are not pursuing nationalist aspirations as the Westerner understands them. They are working toward the resurgence of their respective submerged civilizations. What Western reporters have described as the coming of Western nationalism to the Middle East and Asia is really the return of Islamic or Far Eastern ways and values. For example, at the present moment Pakistan's legal thinkers are throwing out in considerable part at least the law codes they inherited from the British and replacing them with Muhammadan law as laid down in the Quran. It is culturalism rather than nationalism that is the rising fact of the world today.

The contemporary mind of both Islam and Asia has set itself the task of revivifying its own particular cultural traditions and then ingrafting from the West the factors needed to raise the standard of living of the masses. Hence the crucial question arises for both Islam and Asia: Which West—that of the free democracies or that of Marxist Communism?

The final decision on this question will be made by the Asians themselves. They will be guided partly by force and circumstance and partly by persuasion. The probabilities are that the victory will go to that Western ideology with the deepest and most sympathetic understanding of the mentalities of Islam and Asia.

The way of life which we call Western civilization stems from two sources: the religion of the Old and New Testaments; the science and philosophy of the Greeks. Islam has the same two sources and adds to them the revelation of God through Muhammad as recorded in the Quran.

Just as the Christian regards the New Testament with its story of Jesus as the fulfillment of the Old Testament of the Jews with its account of Moses and the prophets, so the followers of Islam regard the Quran with its record of God's revelation to Muhammad as the completion of the revelation of God to man initiated with Moses and carried forward by Jesus. This explains the failure of the Christian missionaries to convert many Muhammadans. The Muhammadan believes that he has within his own religion all the values which Judaism and Christianity can offer and additional divine knowledge as well.

The mentality of Islam is grasped in its essentials, therefore, when the beliefs common to the three Semitic religions— Judaism, Christianity and Islam—are specified and when the unique revelations which Islam believes God to have given man through Muhammad are added. We find two basic common principles: First, both nature and man are the creation of an omniscient and omnipotent personal God who is immortal and *determinate* in character. (By *determinate* is meant anything

definite with characteristics different from those possessed by
something else. For example, the sensed sun has the determinate
shape of a circular disc, and this page has the determinate
shape of a rectangle.) Second, each individual person has a determinate immortal soul, different from that of any other
person.

But beyond this Islam also believes that God merits and desires in this world a much more active and immanent role in
daily life than Judaism or Christianity have given to Him either
in theory or in practice. To the Muhammadan the separation of
church and state in Protestant Christianity and in modern Western political liberalism is the rankest heresy, resulting in the
forceful conduct of international relations uncontrolled by
religious or ethical principles. The Muhammadan affirms that,
in this matter, Roman Catholicism differs from Protestant Christianity only in degree rather than in kind.

The essential connection between the military and the religious in Islam has often been noted. To Islam this identification
of the military with the religious is good and but another proof
of the immanence of God, how He operates through His followers every day of the week in every phase of their daily
activity.

Another Islamic characteristic is the conception of religion
as passion as well as reason, a conception that the Moors left
behind them when they were driven out of Spain, and which
distinguishes the Roman Catholicism of Spain (and Mexico,
too) from that of Italy and France as the Spaniard, Salvador de
Madariaga, has noted.[2]

With a repetition which impresses the Christian reader as
monotonous, the Quran rings out a solitary theme: "There is
no God but God." Muhammad adjures his followers:

O ye people of the Book! do not exceed in your religion, nor say
against God aught save the truth. The Messiah, Jesus the son of
Mary, is but the apostle of God and His Word, which He cast into
Mary and a spirit from Him; believe then in God and His apostles,
and say not "Three." Have done! it were better for you. God is only
one God. . . .[3]

This pure, unqualified monotheism shows in any mosque of Islam. There are no idols, images or symbols. There is no written mark or sign except for the script, "There is no God but God."

The belief of Muhammadans, Christians and Jews that both God and the immortal soul of man are determinate in character has the practical consequence of making the moral man in any sphere of action one who commits his will to, and if necessary gives his life for, certain determinate principles. This is part at least of the significance of Socrates' drinking of the hemlock and Christ's death on the Cross.

From this conception of God and man and from the discovery in Greek science and philosophy that each individual fact or event is an instance of technically formulated universal laws there arose the Western concept of justice. For Islam, then, as for the West, justice consists in governing individual persons and disputes under codes, commandments or rules which are assumed to be universal and which make all men equal before the law.

The Far Eastern concept of the Divine is foreign to the Western mind. To grasp its significance we must wrench ourselves away from all our previous beliefs and conceptions and think in terms of what we immediately observe.

Let us begin by concentrating our attention upon what we experience directly with our own senses. This is part of what we can call immediacy. Let us consider the sky and recall what we see—not what we have been told and learned—through the course of twenty-four hours. Let us begin, as do the Hindus, before dawn.

What we see then is an all-embracing blackness which we call night. Gradually this blackness thins out. It becomes thinner and thinner. Streaks of brightness appear more in one place in the all-embracing immediacy than in another. Gradually a thin bright curved shape appears. This curved shape becomes larger and larger until it takes on the form of a semicircle. Then it increases its size, becoming narrower and narrower at its lower edge until it is a yellow, flaming circular patch surrounded by the all-embracing brightness which we call the light of day. At one point this brightness is overhead and reaches its utmost intensity. This event the men who first saw it called noon. Then the brightness grows thinner and thinner. Finally comes the dusk with the shrinking and final disappearance of the yellow circular patch. Forthwith there is the all-embracing darkness again.

This cyclical sequence goes on and on and on. It never ceases. However much any other directly observed events may vary from time to time and surprise us, this sequence of night and day from darkness to brightness and then back to darkness again never fails.

One notes, moreover, that the flaming yellow patch called the sun rises at a different point on the horizon each morning From morning to morning the point at which it appears marches across the sky, creating another cycle which brings it back to its starting point. This second cycle the first primitive man who looked at nature called the year.

In the darkness of night he also noted another two-dimensional patch in the sky sometimes crescent in shape, sometimes a semicircle, sometimes a full circle. This he called the moon. This too he found to move through a cycle which we call a month.

Then man looked at man. He saw his childhood, the springtime of life. He saw the growth to middle age, the summer of life. He saw the decline from middle age, the fall of life. And he saw this decline accelerate until death, the winter of life. But he also saw this sequence pick up again in the next generation. Cycles, he concluded, are everywhere. Thus there arose one of the basic beliefs about man and nature of Far Eastern mentality: the cyclical theory of time.

To discover, as we have, the observable evidence for this theory is to appreciate the Asian's lack of enthusiasm for the improvement of human and earthly conditions which seemed so vital a moral value to nineteenth century Westerners and which is so evident to most contemporary Americans. In Chinese

Taoism the deprecation of the life of action is explicit. The Taoist classics teach that the best action is non-action. In a similar vein the Hindu Bhagavadgita affirms that the only moral attitude toward the worldly deeds in which one participates is that of non-attachment and of indifference to the outcome.

Now we can understand how it is that in the very heart of Hindu India's most sacred temples at Benares the sacred cows and priests, both indifferently cleaned, walk, squat and meditate unperturbed amidst the dirt and filth of this very earthy world. Gandhi, who can hardly be charged with prejudice in this matter, referring to Indians in his *Autobiography*, writes of

. . . our indifference to the laws of hygiene and sanitation, our slowness in keeping our surroundings clean and tidy, and our stinginess in keeping our houses in good repair. . . .[4]

and describes his visit to the Hindu temples of Benares as follows:

Numerous Brahmans surrounded me, as soon as I got out of the train, and I selected one who struck me to be comparatively cleaner and better than the rest. . . . I went to the Kashi Vishvanath temple for *darshan*. I was deeply pained by what I saw there. . . . The swarming flies and the noise made by the shopkeepers and pilgrims were perfectly insufferable.

Where one expected an atmosphere of meditation and communion, it was conspicuous by its absence. . . . I did observe devout sisters, who were absorbed in meditation, entirely unconscious of the environment. . . . When I reached the temple, I was greeted at the entrance by a stinking mass of rotten flowers. . . . The floor was paved with fine marble, which was however broken by some devotee innocent of aesthetic taste who had set it with rupees serving as an excellent receptacle for dirt. . . . The surroundings of the *Jnana-vapi* too I found to be dirty. . . .

Since then I have twice been to Kashi Vishvanath, . . . the dirt and the noise were the same as before.[5]

At holy Hardvar and Hrishikesh and even in "the sacred water of the Ganges" the dirt, Gandhi writes, of "people performing natural functions . . . filled me with agony."[6] The traditional

Hindu blandly accepts the ugliness of the world around him and usually aims merely to attain spiritual equanimity within it.

Gandhi again says in his *Autobiography* that it was from Ruskin's *Unto This Last* that he got the idea

That the life of labour [and action], i.e., the life of the tiller of the soil and the handicraftsman, is the life worth living.

This idea of action and labor being a primary value, he adds, "had never occurred to me," [7] notwithstanding all his mastery of the values of the Buddhist and Hindu classics. Thus Asian values alone, Gandhi tells us, simply did not give him the motive to transform the actual world of daily life by belief, action and labor.

If the nature of things is such that everything runs in a cycle, coming back at some later date to precisely where it is now, what is the point in trying to change the present state of affairs? One merely hastens, if this be possible, the time when tomorrow becomes today. A very wise Christian missionary in Thailand may have been right when he said to me, "There will be no end to the corruption that accompanies the Asians' casual handling of Western reforms so long as the Asians retain their cyclical theory of time." This does not mean that there is no corruption in handling reforms in the West. Its occurrence there is due, however, to causes other than the pointlessness of change because of belief in the cyclical theory of time.

More than the cyclical theory of time is, however, behind the tendency of Buddhist-Gita Asian values to aim at equanimity within the world as it is rather than at the transformation of that world. There is also the traditional Asian thesis that all definite, determinate things are transitory. If this be the last word, then there is little point in learning the determinate scientific laws necessary for the effective transformation of these things. Being transitory and fleeting they are not deserving of unswerving attachment on the part of man, himself in part a transitory phenomenon. Non-Aryan Hindu or Buddhist or Taoist Asian mentality acknowledges only one thing in man

and nature to which attachment should be absolute. This is
Brahman or Nirvana or their Taoist equivalent.

We can pass from the directly observed cyclical sequence of
phenomena to the meaning of Brahman or Nirvana by means
of the words of the Bhagavadgita:

On the advent of day, all perceptible things are produced from
the unperceived; and on the advent of night they dissolve in . . .
the unperceived. This same assemblage of entities, being produced
again and again, dissolves on the advent of night, and . . . issues
forth on the advent of day, without a will of its own. But there is
another entity, . . . which is not destroyed when all entities are
destroyed. It is . . . the indestructible. . . . Attaining to it, none
returns.[8]

To grasp the full meaning of this description of immediacy,
we must distinguish within the totality of immediacy between
the sensed objects or qualities which are known with immediacy
by means of the senses, and the remainder of immediacy, out of
which the sensed objects or qualities arise and into which they
dissolve. This remainder of immediacy, within which the transitory sensed objects are immersed, is not given by the senses.
In fact, the senses are themselves transitory differentiations of
the immediacy out of which they, like their objects, arise and
into which they also dissolve. This remainder of immediacy,
other than the sensing and the objects sensed, is what the foregoing passage from the Gita calls "the unperceived." It is unperceived in the sense of not being perceived by the senses, but
it is not unperceived in the sense of not being existentially immediate.

Furthermore, it must not be thought of as an object of immediate consciousness other than the knower. It is that out of
which the transitory subjective sensing arises and into which
it dissolves as much as it is that out of which the objects sensed
arise and into which they dissolve. In fact it is in itself both
the subject of consciousness and the object and neither, since,
being formless immediacy without qualities to distinguish one
portion of it from another, there is no difference in it and hence

no distinction between subject and object. In other words, it is undifferentiated immediacy consciousness, called in Hinduism *Chit* consciousness,[9] and termed in my *Meeting of East and West*[10] "the undifferentiated aesthetic continuum." The word "aesthetic" was used there in the sense of immediacy, but not in the sense of sensed immediacy. Failure to note this difference caused several Asian and Western scholars to misinterpret what *The Meeting of East and West* affirmed. *Chit* consciousness, or in other words the undifferentiated aesthetic continuum, is to be distinguished from sensing subjective immediacy consciousness and sensed immediate consciousness of sensed objects, which are its differentiations. Thus the totality of immediacy made up of the *Chit* consciousness together with the subjective and objective differentiations which mask it is appropriately called "the undifferentiated aesthetic continuum."[11] The *Chit* consciousness, apart from the subjective and objective qualities which mask it, is, according to Gandhi's Buddhist-Hindu Gita, one's true self and God. It is to be noted, therefore, that in this immediacy intuition of divinity one's true self is identical with the true self of all other men and is identical with God. This is why there is no immortality of the differentiated individual person in this non-Aryan Hinduism.

We can think of Brahman or Nirvana, therefore, as the ocean of immediacy which is the immortal formless (because undifferentiated) part of man, within which the subjective sensing part of man is a wave and the sensed object is another wave. The waves come and go, but the ocean which is the immortal part of man never ceases to be. The sensing and sensed part of a man lives and dies, but Brahman, his true self, is formless and timeless and hence "escapes the ravages of death." To the Hindu, Brahman is as immediate and therefore as directly apprehended a part of the world and of one's self as is anything which is born and dies, even though its immediacy is not given through the senses. What is Brahman in Gandhiji's non-Aryan, Buddhist Hinduism is Nirvana in Buddhism, Tao in Taoism, and the source of *jen,* the intuitively felt man-to-manness, in Confucianism. There are, to be sure, important differences between these philosophies and religions. It is often argued that Chinese Confucianism has very little in common with the other three. Confucianism, according to this view, seems hardly to be a religion as we understand the term; it has almost no other worldly content, confining itself to practical maxims on the sensible conduct of life in this world.

Such a conclusion, however, requires supplementation in two ways. First, while the major concern of Confucianism is with practical human relations, it is essential to Confucianism that practical affairs will be on an effective basis only when all men are infused with the spirit of *jen* and this spirit of *jen,* although radically different from the Christian deity, is unequivocally religious in the sense of Brahman above as experienced in an intuitive natural piety and in warm human relations. The contemporary Confucian, Chiang Monlin, former Vice Chancellor of Peking University and present associate of Chiang Kai-shek in Formosa, writing of his Confucian youth says:

Moral ideas were driven into the people by every possible means—temples, theatres, homes, toys, proverbs, schools, history, and stories —until they became habits in daily life . . . [and even festivals and parades] were always religious in character.[12]

Second, this religious character of all the moral manifestations of Confucian culture has its source in an immediately felt factor in nature. Thus, Chiang Monlin continues: "From nature the Chinese learns the sublime nature of man."[13] Describing his experience at the top of the Confucian Temple of Heaven in Peking, Chiang Monlin adds: "I . . . felt as if heaven, earth and myself merged in one vastness. . . . Nature and man are one and inseparable."[14] This "one vastness," with the different objects within it neglected, is the same all-embracing ocean of immediacy which is the Brahman of Hinduism and the Nirvana of Buddhism. It is the constant theme also of Buddhist-Taoist-Confucian landscape painting.[15] The Chinese, to be sure, are essentially a this-worldly and practical people. But as Chiang

Monlin says: "The Chinese is contented with his immediate world and has never wanted to speculate far and deep in nature." [16] He is contented also more with enjoying immediacy than transforming it.

Moreover Confucianism in China is merged with Taoism and Buddhism. Both Taoism and Buddhism are definitely religious. Also Taoism and Zen Buddhism are creations of the Chinese. Furthermore, Confucianism shares with Hinduism, Buddhism and Taoism an emphasis upon peace-making by the give and take of mediation. For our purposes, therefore, in analyzing a subject as vastly complicated as the mind of Asia, the differences separating Confucianism and the other Far Eastern ways of life are less important than the similarities uniting them.

We have already come upon the Asian concept of the Divine in Hindu India's most influential epic, the Bhagavadgita, which tells how Arjuna finds himself on the field of battle about to kill members of his own clan on his enemy's side. He recalls the teaching of his Hindu sages which brands the taking of the life of any creature—human or animal—as evil. To Arjuna in his quandary the God Krishna appears and to Krishna he puts his problem: Since to act is evil, should he act? Krishna answers: The good is not to act.

The good is to dedicate one's self to the indeterminate, all-embracing immediacy which is Brahman and to give up determinate desires and actions, treating them as the worldly and transitory things which they are. But man is in part transitory and determinate as well as in part the indeterminate, unlimited formlessness which is his true self or Brahman. Thus man on earth must acquiesce in the transitory, determinate earthly state of affairs as well as the timeless, divine formlessness. Hence Krishna tells Arjuna that he must act.

However, his action must be of a particular kind. To act so as to accept the world, cherishing the victory of battle or regretting the defeat which it may bring, is evil. This is to turn the relative and the transitory into the absolute and the timeless.

Arjuna's action will be good, Krishna tells him, only if he acts with non-attachment. In other words, one accepts the determinate, earthly deeds and facts of life for whatever they may be, ugly or beautiful, with indifference or non-attachment. One is in the dirt of the world, but not of it.

Buddhist Thailand and Ceylon illustrate the Asian mentality in another way. In every city and village there are Buddhist temples, and within each temple there sits the image of the Buddha himself, legs crossed, body erect, eyes half closed, benign, compassionate, calmly joyful, spreading the equanimity and the beauty which is the formless, immediately felt Nirvana over everyone and everything around him. Every vivid color, noise and odor is there about him, untouched, unaltered. Into all this earthly, transitory, richly sensuous concreteness he brings a timeless divine serenity.

This Thai Buddhist sense of the beautiful is so rich in the diversity of its coloration that initially it shocks the Westerner with its lusciousness and richness. The different artistic manifestations of India's Hinduism and of China's Buddhist-Taoist-Confucianism have the same effect.

However, we should now be able to understand without being shocked, for we have already noted that nature too is a cyclical sequence of flaming reds and yellows and of contrasting brightness and darkness. It is in addition the differentiated mass of brilliant colors, clanging sounds, contrasting flavors and pungent odors which at any moment of the day we can, if we will, sense it to be.

To put the matter in Western terms, the Oriental approach to nature is that of the modern French impressionist with his rich continuum of diverse colors and fuzzy shapes rather than that of the classical Western artist with his three-dimensional, sharply contoured solid persons and objects. As Confucius put this difference, "There is no one who does not eat and drink. But few there are who really know flavor." [17] The Asian mind, whether Confucian, Taoist, Hindu or Buddhist, focuses attention on the flavors before merging himself and them in the all-embracing vastness out of and into which the transitory part of himself and they come and go.

From this focus of attention upon the aesthetic fragrance and quality of experience arises the softness, the tenderness, the refinement and lightness of touch of the Chinese and much Buddhist art. From the all-embracing formlessness or vastness arises also the moving beauty of the compassion of the Buddha which is the divine Nirvana. They savor experience rather than devour or manipulate it.

In their concern with the diverse, vivid, aesthetic qualities and objects which are apprehended directly by the senses, they note that all of them die. Each color appears only to vanish. Each sound speaks and then ends. So with the dawn, the brightness of day, dusk and even darkness. So with all sensed creatures and things. So even with the *determinate* individual person himself.

From this obvious fact of the death and transitoriness of all determinate things, the Far Eastern Oriental draws a far-reaching moral implication. This moral implication is that any rule built out of determinate meanings, whether it be a rule of law for society, a rule of personal conduct or a rule of religion, must by the very nature of the meaning of its terms, be something that cannot hold at all times for all men under all circumstances. As Gandhi has told us before,

I think it is wrong to expect certainties in this world, where all else but God [i.e., the all-embracing formlessness which is Brahman] . . . is an uncertainty. All that appears and happens about and around us, is uncertain, transient.[18]

In short, there cannot be timeless, determinate rules of conduct since all determinate things are transitory.

The Far Eastern Asian concludes, therefore, that to use determinate rules to settle disputes between men regardless of time, place, person or circumstance is to act immorally. What is moral for tomorrow depends on tomorrow's facts and circumstances and these we will not know until tomorrow comes. Determinate rules are relative to persons, circumstances and occasions. Moreover they are built out of meanings derived from determinate facts which are transitory. Hence they are things to be compromised through mediation between the disputants.

Clearly there is a basic difference in the conception of legal and moral action between the Far East and either Islam or the West. This difference centers in the fact that the Far East *per se*, apart from ancient Aryan, medieval Muslim, or modern British influences, tends to conceive of the Divine and what is common to all men as indeterminate or formless, whereas Islam and the West regard it as determinate or fixed. As Gandhi writes: "A votary of [the Hindu doctrine of] *ahimsa* . . . remains true to his faith if the spring of all his actions is compassion, . . . underlying *ahimsa* is the unity of all life. . . . When two nations are fighting, the duty of a votary of *ahimsa* is to stop the war. . . ." [19] What he clearly means by drawing upon compassion and "the unity" of all life to stop war is an appeal to the inexpressible, intuitively felt Brahman formlessness which makes all men and nature one rather than an appeal to determinate moral legal or religious principles, against which disputants are measured to distinguish between the guilty and the innocent. Contrast this with the concept of justice in the Old Testament, Islam and the Christian and Roman West with their determinate moral commandments used in the settling of disputes, whereby all men are measured and made equal before a common law and the virtuous are distinguished from the sinful. For the Gandhian Asian there are the sinful also, but they are those who insist upon their legal rights and do not mediate and compromise.

Even so, Protestant Christianity with its doctrine of toleration and freedom of religious belief, Western science with its tentative acceptance of theories, and liberal Western democracy with its free debate of definite alternatives followed by compromise as given in a majority vote, have much in common with this Asian concept of the moral and social leader.

Certainly no mentality is more completely Western and foreign to traditional Asian thought than Marxist Communism with its uncompromising determinate blueprint for man and society spelled out to the last letter after the manner of the determinate codes of constitutional Roman law or the Thomistic doctrine of Roman Catholicism. One must ask, therefore, why it was that Protestant democratic liberalism failed in China under Chiang Kai-shek and that Marxist Communism has temporarily at least succeeded. The major reasons are four in number.

First, the Communists give great initial attention to understanding any culture they hope eventually to take over, paying attention to its inner, basic beliefs and mentality as well as its outer needs and forms.

Second, they put themselves on the side of the resurgence and revivification of the indigenous cultural beliefs instead of merely imposing foreign ideas, as previous imperialisms have done. Every movement for the resurgence of Asia or of Islam is infiltrated and vigorously supported by Communists. For example, one of the most important centers for the spread of Communism in Islam is the oldest center of Islamic education, the El Azhar University in Cairo. Similarly, when the Communists took over Peking their parades thrilled hundreds of thousands of Chinese jamming the streets because the Communists were singing old Chinese folk songs. The Communists won China in part because they first made the Chinese feel that they were taking them back to their own traditions and making them vital Chinese and vital Asians rather than artificial imitations of Americans and Westerners.

Third, when the Communists turn to the introduction of their own mentality they begin not with a heavy gift of arms or of technicians or of money but with their Marxist ideas. This is why indoctrination is the essence of Communist practice. The Marxist knows that if you do not capture the mind anything else you do will not succeed.

Fourth, the Communists succeeded in China because Chiang

Kai-shek failed long before the Americans stopped backing him. He failed because he was unable, while under the pressures of instituting social reforms and resisting military invasion, to make compatible the doctrine of filial piety of his Chinese Confucianism with his Methodist Christianity and Western liberal constitutional nationalism. Filial piety places family obligation above loyalty to the nation and this inevitably leads to the enrichment in the name of nationalism of a few families and to a lack of integrity in the handling of national finances in the national interest. The continuation of the Communists' present hold on China will depend on whether they can overcome the incompatibility between the extreme loyalty to the community which Marxism requires and the Confucian primary loyalty to the family.

This primacy of the family over other determinate social obligations, like other elements in Asian mentality, goes back to facts in immediate experience. It is a fact that one cannot be a person without having had parents. This is a social relation that has to be, not one like other social relations which merely may be. Secondly, it is a fact that one's attachment to the members of one's family is stronger than one's feeling for strangers. Hence, to treat all men making up the entire community with a higher loyalty and emotional attachment than one gives to the intimates of one's own family or to one's parents is to falsify both nature and human nature and therefore to act immorally.

Even so, parents, sons, daughters and even families are mortal. Like other determinate things, they are transitory. Moreover, the determinate feelings and interests of one family are not necessarily those of another.

From these two immediately experienced facts of the transitoriness and relativity of all determinate things, the Far Eastern Asian, whether he be Confucian, Taoist, Buddhist or Gandhian Buddhist-Hindu, arrives at his conception of the superior man and the social leader as a mediator. This is the reason why Prime Minister Nehru carries most of non-Islamic Asia with him when he refuses to take sides in the Korean affair or in the

Western conflict between liberal democracy and Communist totalitarianism, and offers instead again and again the services of the compromiser and the mediator following "the middle path."

To Westerners the notion of an immortal, ineffable, indeterminate formlessness out of which one's determinate self comes as a transitory differentiation at birth, and into which it fades at death, seems at first to be the negation rather than the fulfillment of human and divine personality. The Muslim or the Westerner has never learned to think of himself or of God in other than determinate, definable terms. For him, for anything to be is for it to have definite properties. But the Orient's discovery of the all-embracing formlessness in one's self, in all other persons and things and in God cannot be dismissed. Moreover the Oriental tells us that to give up one's transitory determinate self for the realization of this all-embracing formlessness, which he terms Brahman, Nirvana, Tao or the source of *jen*, is not a loss of personality but a gain. This gain, he affirms, consists in passing from a personality with limited, transitory, fitful pleasures mixed with equally transitory pains and tragedies to a personality or consciousness which is unlimited or infinite and which therefore brings unlimited blissfulness.

The Communists have done their best to make the time in which we live a desperate and tragic one. For how tragic it is that these glorious civilizations which are Asia and Islam, now in resurgence, cannot draw at their leisure in their own way upon the equally glorious civilization of the Hebrew-Christian, Greco-Roman, modern liberalized West, and even upon Karl Marx's original thought, without having their hands and our hands forced by North Korean, Moscow and Peking Communists. But if the result of the present Communist behavior is not merely to call forth our military containment of their imperialistic materialism but also to drive the rest of us, East and West, to the deeper understanding of ourselves and of one another, perhaps all is not in vain.

If the result is the rediscovery and reaffirmation of our own liberalized, Hebrew-Christian, Greco-Roman concept of the divine and the just, together with the cultivation in ourselves of a vision of the Divine as passionate in feeling and forthright in deed as that of Islam and as ineffably immediate and infinitely blissful as that of Asia, perhaps we have been unnecessarily pessimistic about our times. For if this is what happens, then posterity may well look back upon our era as a period not of self-pity and lack of nerve but of world-embracing self-knowledge and enlargement of faith and courage.

6

THE DOMESTIC POLICY AND NEEDS OF FREE INDIA

India's domestic policy affects the rest of the world in two ways. First, like all Asian nations, she is not merely giving expression to Asian mentality but also choosing ways and values from the West. Second, she has economic and other needs which she alone, however great her efforts, cannot meet.

Previous chapters have shown India's foreign policy, especially with respect to the United Nations in Korea, to have been determined predominantly by Gandhi's way to peace and that this way derives from Gandhi's religion. Actual Hindu Indian culture, is, however, something much more than this. It involves a caste system, an incredible plurality of mortal, religious divinities, ruling Maharajas with fabulous wealth, a codified legal system as well as the intuitive mediational Gandhian method of settling disputes and a most brazen power politics ethics, the very antithesis of that for which Gandhiji stood. It will be recalled that Gandhi was able to make his Bhagavadgita support his way to peace only by ignoring its tribal and caste elements and its injunction by Lord Krishna to Arjuna that he (Arjuna) should not be a neutralist and non-participating pacifist in the battle confronting him, but should instead indulge in the force and slaughter of battle.

It was natural and inevitable, therefore, when Prime Minister Nehru's Congress Party accepted the responsibility for governing Free India on August 15, 1947, that they would have to pursue a domestic policy which operated with Hindu culture as it is in its entirety, rather than with the merely pacifistic Buddhist-Gita piece of it which Gandhi used as his canon for action. Gandhiji's way to peace by non-cooperation without recourse to backing with force might work very well, as it did to break the hold of the British on India, and as a norm with popular appeal in India for judging the United Nations and its majority supporters in Korea. But when applied to Free India, it failed with results that were tragic, notwithstanding all that Gandhi and his followers could do. Massacres of Hindus, Sikhs and Muslims broke out almost everywhere. Tens upon tens of thousands were butchered in cold blood. Constitutional processes backed by police power were required to bring the situation back into a semblance of order. Moreover a positive, definite program, not mere mediation between disputants with their respective conflicting programs, was required to transform and reform into federal unity what had been inherited from the British.

The mere intuitive approach of the mediator between disputants without recourse to the determinate legal principles of a specific constitution implemented with police power was not enough. Of necessity the new government was one of the disputants. For it to have remained merely an intuitive mediator would have left the situation in chaos. In fact it was in chaos.

For consider who the disputants would have been had the Congress Party Government not taken a firm line of its own about what the new India was to be and expressed this firm line in a new constitution backed with the police power not merely of the policeman but also of the Indian army. The disputants would have been and were Hindus, Muslims and Sikhs at one another's throats in bloody massacre. Even Gandhi's presence could save only pieces of the situation. He and his followers were quite impotent before the wave upon wave of hatred and bloodshed that burst forth. The non-Gandhian portion of Hinduism took over and he was assassinated by one of its hands.

The Aryan Hindu of the militant Mahasabha with his political ethics of codes and power politics, rather than of Gandhi's Buddhist-Gita non-caste, politically pacifistic purely Asian Hinduism, was making its rule of force and terror the law. Similarly, the Muslims of the Muslim League, whose ethics also was not that of Gandhi, were doing the same thing, although as Gandhi saw and said, they were far less to blame being in a minority of one to eight with respect to the Hindus.

Let no one have any misconception about what the political ethics of the Aryan Hindu is. To understand it, the four stages of life and the four castes must be kept in mind. All too many Westerners and Hindus interpreting Hinduism to the West equate Hinduism with but its Gandhiji, purely Asian Buddhist-Hindu portion. There is this latter component in actual Hinduism but it is, as the previous chapter has indicated, the purely indigenous part, identical for all practical purposes with Buddhism, Taoism and Confucianism. As the Indian sociologist, N. G. D. Joardar, the Indian student of history, Nirad C. Chaudhuri, and the distinguished Indian linguist, S. K. Chatterji, have indicated, to this purely Asian Gandhian component of Hinduism there was added at successive times in Indian history non-Asian contributions from the West.[1]

The first addition came around 1500 B.C. when the inhabitants representing the equivalent of the purely Asian pacifistic mediational Hinduism were conquered by the Aryans. Actual Hinduism is the synthesis resulting from this conquest. It combines the Sanskrit language, the codified legal method of settling disputes, the power politics theory and practice of the Aryan Western conquerors with the pacifistic Asian mediational way of settling disputes of the native Indian Asians. Dr. Joardar has pointed out that Buddhism with its emphasis upon pacifism and its rejection of caste occurred when the Aryan conquerors, established in the Ganges Valley, were attacked from, and forced to turn their attention back to the West. Sir C. P. Ramaswami Aiyar has pointed out also that in the Hindu Upanishads, written immediately after the Buddha's influence, caste is pushed aside and the man with true wisdom in the Hindu community is found in a very humble laborer lying on his back under a cart which he is repairing.[2]

The relationship is very complicated, but as a first approximation it can be said that the synthesis of these contradictory or at least radically different practices and norms of the native Indians and their Aryan conquerors was achieved by assigning the indigenous native Asian values to the top caste Brahmans with merely priestly teaching functions and by giving the method of settling disputes by legal codes, the police power necessary to make it effective and the power politics army to the second caste Aryan conquerors. Similarly in the life of each Aryan Hindu individual there are four stages called: studentship, householder, hermit and ascetic. Roughly to the first, third and fourth stages the more intuitive communion with the Hindu Brahman formlessness was assigned and to the householder stage of active life, comprising the period beyond the twenty-fifth year to the time when the eldest son takes over the responsibilities of the joint family, the more Aryan ritualistic and legalistic concern with determinate, worldly affairs, wealth and power was assigned.

The power politics of the Aryan Hindu politician is such as to make Machiavelli seem almost like a sweet little shepherd girl nursing a lamb. Its specifications for the ruler are given in the Hindu Laws of Manu, along with the more pacifistic values for the priest, and are as follows:

A king who, while he protects his people, is defied by (foes), be they equal in strength, or stronger, or weaker, must not shrink from battle, remembering the duty of Kshatriyas [i.e., his caste].

Not to turn back in battle, to protect the people, to honour the Brahmanas, is the best means for a king to secure happiness.

Those kings who, seeking to slay each other in battle, fight with the utmost exertion and do not turn back, go to heaven.

Chariots and horses, elephants, parasols, money, grain, cattle, women, all sorts of (marketable) goods and valueless [sic] metals belong to him who takes them (singly) conquering (the possessor).

Thus has been declared the blameless, primeval law for warriors;

from this law a Kshatriya must not depart, when he strikes his foes in battle.

What he has not (yet) gained, let him seek (to gain) by (his) army; what he has gained, let him protect by careful attention; what he has protected, let him augment by (various modes of) increasing it; and what he has augmented, let him liberally bestow (on worthy men).

Let him be ever ready to strike, his prowess constantly displayed, and his secrets constantly concealed, and let him constantly explore the weaknesses of his foe.

Of him who is always ready to strike, the whole world stands in awe; let him therefore make all creatures subject to himself even by the employment of force.

Let him plan his undertakings (patiently meditating) like a heron; like a lion, let him put forth his strength; like a wolf, let him snatch (his prey); like a hare, let him double in retreat.[3]

Let (the king) consider as hostile his immediate neighbour and the partisan of (such a) foe, as friendly the immediate neighbour of his foe, and as neutral (the king) beyond those two.

When (the king) knows (that) at some future time his superiority (is) certain, and (that) at the time present (he will suffer) little injury, then let him have recourse to peaceful measures.

But when he thinks all his subjects to be exceedingly contented, and (that he) himself (is) most exalted (in power), then let him make war.

But if he is very weak in chariots and beasts of burden and in troops, then let him carefully sit quiet, gradually conciliating his foes.

But if the king undertakes an expedition against a hostile kingdom, . . . let him instigate to rebellion those who are open to such instigations, let him be informed of his (foe's) doings, and, when fate is propitious, let him fight without fear, trying to conquer.[4]

Having thus pursued his foreign policy, the Hindu statesman then returns to domestic rewards.

For times of need let him preserve his wealth; at the expense of his wealth let him preserve his wife; let him at all events preserve himself even by (giving up) his wife and his wealth.

Having thus consulted with his ministers on all these (matters), having taken exercise, and having bathed afterwards, the king may enter the harem at midday in order to dine.

Well-tried females whose toilet and ornaments have been examined, shall attentively serve him with fans, water, and perfumes.

When he has dined, he may divert himself with his wives in the harem; but when he has diverted himself, he must, in due time, again think of the affairs of state.

Having performed his twilight-devotions, let him, well armed, hear in an inner apartment the doings of those who make secret reports and of his spies.[5]

It may be said that this ethics of intrigue, deception and force as specified in the Laws of Manu refers only to the ancient past and not to the Aryan Hinduism which Prime Minister Nehru's Congress Party government faced in 1947. Three considerations must give one pause, however, before accepting this thesis.

First, there was the fact already noted that the Hindu Mahasabha was acting on exactly such an ethics at the time Free India came into being. Second, there were the actual Aryan Hindu Maharajas with their very efficient armies left by the departing British as independent princely states. Many of these Hindu Maharajas were then living in 1947 exactly as the Laws of Manu prescribe in the following passages which occur immediately preceding those on foreign policy cited above:

Inhabiting that, let him wed a consort of equal caste [i.e., color], who possesses auspicious marks (on her body), and is born in a great family, who is charming and possesses beauty and excellent qualities.

Let him appoint a domestic priest (purohita) and choose officiating priests (ritvig); they shall perform his domestic rites and the (sacrifices) for which three fires are required.

A king shall offer various . . . sacrifices at which liberal fees (are distributed), and in order to acquire merit, he shall give to Brahmanas enjoyment and wealth.

Let him cause the annual revenue in his kingdom to be collected by trusty (officials), let him obey the sacred law in (his transactions with) the people, and behave like a father towards all men.[6]

With the British Raj no longer there to keep the armies of these Maharajas in their place, was there any assurance that they would not make their foreign policy correspond to the Laws of Manu as did their domestic life? Their Aryan Hindu code being what it is, the chances were indeed unlikely.

In any event this is how Prime Minister Nehru and his Congress Party colleagues decided. Their realistic Hindu Deputy Prime Minister and Minister of Home Affairs, Sardar Vallabhbhai Patel, made amicable but firm calls on the Aryan Hindu Maharajas and their Muslim counterparts in the princely states while quietly also marching in his stronger Indian army. Thereby the merely British ruled provinces of India which were all that New Delhi inherited from Great Britain at midnight on the night of August 14, 1947, were merged with the princely states to constitute present Free India.

Gandhiji wept when he saw this happen. There are those who have suggested that in these acts Nehru and his Congress Party colleagues betrayed the saint and father who gave them their power.[7] What such a moral judgment overlooks is that actual Hinduism is much more than Gandhiji's purely Asian Hinduism. It was the former, not the latter, with which Prime Minister Nehru and his Congress Party colleagues were actually confronted when they took office. As we have already noted, notwithstanding Gandhi's presence and influence, his method had failed. Massacres were occurring and were to continue to occur on an almost unbelievable scale. Only the strongest use of law backed with police action succeeded in restoring order and bringing the horrible bloodletting to an end.

It follows that Gandhiji's way to peace is recognized even by Pandit Nehru and his Government to be inapplicable to any political situation where peoples or nations governed by any ideology other than Gandhiji's live, act and operate. If Gandhiji's way to peace will not work even with Indian Hindus or with Aryan Hindu Maharajas, is it fair or appropriate to use it on Communist North Koreans actually engaged in militant aggression or with respect to their Communist Chinese and Soviet Russian supporters, in judging the use of law backed with police power by the majority of the United Nations in Korea? Certainly the Communist North Koreans, Chinese and Soviet Russians are not less materialistic and militantly and avowedly aggressive in their ideology than are Aryan Hindus in

India or the Aryan and Muslim rulers of the princely states of India. If law backed by police action rather than Gandhiji's principles was required and justified in stopping massacres and taking over the princely states in India in 1947–1948, it is also justified in stopping a dialectical materialist aggressor and his colleagues in Korea.

No political leaders can claim to be governed by moral principles unless they apply the moral principles, which they use to judge the other fellow, to themselves. Conversely any nation whose domestic and foreign policy faces an actual situation which requires law backed with police power to justify what is done—if it is to claim moral principle in support of its judgment of other nations and the United Nations majority—must use the moral principles for such a judgment which it applies to itself in its own conduct.

One other fact demonstrates that the actual India which Prime Minister Nehru's Government faced in 1947, and still faces, is not that of Gandhiji's merely Asian, non-caste, mediational, pacifistic Hinduism. All over India one can still see not merely the picture of the beloved Gandhi, but also that of Subhas Chandra Bose. His Hinduism was and still remains militant, revolutionary and aggressive. In 1942 he led an Indian army, organized at Singapore after its capture by the Japanese, which succeeded in invading India before it was finally beaten back by Lord Mountbatten's command. Authentic evidence seems to indicate that he was killed when trying to escape to Japan on a Japanese airplane that crashed on Formosa. His present hold on Hindu India is indicated in the following report by an American correspondent from Bose's home city of Calcutta.

Today, the memory of Bose inspires a fiery and almost religious fervor in the heart of millions of Indians who, like Bose, believe that the path of India should be along forceful lines.

Many of these millions believe their fabulous leader didn't die in the wreckage of the plane on Formosa. They place him variously in China, Russia, Indo-China, and Malaya. And the believers are confident that he is not only alive but will return to save India at some critical time. . . .

And so strong is the Bose cult, that Nehru, whose dislike of the fiery Nationalist is an open secret, has felt compelled to describe him publicly as a "great Indian patriot." . . . Few cities of India do not have a street named for him. His birthday is observed as a holiday in West Bengal. In Calcutta and other cities his picture is hawked on the street corners.

Bose is dead. But in death his strength is greater than it was in life.[8]

Clearly present India is Aryan Hindu India with legal codes and soldiers; it is not merely Gandhiji's Asian Hindu India.

But more than Aryan Hindu India confronted Prime Minister Nehru's Government on the morning of August 15, 1947. In A.D. 1192 invading militant followers of Islam from the West conquered Aryan Hindu India to create and maintain there for the subsequent 565 years one of the architecturally and artistically richest cultures this world has seen—Muslim India. Needless to say its theory of good government is that of theocentric law backed with police power. Even after the partition which had placed two-thirds of these Muslim Indians in a new nation called Pakistan, forty million of them remained in Free India. Also there were Sikhs, Jains, Christians and some Buddhists.

Clearly under such circumstances a monistic religious state, such as that of Pakistan, was out of the question for Free India. Prime Minister Nehru's Government introduced, therefore, by means of its constitution a secular state modeled after that of the United States with its freedom of worship. But this meant that a political and ethical norm introduced by legal constitutional means at the national level was required to supplement and also to alter the traditional intuitively given ethical and religious norms and the traditional Asian joint family and village community of elders. To use the language of Sir Henry S. Maine, contract as well as inductively given status was required to define the religiously and the ethically good.[9] The importance and the difficulty of such an achievement of adequate moral and religious norms in contemporary Asia has not received the attention it deserves. In traditional Buddhist, Confucian and Hindu Asia the joint family is the key social unit. It is through this joint family, whether it be Taoist, Confucian, Japanese Bushido, Buddhist or Hindu that the main values of a traditional Asian society are transmitted. Consequently to shift the norms of the community from intuitively given status at the joint family level to constitutional code and contract at the national level involves a tremendous change.

It also entails a transformation in personality structure and in the object to which one looks for the force of moral and religious personal values. Forthwith in part at least these values become located not in the intuitively felt warmth, intimacy and man-to-manness of one's family or even in the mediationally achieved advice of village elders, but in the dry, technical legal propositions of a constitution written by Western-trained lawyers in a book too dull to read, located at Nanking, Bangkok or New Delhi.

This moral transition required of the Asian individual, if contemporary developments in Asia are to be effective, is precisely the difference between Gandhi's family and village political and economic program for India and Prime Minister Nehru's constitutional political and Five Year Plan economic program. This difference goes much deeper than the question of local versus national development and control. It means also that, whereas the spiritual sources of the one are in the warmth of the traditional family and in what Gandhiji termed "the communal unity of the heart," [10] the nearest principles of the other are in the pages of strange books called constitutions or Five Year Plans with their roots in the spiritual foundations of a Western civilization far away.

Such, at bottom, is the heart and the difficulty of the Asian problem of imposing Western economic and political ways on an Asian society. Need one wonder that so far every attempt by either Western or Asian leaders to achieve this has failed?

Yet face the problem and attempt to solve it, the Asian must.

A Free India composed of Aryan Hindu, Gandhian purely Asian Hindu, Muslim, Sikh, Christian, Parsi and Buddhist communities simply cannot build itself on a monistic religious state after the manner of the Muslim nation of Pakistan.

Clearly under such circumstances a political and cultural nation built on traditional Asian localized joint family and village elder values breaks down. National, religious and cultural as well as economic and political norms must be introduced at the national level, and for this consciously constructed legal constitutions must be introduced; intuition and traditional statutes are not enough. Thus even in the purely spiritual and cultural sphere Gandhiji's intuitive method of merely warm, personal contact and heart-to-heart fellow feeling, necessary and valuable as it is, will not suffice.

But facts other than the pluralism of religious communities require novel constitutional norms and economic plans at the national level. Even before the War India was the seventh largest industrial nation in the world. The Asian intuitive ethics of its joint family works at the village, non-scientifically run agricultural level. But industrialization and the education that goes with it pulls members away from the local guru or teacher and the joint family into the larger cities. Again the traditional family and village-centered political bonds cease to be sufficient. Codified constitutional law not merely for commerce and industry but also for marriage, divorce, the treatment of daughters on an equal basis with sons and of sons equally with the eldest brother, have to be introduced. Also the old way of having the marriage arranged by the heads of the respective joint families becomes not merely inappropriate but also unworkable. The youth meet at distant universities rather than in the home village where they are known by the respective joint families. Similarly industrialization necessitates corporation law of which even the Aryan Hindu codes and the later Manchu Chinese codes never dreamed. Also in China and India population has continuously outrun production so that starvation and famine become worse and worse. Greater scientific efficiency of the

Western type in both agriculture and industry becomes inescapable, the mass pressure for well-being being what it is the world over. But scientific technology requires capital expenditures derived from countless families, too far apart to determine the terms upon which it is given by intuitive, immediate contact. Again the more impersonal codified law at the national level becomes a necessity.

To achieve this with effectiveness is not quite as easy as it might at first seem. More than the specification of the codes and the contracts is required. Loyalty to these national codes and contracts is also essential. But such a loyalty, if it is to be forthcoming, entails putting a nationally defined, communal loyalty ahead of the traditional Asian Asian's primacy of loyalty to the local joint family. As the next chapter will show, in the case of Chiang Kai-shek's China this shift of loyalty was not forthcoming. The joint family and the local village and provincial interests triumphed over the national interest.

The introduction of Western scientific efficiency to solve the food and population problem also requires scientific education. This education brings with it, as the sequel will show, new outlooks and new personal and social norms. When this process starts a very real danger arises. The coming of the new norms tends to cause the youth to break completely from the traditional ones. At the same time, apart from the very few who get precise training in the new Western norms abroad, the basic Western spiritual values and understanding necessary to make the new Western political, financial and economic constitutional legal codes effective are not grasped. Nor is even the need for going beneath these Western constitutions and five year economic plans to the Western philosophical and spiritual roots necessary to make them effective fully appreciated even by the leaders who introduce these constitutions and plans. Thus what has usually happened in the past is that the youth and their leaders tend to fall between two moral stools. They run the risk of not having the spiritual roots and foundations necessary to build any effective society of either their own indigenous cul-

ture or of the new political and economic Western plans and
ways which they are trying to impose upon it. When this happens the entire program breaks down and a military, political
leadership takes over; or an aggressive imperialist from outside
comes in to conquer and forthwith run the show. Contemporary
Thailand and most Latin American nations are examples of the
former of these two phenomena. South Korea, had not the
United Nations acted, would be an instance of the latter.

Any wise foreign policy for the United States and any effective
program for peace in this world must find the solution to this
unsolved problem. It will concern us in the next chapter. For
the present we must pursue Prime Minister Nehru's method
of attack upon it.

It has already been noted that he and his Government have
introduced a Western type of constitution and five year economic plan. Having agreed upon this, they faced a crucial question. There are several types of Western political constitutions
and economic plans which Free India could take as her model.
The designation of contemporary India as Free India gives the
answer to this question. She has chosen that of the free democracies and in particular that of the United States.

Prime Minister Nehru did not utter mere words when, in the
address to the Congress of the United States, he said, "I always
had much love for this great country and I have been an ad-
mirer of your leaders since my childhood. Some of them have
been my heroes." Or when he added,

It may interest you to know that in drafting the Constitution of
the Republic of India we have been greatly influenced by your
Constitution.

The preamble of our Constitution states that "We, the people of
India, having solemnly resolved to constitute India into a Sovereign
Democratic Republic and to secure to all the citizens: justice, social,
economic and political: liberty of thought, expression, belief, faith
and worship: equality of status and of opportunity: and to promote
among them all fraternity assuring the dignity of the individual and
the unity of the nations: in our Constituent Assembly do hereby
adopt, enact and give to ourselves this Constitution."

You will recognize in these words that I have quoted an echo of the great voices of the founders of your Republic. . . . Like you we shall be a Republic based on the federal principle, which is an outstanding contribution of the founders of this great Republic.

Since then one of the largest free elections, with many parties entered, which this earth has ever experienced has been carried through after free and open discussion and criticism. These elections can well serve as a model for their orderliness and honesty to some countries with a much longer experience in these matters.

In Free India's Constitution there is not merely the guarantee of freedom of religious belief and worship and of freedom of speech and expression, but also of freedom "to form associations or unions" and "to acquire, hold and dispose of property." [11] In India's Constitution moreover, "Any section of the citizens residing in the territory of India . . . having a distinct language, script or culture of its own shall have the right to conserve the same." [12]

Moreover distinctions due to caste are outlawed. On the latter point Free India is returning from Aryan Hindu India to Gandhi's Asian Buddhist Hindu India. But Free India's Constitution does not conceive of freedom in merely political terms. Its Preamble guarantees not merely Justice, Liberty and Fraternity but "also equality of status and opportunity."

Furthermore, to give implementation to these words a Planning Commission under Prime Minister Nehru's chairmanship has brought forth its Five Year Plan. This defines in detail the economic program of Free India.

Before considering its provisions it is necessary to consider the situation it is designed to meet. As India's expert and able Minister of Finance, Mr. Chintaman Deshmukh, said to the writer: "The War brought independence to India. The British saw that if we were of sufficient worth to defend the free world in times of war, we were also of a worth sufficient to live as free men in it in times of peace. But the War also gave independence to India under the most unfavorable of circumstances." For a war wears down the economic equipment of a country and stops even the previous normal replacement of capital resources and housing. Consequently receiving an economic system after a world war means gaining it in a wornout and rundown condition.

But in addition to this there came partition. The average annual increase of population per year in Free India is around four millions. Partition suddenly threw at least eight million more refugees from Pakistan upon the war-worn economy of Free India. Also it almost stopped, and at times did stop, trade between Pakistan and India even though the traditional source of supply of raw jute for India's jute mills is now in Pakistan as are also two major areas of the surplus production of British India's food.

A converse story can, of course, be written for Pakistan. Her influx of refugees has been put at six million. She had the raw jute and India had the mills to process it.

Partition and the tension over Kashmir, which followed upon it, also necessitated that a disproportionately large section of the government money must go for military defense on the Indian-Pakistan frontiers. One needs to look merely at the present boundary line of Free India to become aware that its extremely circuitous length has nothing to do with natural or militarily defensible considerations. The boundary of present India is far longer and more difficult to defend than was the old boundary of Pakistan and India combined.

With such domestic military requirements, one can well understand, therefore, why India did not feel able to take on additional policing obligations under the United Nations in Korea. This does not, however, excuse India from her failure to give those who did take on such obligations her wholehearted moral support.

Such was the economic system which Free India inherited suddenly from Great Britain. Forthwith it had to be operated by Indian rather than British decision-makers. To be sure the British had trained in India an Indian Civil Service, but even so the main policy decisions had been made by the British. As Mr. Deshmukh said to the writer in 1950, "The type of expertness necessary to make correct decisions in a free economic and political democracy can be learned only by experience. No amount of book learning, however necessary it is, can take the place of making the decisions actually and learning from one's own experience." This type of expertness, by the very nature of the case, can only come with time. Moreover if native Indian leaders were to get the type of training and experience necessary to run a Western type of political and economic society, it was for the most part necessary for them to remain with the British during the long period of India's fight for independence. This meant when independence came that leadership had to go naturally to those Indians who had paid the price of going to jail under the British. Thus at the outset of Free India those Indians with the best training in Western ways could hardly be used in the topmost decision-making positions.

Beneath all these difficulties are other hard facts. There is a population two and four-fifths that of the United States [13] in an area less than two-fifths that of the United States. Of this much smaller area "two-thirds . . . is either semi-desert or for months in the year parched land." [14] The resultant shortage of continuous minimum water requirements results in a shortage of trees. The shortage of trees causes the soil to be washed away in the heavy monsoon floods which come over short periods; it also forces the use of cow dung rather than wood by the peasants for fuel. Thus by both erosion and the absence of fertilizer the efficiency of the available soil continuously decreases. Upon this relatively small amount of inefficient soil approximately 360 million people depend for their food and about 240 million live.[15] The consequence is that whereas on his much larger and continuously enriched soil the individual American farmer cultivates on the average 145 acres and his British cousin 21 acres, the individual Indian farmer on the average cultivates less than five acres.[16] Also whereas Japan grows 1,713 pounds of wheat per acre and Egypt 1,918 pounds, India achieves 660 pounds.[17]

Relate this situation to a population increase at the present moment of four million per year and the following picture emerges. In the thirty years from 1911 to 1941, the amount of cultivated land per person of the total population dropped 20 per cent from .9 of one acre to .72 of an acre.[18] This trend is continuing. One grasps what this means in terms of human suffering when one realizes that 1.2 acres per person of population is necessary to avoid starvation by an emergency restricted diet. An adequate diet requires at least 1.8 acres per person.[19] The result is youthful starvation and an early death as told by the following comparative figures of the expectancy of life in the various countries. In New Zealand in 1931 it was 65 years, in the United States in 1940 it was, for the white population, 63 years, in Japan in 1930 it was 49 years, and in India at the latter date it was but 27 years.[20]

Clearly the economic problem of contemporary India is one which the local farmer or individual industrialist or even the community of village elders cannot meet alone. Reforestation and irrigation projects on a vast scale are obviously necessary even though India already has an amount of land under irrigation "more than twice as large as any other nation in the world." [21]

Faced with such cultural, political and economic problems Prime Minister Nehru's Government might perhaps have been excused if, when they took power, they had decided that reviving an economic system in India was too much for her people to attempt without rigid dictatorship. Consider, however, the report of its Planning Commission signed by Jawaharlal Nehru, its Chairman.

Now, what kind of an economic system do we need to achieve our aims? The prevailing inequality, economic stagnation and poverty indicate the necessity for change.

What are the alternatives?

At one extreme is some kind of totalitarianism. To many its appeal lies in its promise to satisfy quickly the basic human needs. It achieves results because under a totalitarian system the mobilization and direction of resources are in the hands of an all-powerful central authority. We know, however, that totalitarianism brings in its train violence, conflict, regimentation and the suppression of the individual. Now these things are repugnant to our national instincts and tradition. We cannot, therefore, give up the democratic ideal even if it were less profitable from the practical point of view. But is it really so?

Economic progress under democratic planning is perhaps less spectacular, but surely more enduring. . . . To carry out a plan in a democratic state means hard work and participation by every individual. It is a process of education which, while it secures the progress of the country, also raises the quality of the individual. . . . On the whole, therefore, the democratic way is more advantageous even from a narrow point of view.

The question now arises, how can we reach our goal in the democratic way? This can be done if we avoid unregulated private enterprise and replace the acquisitive spirit with co-operative effort. This is exactly what the Planning Commission suggests. The Plan envisages an economy in which the private sector will co-operate with the public sector for the common good of the people under the broad direction of the State. . . . Under the Plan the bulk of the Government's material resources will be devoted to agriculture, irrigation and power, the social services and the completion of industrial undertakings already under way. . . . The Commission is convinced [therefore] that . . . only democratic methods should be employed to achieve the aims of the community.[22]

In short, Free India is to be democratic in method as well as aim. Not even a democratic goal is to be allowed to justify undemocratic dictatorial means in either the political or the economic sphere.

It may be noted parenthetically that Jaiprakash Narayan, a leader of India's Socialist Party, holds exactly the same position. Speaking to the Socialists of India he has said:

. . . I have watched the Soviet experiment with anguish. The revolution has led to a denial of freedom and liberty. . . . It is more than thirty-two years now since the Bolsheviks seized power in order to establish a socialist society. Have they realized this idea? I do not think so. There is a ruthless dictatorship in Russia. No civil liberties exist. . . . If you want to establish a totalitarian state in the name of socialism you can very well do so, but then I will not be a party to any such effort.[23]

The Commission proceeds immediately to spell out this democratic method more in detail. The financial implementation
of the Plan calls for 43 per cent of the Government's outlay
during the five years to go into irrigation, power and rural development for the benefit of agriculture. But 6.7 per cent of
the Government's expenditure will go to government run or
supported industry. Hence, the Commission adds that the "responsibility for industrial development will largely devolve on
private enterprise." [24]

The wisdom of this should be obvious. India's primary problem is the modernization of agriculture in order to meet the
elementary need for food. As has been noted, this requires a
nationwide program of reforestation which no private industry
could undertake. The Government of India, therefore, proposes to use the largest portion of the money it can raise from
taxes in the Plan not merely where the need is the greatest, but
where private industry is least likely to go. Clearly this by itself
will command all the attention and tax raising capacity which
the leadership of India at New Delhi can bring forth. To private
industry and capital, foreign as well as domestic, is left, therefore, the major part of the industrialization of the country.
Already these words have been translated into deeds by agree-
ments, with such foreign companies as Standard Vacuum, guaranteeing their capital investment and exportation of profits in
dollars to the United States with immunity from being nationalized by the Government with remuneration, for a period of at
least twenty-five years. In return domestic and foreign capital
"has to accept the objectives of the nation's social and economic
policy." [25] In other words, Free India has chosen a federally
regulated, free enterprise industrial economy after the manner
of the United States, Australia and countless other free democracies of the liberal democratic West.

The Commission's insistence that "Agriculture takes the
pride of place in the Plan" [26] must not obscure the crucial role
of industry and the introduction of the Western scientific mentality throughout the population if the program is to succeed.

From the aforementioned figures concerning population trends and cultivable land in present India, the expert Indian economist Principal D. G. Karve concludes that

. . . even if all the cultivable land in the country was put under food crops and the best possible system of cultivation was introduced there would not be enough food locally produced for the existing and prospective population if the present trends continue.[27]

This means, as he adds, that necessary as the increase in agricultural land and scientific efficiency of production is, it will not be sufficient; a decrease in the birth rate also is necessary to solve the problem of food.

Is not education, then, in birth control the answer? Principal Karve answers in the negative, for

. . . it is an incontrovertible fact of historical experience that such propaganda has succeeded only with reference to sections of population which were well-to-do and enlightened.[28]

This enlightenment and its fall in the birth rate occurs, he adds, whenever industrialization in the Western manner takes place. Thus increased industrialization is as essential to cure India's food problem as is improved agriculture.

But, as the economist, Karve, adds, what brings the enlightenment is not the industrialization itself but the Western type of scientific mentality which goes with it.

We see again how inadequate is Gandhi's appeal to merely the intuitive mentality of Asia and to merely the traditional Asian village economy to meet India's problem. If "God comes to the poor first of all as food," [29] as Gandhi once said is the case, then He comes to them through the Western scientific mentality and philosophy conceived as *logos* or law as well as in the heart-felt Asian feeling for the spiritual as expressed in the Asian joint family and village community.

Prime Minister Nehru's Planning Commission protects the private property of the peasant as well as that of the industrialist. Landlordism is to be removed. Adequate acreage per peasant for efficient production is to be introduced. Soviet collectivism

is rejected. In this connection the Commission says that the nationalization of land is

. . . an impracticable course and inexpedient from the financial
and social points of view. The peasant is so deeply attached to the
land that nationalization is unlikely to appeal to him. . . . [In-
stead,] the best solution of the problem of Indian agriculture . . .
lies in some form of co-operative management of the village.[30]

At this point the national policy from the top ties to the Asian
village at the bottom of India's political and economic system.
It is at this point also that the Point Four aid program of the
United States, recently agreed upon by Ambassador Bowles and
Prime Minister Nehru, makes its contribution to the meeting of
India's obvious need.

This tie of the national program at the top and the Point
Four aid from the United States to the Asian village is tre-
mendously important. For no Asian society can completely
transform itself into an image of the West without losing the
enthusiasm of the masses necessary to make the new program
effective. The more, therefore, the combining of Western ways
with Asian traditions can make use of the joint family and their
elders of the ancient Asian villages, the more are the chances of
success.

Any Point Four program for India is not likely to succeed if
it merely sets up images in India or other parts of Asia of an
individual family or a county agricultural program as they exist
in the United States. One must begin instead with an Asian's
understanding of an Asian joint family and an Asian village of
elders including all the Hindu, Buddhist, Confucian symbols
and other values embodied in these key Asian social units and
then, as far as possible, achieve what needs to be done through
them and by appeal to their values and symbols. Otherwise the
enthusiasm of the people necessary for success which is there to
be tapped, as Gandhi showed, will not be forthcoming, and in
all likelihood even if success is achieved temporarily under the
tutelage of the American experts, the situation will revert back
to its old inefficiency the moment the American advisers leave.

The problem of combining Western ways with Asian people is much more difficult than most Asians or Westerners realize. The problem at bottom is that of first restoring and strengthening the native plant and then introducing the Western graft.

Thus considerations indicate that India's policy is such that her needs can be met. The resources are there and the potential capacities of the people necessary for the task are also present. The problem is to put all these things together within the time that is allowed. As Ambassador Bowles has written, "India is not a poor country; it is merely a country of poor people." To succeed, however, she clearly needs Point Four aid from the United States. Moreover the plans and achievement to date of her present leadership are such as to more than justify this aid. Her achievements in handling the tremendous refugee problem far surpass those of much wealthier Europe with its relatively much smaller similar problem. Recently a sober Britisher who has surveyed the results tells us that the story is one "of solid achievement." [31] Parts of the story are positively thrilling in the combination of idealism and practical achievement which they demonstrate. Imagine how the people and government of the United States would rise to the opportunity with a tremendous outpouring of Point Four aid if there were in China today a government with domestic political and economic aims identical with their own and with leadership that has already demonstrated its capacity.[32] The people of the United States and their representatives in Washington have exactly such an opportunity before them at the present moment in India.

Even so success will not ensue, unless the people of India become more exactly and completely informed by their political and educational leaders concerning the theory and practice of Communism than is the case at present and both Asians and Westerners face and learn to resolve the basic cultural problem. The difficulty is that of combining Asian and Western values and ways. Even with Asian and American resources present, the task is not easy, as Generalissimo Chiang Kai-shek's China clearly shows. The problem demands deeper study.

7

ASIAN RESURGENCE AND
WESTERN WAYS

There is an ominous similarity between the program for India introduced by Prime Minister Nehru in 1947 and that inaugurated for China by President Chiang Kai-shek in the 1920's. Both attempted to combine a resurgent Asian culture with Western political and economic ways. Chiang Kai-shek's attempt ended in failure. We will do well, therefore, to examine the similarities between his policy and that of Pandit Nehru in detail and to note what happened and why in the Chinese example.

Both of these Asian leaders chose as their Western model the liberal, modern, democratic type of economic and political society rooted in the Anglo-American tradition. To this end each introduced a liberal Western type of law and constitution. These Western constitutions attempted to reform the joint patriarchal family common to China and India by proclaiming woman suffrage, allowing the equal inheritance by daughters as well as by sons and legal divorce. Each found his first task to be the military unification of the state. In the case of Prime Minister Nehru, this military unification was carried through by his Minister of State, the devoutly Hindu former follower of Gandhi, Vallabhbhai Patel; in the earlier Chinese instance it was directed by the Generalissimo himself. In both cases public opinion supported this military unification. For example, in

India the Maharajas were bought off, liquidated or combined and their armies were incorporated into or replaced by the Indian army. In response to invitations or by other means, India's army took over Kashmir and Hyderabad State. Unquestionably Indian public opinion, especially of the overwhelming Hindu majority, supported this move. The Generalissimo's military unification of China had an even more popular response. His armies were welcomed by a happy populace as they marched north from South China. Their coming had been preceded in almost every village by young men preaching the ideological program of Chiang Kai-shek's new China which was to fulfill the earlier hope of Sun Yat-sen.

Next they turned to the economic problem. In both instances the decision was in favor of a federally controlled free enterprise economy, except where large projects necessary for national welfare could not be carried through by private capital. Both governments had many foreign advisers and native planning boards.

Moreover each Asian leader came into power under the halo of a greater one who had preceded him. In the case of the Generalissimo this greater one was Sun Yat-sen; in the case of the Pandit, it was Gandhiji. This meant that their coming was an anti-climax. Sun Yat-sen and the Mahatma had directed the shorter, more spectacular venture of carrying through the revolution to gain democratic independence. Union among their respective followers was relatively easy because it demanded of any one merely the negative virtue of being against the Manchus or the British. With independence achieved there then fell to President Chiang and Prime Minister Nehru the more difficult task of deciding what to do with one's independence now that one had it. Harmony among one's followers on this positive, particular objective was more difficult because it required an agreement upon the Asian ways to be kept or removed, upon the particular Western ways to be introduced and upon the reconciling of the two.

Moreover the revered predecessors had filled the minds of

the masses with images of great expectations. Their present representatives had the hard step by step, long-term task of matching these easily conjured up subjective images with their objective political and economic counterparts in millions upon millions of Asian villages. Whereas Sun Yat-sen and Gandhi could succeed in their task of winning independence by merely capturing the imagination of the people for non-cooperation with the previous rulers, President Chiang and Prime Minister Nehru had to deliver the goods on the revolutionists' promises if they were to succeed.

Delivering the goods is a slow, painful, dull job requiring hard work upon the part of everyone. In such an undertaking people with excellent, easily excitable imaginations are not so effective. When paradise does not come merely by imagining it, such followers tend to lose interest. They even begin to blame the present leadership. This became the popular mood in China about fifteen years after the Generalissimo's triumph. It was already the mood of contemporary India in 1950, less than three years after the Pandit took power. Prime Minister Nehru and his government had plans, many plans, but as Asoka Mehta, the Secretary of the Socialist Party, pointed out in 1951,[1] the people lacked enthusiasm. At least the Generalissimo was given the time and the chance to produce an approximation to what was promised. He lost his hold upon the Chinese people because he failed. It will be well to examine his failure more in detail.

In examining his failure, we shall draw for our evidence not upon his critics, but upon his Chinese supporters, friends and present colleagues. None has been more informed about both China and the West and faithful to the Generalissimo than Chiang Monlin. Chiang Monlin came of a Confucian patriarchal joint family in a typical Asian village. From childhood through his passing of the imperial examinations at Peking he was steeped in Confucian values, ways, beliefs and culture. Then he attended the University of California at Berkeley where he became acquainted, most significantly as the sequel will show, with Greek scientific and philosophical thought. Later Chiang

Monlin went on to Columbia University to study under the late John Dewey and others. Throughout his American education he took courses in natural science as well as in Western social science and philosophy.

One deep-seated contrast between Asian and Western ways of thought became evident to Chiang Monlin as a result of his native Confucian and American studies. This basic contrast is so crucial for the topic of this chapter that we will do well to examine what he tells us about it in considerable detail.

Chiang Monlin noted first that the social values and norms of the two cultures are different. Many other scholars have seen this. What makes Chiang Monlin notable is that he found the difference in cultural, social and moral norms to have its basis in two fundamentally different ways of knowing nature. The Asian way of knowing nature which his Confucian training illustrated he characterizes as the way of "naive observation." [2] By "naive observation" he tells us is meant something given in "immediate personal experience." [3] It is the kind of experience one has when one sits in the moonlight observing the shadows and listening to the chirp of the crickets as these sounds and visual images differentiate the all-embracing equanimity and stillness of the evening. He describes it as follows:

> The Chinese people are devoted to nature, not in the sense of finding the natural laws but in the sense of cultivating the poetic, artistic, or moral sense of lovers of nature. To be under the pine trees steeped in the moon and listen to streams flowing gently over the rocks gives one a placid mind and a tranquil heart To see the spring flowers in bloom makes one feel the universe filled with the spirit of growth; to observe autumn leaves falling serves as a warning of the approach of autumn days. . . . The [Confucian] conceptions of Yin and Yang and the Five Elements undoubtedly grew out of naive observation of nature. They were good enough for rationalizing the conduct of nature and man. No minute calculations were necessary. . . .[4]

This naive way of knowing nature reaches its culmination when Chiang Monlin has the immediate experience of standing at the top of the Temple of Heaven in Peking. He describes this experience as follows: "I . . . felt as if heaven, earth and myself merged in one vastness." [5]

The Westerner's way of knowing nature is different, Chiang Monlin tells us. He designates it as the way of the "all-piercing intellect." [6] What he means is that the Westerner pierces beneath the immediately felt phenomena of the Chinese naive observation and even behind the one all-embracing immediately felt vastness within which the sensed sounds and shadows come and go, to their underlying causes and the specific determinate laws and principles of which the sensed and felt phenomena are an illustration. For this Western way of knowing nature, "immediate personal experience," [7] which sufficeth for the Chinese is not enough, he adds; instead the mind must become "used to handling abstractions and generalizations." [8]

What he has in mind will be grasped if we recall that in the scientific knowledge of nature of the West no inductively observed fact is considered to have been put upon a scientific basis unless the universal law which it illustrates and of which it is an instance is discovered. In nature as given to the Confucian Chinese mind by naive observation, each particular image and sound is unique. To use the language of professional philosophers, it is a particular, it is its own unique, here-now, immediately felt self and nothing else; it is not a universal.

To the Western mind, however, rooted as its Greek and modern philosophy are in Greek geometry and mathematical physics with its determinate postulates holding for all instances and their deduced theorems, any particular fact or event such as a stone falling to the ground behaves according to the very same determinate law as does any other stone, no matter how unique as given inductively in naive observation, the particular stone may be. Again to use the language of the professional philosopher, particular things as known by the Western way of knowing nature are universals rather than particulars, or, in other words, they are always instances of universal laws.

From this unique difference between the Western way of knowing nature in terms of the determinate laws of indirectly

verified, deductively formulated, scientific theory, the unique
legal, political, moral and even Christian religious values of
the West follow. It is because ultimate knowledge is identified
with the logic of the laws of deductively formulated scientific
theory that the divine in the Greek Christian West of the
Fourth Gospel and the Epistles of St. Paul is identified with the
logos. It is because this Greek Western scientific way of knowing
nature entails the conception of the individual when truly
known as an instance of a universal rule or law that moral man
in the classical and the contemporary Western moral and
political tradition is identified not with inductively given particular man but with universal man. As a subsequent chapter
will demonstrate in detail, it is because fundamental moral
man is universal man, i.e., an instance of universal determinate
principles or laws, that to be moral in the West consists in
standing for certain determinate principles which in the last
analysis cannot be compromised. It is moreover this conception
of a truly known individual person or event in nature as an
instance of determinate principles, laws or rules which, passing
over from Greek natural science through Greek philosophy into
Roman Stoicism, created the Western type of law, religion and
morality, according to which the just method of settling disputes is to measure the disputants and the facts of the particular case against determinate statutes or rules, thereby making all
men equal before the law. It was not until this new way of
knowing nature, first discovered by Greek scientists, brought
its impact to bear upon human morality and social practices
that there were any legal codes in the world, East or West, other
than those such as the later Chinese and the Aryan Hindu
Manu which are based on the inductively given status of the
individual in the joint family and of the family in its respective
tribe or caste.

These additional comments fill in Chiang Monlin's acute observation that the basic difference between the social, moral,
religious and legal norms of the Orient and those of the Occident arises from their different empirical, and hence scientific,

ways of knowing nature. Recently a Western scholar, Joseph Needham, has reached the same conclusion.[9] Truly, Chiang Monlin concludes: "Civilizations are built around different systems of the universe as men conceive it." [10]

Previous attempts to merge Asian resurgence with Western ways have failed because these basic differences have not been appreciated and taken into account. At this point Chiang Monlin's description of the failure as it occurred in China under Chiang Kai-shek's regime becomes significant. His testimony is all the more telling because he has remained loyal to Chiang Kai-shek and is at the present moment working with him in Formosa on a more constructive solution of this basic problem.

Let us first consider the fate of Chiang Kai-shek's modern liberal, democratic Western constitution. Of it Chiang Monlin writes:

The Constitution of China was a copy of imported ideas, adopted according to the fancy of those who drafted the document and alien to the habits and ideas of the Chinese. . . . For China to follow the constitutional pattern of the West without its background was to hitch China's wagon to the Western star. It was small wonder that the experiment failed miserably.[11]

How did the failure show? The first effect was corruption of a form and magnitude completely alien to pre-Westernized Confucian Chinese society. So bad became this corruption that Chiang Monlin writes, "the corrupt National Assembly . . . had become a headache to the entire country." [12]

The crucial question now arises. Why did the introduction of Western political and legal ways issue so quickly in corruption? To answer this question we must recall what we already know about the character of Asian society and the locus of its traditional moral and social roots. The key fact is that Asian society centers in the joint family. Its social ethics, whether the ethics be Hindu, Buddhist, Taoist or Confucian, centers in and is propagated largely, even in India, through this joint family. After the Hindu has passed through his spiritual and moral tutelage under the Hindu sage or *guru*, he then enters the householder's stage of life; in other words he takes his place in the joint family. If he is the eldest son of the head of the family he takes over the headship himself and his father departs not merely from family life but from political and economic concerns to retire to the forest and to prepare, after the manner of a saint and recluse, for the fading back into the all-embracing, intuitively felt vastness or Brahman which is the primary concern of the last two stages of the Hindu's life. The Buddhist Asian behaves roughly in the same way except that in the equivalent of the studentship stage of the Hindu he puts on the yellow robe of the Buddhist priest and passes at least three years under the spiritual tutelage of the elder, more professional priests of the Buddhist temples and monasteries. Today on any morning in Bangkok, one can see thirty thousand young priests in their yellow robes going forth to homes and to the market place to receive the gifts of food and pieces of cloth from a devoted Buddhist populace. All traditionally trained Thai statesmen have been through this tutelage. Following this, the Buddhist Thai returns to his joint family. It differs from the Hindu joint family only in that the absence of an Aryan factor in Buddhism frees Buddhism from the second caste Aryan Western values of Hinduism with this second caste international ethics of force and in that daughters and sons share alike in the Buddhist joint family. This happens because all people are equal before the Buddha's intuitive formlessness which is called Nirvana and because the Buddha admitted nuns as well as priests to his holy order.

The Chinese joint family is patriarchal and hence similar to the Hindu so far as the inheritance of sons only is concerned. It differs from the Hindu and Buddhist joint family merely in the fact that the moral tutelage is given more completely from the beginning in the ancestral home of the joint family, except as it is supplemented by community parades and ceremonies or by the tutelage of Buddhist and other priests. The Korean joint family is Confucian also and is similar to the Chinese. The Japanese is also, except that it is also located in the Shinto

CHART OF BLOOD RELATIVES THROUGH THE MALE LINE

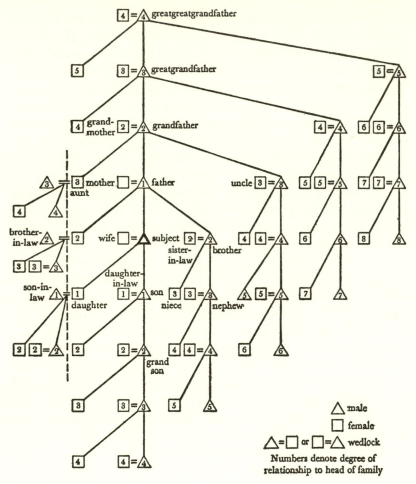

aristocratic feudal hierarchy of families of higher and higher hereditary status which culminates in the Emperor.

Included here is a diagram of a typical Asian joint family. I am indebted for it to my friend, Judge Kyung Keun Chang, of contemporary South Korea.

It is to be noted that the head of the joint family is represented by the triangle at the center of the chart. The difference between the Western and in particular the American concept of the family and this Asian joint family is obvious. Triangles represent male members of the family. A rectangle represents females. Different generations are located on horizontal lines; brothers, wives and brothers-in-law on horizontal lines. A single family may embrace eight generations, including brothers, uncles, great-uncles, sons, nephews and nephews' sons. All these usually live in a single ancestral home. Sons and daughters-in-law live in the father's or the grandfather's home. As many as thirty male parents with their offspring, each with their ancestors and offspring even unto grandparents and grandchildren, may live in a single joint family home comprising but one single family. Throughout the whole of Asia this social unit is the custodian of religion, ethics and morality and the instrument for their application to national as well as to family and individual life.

Moreover the basic social and moral principle of this joint family is filial piety—where by filial piety is meant not merely loyalty to one's father and mother, but loyalty to this joint family. Hinduism and Buddhism may not feature the concept of filial piety as do Confucian Asian families, but the fact is nonetheless there.

It is important if we are to understand the difficulty of introducing Western ways into Asian societies that we know what this universal Asian fact of joint family loyalty means. It requires that apart from his primary loyalty to the intuitively felt vastness and oneness of man and nature, which is the source of *jen,* Tao, Nirvana or the non-dualistic Brahman, the primary social obligation of every Asian is to this joint family. If Confucianism has any unique traits as compared with Buddhism, Hinduism and Taoism, it is that the joint family will only succeed as the intuitive vastness, making all men one, comes to fruition in the family. There is, in other words, no short-circuiting of the relation of man to the divine except by way of the Asian joint family. This means that in the literal sense of the word there is in pre-Westernized, purely Asian Asia only a joint family loyalty and morality. There is no other larger and higher social morality. In traditional Hinduism, for example, there is no congregational worship. Shintoism modifies this general rule somewhat in the case of Japan, as does the ancient Aryan factor in the case of Aryan Hindu India. Asian society, therefore, tends to keep itself under ethical control and to free itself from corruption only so long as social activity in the community can be handled at the joint family village level. The moment demands beyond this level appear, power politics and joint family self-interest take over and social ethics breaks down. As Lin Yutang has put the matter, the Chinese are very suspicious of any social idealism which makes ethical demands beyond the loyalty to the family.[13]

This is the reason why the Western, democratic constitutionalism of Sun Yat-sen and Chiang Kai-shek failed in China. As Chiang Monlin notes:

. . . most members of the Assembly were little concerned with national interests. Their preoccupations were either provincial or local, or still worse, personal. National interests they conceived only vaguely, and they themselves were therefore not in a position to have any coherent guiding principles or policy on national issues. Consequently no leadership was possible except in matters of local or personal interest. The Chinese people love freedom but were inexperienced . . . in constitutionalism. They did not see the importance of it.[14]

The primary point to note about any Western constitution, since the time of the Stoic Romans, is that it demands a social loyalty far transcending and in fact quite independent of the family or the village. A British aristocrat can be a member of the Tory Conservative Party, his son can be a Socialist leader in the Labour Party without any sense of immorality. The reason is that in the West being a moral man consists in accepting certain theoretically constructed and indirectly verified, determinate principles with which family status has little or nothing to do. This is one of the things that Christ must have meant when He said:

For I am come to set a man at variance against his father, and the daughter against her mother, and the daughter in law against her mother in law.[15]

What this amounts to is that the ethics of Christianity is not that of the traditional joint family, present then in Judea, Greece and Rome as well as in Asia.

This should help us to understand, therefore, why the introduction of Western constitutions in Asian societies results so frequently in what the West calls corruption. The morality of these societies, because of its essential connection with the joint family, tends to make a man put loyalty to the joint family ahead of this Western type of national loyalty. This is what was meant when we said in an earlier chapter that Chiang Kai-shek's government failed to achieve Western reforms in China not because it was corrupt but because it was moral in the Asian meaning of the word moral.

This point becomes even clearer if one turns to the Asian method for settling disputes between families and examines the bearing of this method upon national unity. A contemporary Chinese anthropologist, Hsien Chin Hu, has recently made an objective study in China of this topic. After noting that the joint family with its "kinship tie" is the key to Confucian Chinese society and that it has its basis in "a 'natural' relationship," he says that all such family institutions "have a common aim: the consolidation of the group for the security and advancement of its members." [16] He then adds,

The security offered is twofold: religious, in that the [joint family] . . . assures the individual that the rites in his honor will be con-

tinued indefinitely; and social-economic, by assuring each member
of assistance in case of need, both from the group and from individual fellow-members.[17]

The religious component of this security demonstrates again
the falsity of the conclusion that Confucian culture is not religious.

He then proceeds to make the primacy of family loyalty over
national loyalty even more specific by adding that this Chinese
joint family

. . . is not entirely compatible with a centralized form of political
control. In fact, in rural districts far from the capital the county
magistrate has to take into account the wishes of the leaders of the
most important [joint families]. . . . For his own sake he often
finds it advisable to refrain from interference with the autonomy of
the group, particularly in judicial matters, until he is formally consulted. Any inquiry into disputes between [joint families] . . . ,
too, is often resented, and where these are strong, the local admin-
istrator will make a face-saving inquiry only in the case of homicide.
. . . Hence, the development of the [joint family] . . . is inimical
to the strengthening of centralized control. . . . Centuries of experience had taught the lesson that even an honest man has such
strong ties within his home province, particularly because of the
[joint family] . . . organization, that he would find it impossible
to administer public affairs with impartiality.[18]

It might be thought that his following remark provides an
important exception to this conclusion:

The encouragement of moral behavior by the [joint family] . . .
is important in fostering in the young those virtues that make good
subjects and citizens, for according to Confucian ethical conceptions, *chung* (loyalty to the ruler) and *hsiao* (filial piety) go together.[19]

This means that loyalty to the ruler becomes reduced to loyalty
to the joint family. It shows in the case of the Manchus who
were little more than model Confucian families setting an example for the local joint families after the manner in which
the politically impotent Royal Family of Great Britain sets an

example for the British populace. The Royal influence is more by example than through political power.

Chiang Monlin makes this clear when he notes that Chinese villages are made up of a few key joint families and adds,

There were hundreds of thousands of such villages in China. . . . The traditions, family ties, and trades which held them together were more or less the same. A common written language, common ideals of life, a common culture and system of civil examinations bound the whole country into a single nation known as the Chinese Empire.[20]

In short, the national unity of traditional Confucian China was in the Confucian family-centered norms and practices of tens of thousands of Confucian joint families.

More than corruption came into China with the introduction of a Western constitution and Western economic and technological ways. The effect of the Western technological ways and economic products was to introduce there, as into all Asia, processes, products and instruments which could not be handled by the social organization of the joint families at the village level. Chiang Monlin describes the change which occurred in his own youth many years before he went to America to study. Before the Western ways came, the major events of society could be handled at the village level, "by elders of the clan with the Ancestral Hall as its seat." [21] When, however, Western economic products were introduced, factors entered the village life not merely from outside the village but also from outside China. Leaders at the provincial rather than at the village level were used as agents or instruments of the Western traders. Forthwith Chinese life passed out of the ethical control of the individual joint family and of the elders of the joint families who made up the village council. Thus Chinese social life passed into an immoral no-man's land. Robber chiefs began to appear. Individuals gaining their income from Westerners, and thereby loosened from the ethical control of the Asian joint family, began to take over. These robber chiefs grew into war lords. These war lords, moreover, presented Sun Yat-sen and the moral Confucian Chiang Kai-shek with their second major difficulty, a major difficulty moreover for any Asian society. Social control had now passed beyond the reach of the joint family or the elders of the joint families of the village.

At this point the introduction of Western democratic nationalism meets its second difficulty. This difficulty also arises from the joint family and centers in the fact that in such a society there is little if any adequate middle officialdom under legal and ethical control to serve as the instrument for joining the national policy and constitutional codes of the Westernized Asian leader at the national capital to the native ethical controls of the joint families of the villages at the bottom of the social hierarchy. The second effect, therefore, of introducing Western ways into China was to create a group of provincial self-appointed robber chiefs and war lords at the middle provincial level who are under the ethical controls of neither the Asian religious, moral and social values of the masses of people in the Asian joint families or the Western national, economic and political and legal norms of the Westernized Asian leaders at the top.

Inevitably, therefore, in taking over the country the Westernized Asian government at the national capital has to capture the provincial war lords either with military force or with political plums. Moreover, as the military and political unification of the nation under Westernized leaders with moral integrity shows signs of succeeding, the ethically unprincipled war lords flop opportunistically to their support. The acceptance of this unprincipled support becomes almost a necessity, since no other more adequately trained middle officialdom with a following is available. At this point corruption becomes compounded by entering the national government.

The corruption of Western democratic liberal constitutionalism in Asia enters also at a third point. This becomes evident when one examines in detail the Asian method, common to China, Buddhist countries like Thailand, Ceylon, Burma and

Tibet and the purely non-Aryan Hindu culture, for settling disputes beyond those within the joint family. There is a morally controlled method for doing this. The significant point about it is that this Asian method is not that of our aforementioned Western concept of justice.

The Western concept of justice, let it be remembered, is that of measuring disputes and disputants against determinate, ideological and legal principles such as those written in constitutions and applied by the supreme court and those written in statutes and applied by courts of lower jurisdiction. The Chinese student of both Confucian Chinese and Western law, Francis S. F. Liu, has pointed out that

> The European judicial system is founded on the following basic concepts, the absence of any one of which will cause the system to crumble:
> 1. The fighting spirit for rights.
> 2. Individualization of litigations.
> 3. Evidence.[22]

With respect to the first, he notes:

> Western jurisprudence leaves it entirely to the litigants to claim their respective rights. To put it more clearly, where a party does not claim his rights, the court will not claim same on his behalf. . . . Where two persons are engaged in a fight, each will exert his utmost to win the battle. Only one party can win, and, consequently, both cannot exist under the same roof. To be conciliatory is to hand arms to the enemy. . . . Thus once there is litigation, compromise is naturally out of the question. . . .
>
> The result of the application of this system is to make the people guard their rights with extreme care, utilizing all the techniques at their command by way of attack and defence, and taking all the necessary steps on the basis of the rights which they think belong to them.[23]

With respect to the second basic concept of Western justice he writes:

> Claim of rights being left entirely to the litigants, the duty and function of the court are strictly confined to the examination of the validity of the claims on the basis of law. . . . The scope of in-

quiry is to be limited to the suit before the court; and no other matter may be introduced. Justice means justice in respect to the particular suit litigated upon. It is not justice reached after a consideration of all the past relationship between the litigating parties. . . . Each transaction is to be analyzed and isolated.[24]

After making similar comments about the Western concept of evidence, he then raises the question, "whether the racial characteristics [i.e., culturally conditioned mentality] of the Chinese people are in conformity with the basic concepts supporting the western system." [25] Upon this question he makes the following comments. In the first place the Chinese conception of justice centers in four notions which he terms, "Mercifulness, Peace-loving spirit, Concept of 'General Justice' and Faith." Of mercifulness he writes as follows, speaking from his personal experience as a practicing lawyer and a judge in China:

. . . I often came across situations where a judgment having been rendered by the court after years of litigation the losing party at the time of enforcement of the judgment asked for compromise through the mediation of friends or relatives. It is found that in such instances not only such friends and relatives are glad to mediate, but also the party who has obtained the judgment in his favor is sometimes willing to negotiate anew and make compromises. This will be most unusual in the west. Under similar circumstances, hardly any person having won a judgment would be willing to give up the enforceable rights obtainable therefrom.[26]

It will be recalled that Gandhi and his Indian client and adversary exhibited exactly this same behavior in South Africa.

Mr. Liu then turns to the explanation.

It cannot be said that the Chinese people are not conscious of the existence of their rights. The true explanation would seem to lie in their aversion to extremes. Strict insistence upon rights violates the spirit of mercifulness. . . . To cast away this virtue and to advocate the course taken by the western people so as to make our people keen on their rights in disregard of the hardship that may be occasioned to others will cause our solid society to crumble like a volcanic mountain. . . . The concept of rights and of compromise are mutually contradictory. The spirit of mercifulness is the neutralizer.[27]

With respect to the Chinese peace-loving spirit, he continues in the same vein.

The peace-loving spirit appears before the commencement of litigation. Mercifulness occurs after the litigation is over. The former, therefore, prevents litigation before its occurrence; whereas the latter serves to prevent the struggle from spreading too far. . . . No matter how clear the rights are, the Chinese people more often than not would request a third party to effect a compromise in order to avoid litigation. It is a mere superficial remark to say that the Chinese people lack a clear sense of rights. One must note that the evolution of the human being is one from war to peace. To litigate is to engage in a fight. To fight is to destroy. On the other hand to be compromising is to rest in peace, and to rest in peace is essential to progress . . . justice achieved by looking only into one single, particular transaction is specific justice with respect only to that particular transaction. What I call "general justice" is that which is achieved after a careful consideration of all the relationships of the parties. It has often been seen in our country that when two persons resort to the respected elders of the community for a settlement of their differences arising from their conflict of interests in a particular matter such elders would invariably look into the entire past relationship of the parties in order to arrive at a just decision. The particular event giving rise to the dispute is regarded merely as a cause of the dispute rather than the basis for the decision. . . . This is because the entire relationship of the parties is regarded as one compact and correlated whole and no one single event should be isolated from the rest of the chain of relationship. Modern [i.e., Western] jurisprudence, however, is otherwise. . . . It runs counter to the ideal of the Chinese people not to achieve justice with respect to the entire relationship of the parties. The former often causes enmity and hatred in the hearts; whereas the latter makes the people satisfied and willing to comply . . . the former makes the people selfish and cruel while the latter coaxes them to be kind and well intentioned.[28]

He adds: "That our people have grown to be more mischievous of late is partly caused by the Europeanized administration of justice."[29]

Of faith he writes:

It has been said by westerners that "The word of a Chinese is as good and weighty as a written guaranty." . . . But this is no longer true today. The cause lies in the introduction of the westernized method of justice administration. To the Chinese, to bring suit is an evil, and to be charged in a suit is a shame. . . . The attitude of the Chinese people toward government is that they should have as little to do with government as possible. . . . A court is regarded as a trap, the avoidance of which is even more desirable than the avoidance of a major disaster.[30]

Chiang Monlin supports Francis Liu on these points. He writes:

Modern legal sense as the West understands it is not developed in China. Avoid the courts if you can. Let us settle our disputes without going to law. Let's compromise. Let's have a cup of tea and sip together with friends and talk things over.[31]

He adds that beside highways throughout China one finds signs reading, "Do Not Go To Law." [32]

In Buddhist Thailand in 1950 the same state of mind was to be found.[33] There are evidences in India also that, as the Western British type of law is becoming more and more administered by Indians not educated at Oxford or Cambridge or in the Inns of Court in London, corners are being cut and it is beginning to break down. The reason is not that the people administering it are immoral, but that as more and more native Asians take over the administration of a Western type of law without the training in Western values necessary to appreciate it, their own Asian morality causes them to behave in ways that to a Westerner seem corrupt.

The reason for the Asian concept of the proper way to handle disputes should now be clear to us. It centers in a morality derived from a knowledge of nature by means of naive observation and immediately felt immersion in the all-embracing vastness of nature. From this standpoint all different things in nature are found to vary from occasion to occasion and from person to person. Furthermore, as Confucius, Buddha, Gandhi and countless other Asians have noted, all directly observed determinate persons or things are transitory. In other words all definite knowledge of nature given by mere observation is knowledge of a particular rather than of a universal, and of a particular which is transitory. From this it follows that there are few determinate rules other than those of the inductively given father-child relationship holding for all men under all circumstances.

At first one might think, therefore, that there can be no other absolute standard. Such a conclusion overlooks the following fact, pointed out again and again in connection with our examination of Asian beliefs and ways. We immediately feel and apprehend directly in ourselves and in our objects of desire not merely the differentiated relative, transitory part which distinguishes one person with his particular desires from another person with his different, determinate objects of desire thereby generating disputes and conflict, but also another part of one's own self, the same in all persons and objects, namely the undifferentiated all-embracing vastness or continuum. In other words, we do not immediately apprehend ourselves as merely this definite person with these specific properties or characteristics different from those of other persons and objects. We also immediately apprehend these transitory properties of ourselves which make one of us different from another within an all-embracing consciousness, vastness or continuum within which the other person or object is similarly immersed and from the standpoint of which he also apprehends his particular objects and is conscious. Hence, in addition to the parent-child-relationship, with its attendant doctrine of filial piety which is a necessity of any person's existence and therefore an absolute holding for all people, there is also the all-embracing continuum of immediacy in its undifferentiated sameness in all persons and things out of which our differentiated consciousness and objectivity arises at birth and into which it fades at death. Because this undifferentiated consciousness and all-embracing continuum of immediacy is common to all persons and things not merely spatially but also temporally, it also is a timeless or non-transitory absolute.

Furthermore, because the Oriental tends to restrict his valid empirical scientific knowledge to nothing but what is immediately apprehended, the parts of all immediately apprehended things which have different properties are both relative and transitory; they do not give meanings for the expression of definite laws or codes the same for all men and occasions. Hence, the antipathy to all settling of disputes by recourse to laws and to processes of litigation. Also because the factor in their valid knowledge, given not by sensed immediacy, but nonetheless with immediacy, which is common to, identical in and thus the same for all, is an immediately felt thing which is undifferentiated and hence devoid of any determinate properties, it cannot be said in any proposition or code; it can only be cultivated inarticulately and felt. This is the reason for Gandhi's, the Buddha's and Confucius' injunction against the use of codes and litigation, and their cultivation instead of the intuitive, immediately felt communion of the heart or man-to-manness which the Confucian calls *jen*.

Thus the way of absolute morality for the non-Aryan Asian is always that of the middle path between the determinate rights pro and con with respect to the legal code of the two parties to the dispute. One cultivates this middle path by bringing into the foreground the legally inexpressible felt formless vastness which is the true, permanent self identical in the disputants and by pushing into the background the transitory, relative differentiations setting one party to the dispute against another.

This is what the Confucian Liu and the Asian Hindu Gandhi mean when they say that the Hindu and Chinese way is the way of the peacemaker. This is also what Gandhi means when he adds that his political program derives from his religion. The root of Asian religion, whether it be that of the natural piety of Chiang Monlin's Confucian all-embracing vastness, that of the Buddhist's middle path to Nirvana or that of Gandhi's pacifistic Asian Hindu Bhagavadgita, is the all-embracing, in itself undifferentiated, continuum of immediacy within which the transitory particular part of individuals and of their different objects of desire come and go.

How to combine this Asian intuitively felt, all-embracing, undifferentiated component of divinity and justice with the Western indirectly verified, theoretically constructed concept of the moral and just man is the heart of the legal problem of merging Asian resurgence with Western ways. This will become clearer when we examine the spiritual foundations of Western civilization and its technology.

There is a practical difficulty involved in the introduction of Western know-how into Asian cultures. Western know-how is a consequence of the deductively formulated theories and laws of Western mathematical physics. The atomic bomb, for example, was revealed to men as a possibility when Einstein developed his special theory of relativity in order to clear up an abstract theoretical question concerning the relation between space, time and matter in Newton's mechanics and Maxwell's electromagnetics. When he found the solution to this very abstract theoretical question, a formula relating mass to energy was found to follow by logical deduction. This formula revealed the possibility of deriving energy, not from other pools of energy, but directly from the breakdown of matter itself. Without this mathematically formulated, abstract theory, discovered by Einstein, the practical possibility of releasing atomic energy and making an atomic bomb would not have occurred to any engineer.

Furthermore, as Chiang Monlin has already indicated to us, this theoretical way of knowing nature in terms of abstract, precise, determinate laws and principles was the discovery of the ancient Greeks. With them arose the abstract, logically formulated, theoretical way of thinking about naively observed, personally sensed and felt natural phenomena, which requires quantitatively exact experiments for its verification. Einstein confirms Chiang Monlin's judgment when he writes:

We reverence ancient Greece as the cradle of western science. Here for the first time the world witnessed the miracle of a logical system which proceeded from step to step with such precision that every single one of its propositions was absolutely indubitable—I refer to Euclid's geometry. This admirable triumph of reasoning gave the human intellect the necessary confidence in itself for its subsequent achievements. If Euclid failed to kindle your youthful enthusiasm, then you were not born to be a scientific thinker [in the Western meaning of the word].[34]

This is what Chiang Monlin noted when, in his first acquaintance with the Western science of nature in America, he found it to be steeped in formal rationalism. It may be noted that he found purely inductive, descriptive Western science quite congenial to his antecedent Chinese temperament.

This shows that the difference between Asian and Western thought is not that between knowledge which is scientific and knowledge which is not scientific. Both Asian and Western knowledge is scientific. The difference is between scientific knowledge which restricts itself to what is directly apprehended and that which in addition introduces theoretically constructed laws involving a speculative leap beyond immediacy for their discovery and indirect verification through their deduced consequences, for the determination of their truth or falsity.

This difference has immediate practical relevance with respect to the introduction of Western know-how into Asia. As Chiang Monlin called to my attention, the Asian tends, when confronted with Western scientific instruments and processes, to look at those instruments from the standpoint of the only concepts of nature he possesses, namely those given by what Chiang Monlin has termed the naive observation of nature. In other words the Asian tends to suppose that the Western ways and instruments can be understood in terms of the immediately felt impressions and the directly sensed images which the objects impress upon his mind. The idea that Western machinery, processes and instruments can be understood only in terms of unobservable scientific objects and processes which obey determinate laws and mathematically exact formulae never occurs to the un-Westernized Asian.

Some concrete examples will make this clear. In the interior of northern Thailand 450 miles from Bangkok a Thai friend of mine, educated in the Yale School of Engineering, is now engaged in selling rice-hulling machinery to Thai farmers. The importance of this in the contemporary Asian situation can hardly be exaggerated. The milling of rice has been traditionally in the hands of Chinese mill owners. With China now in Communist hands and with Communist Chinese armies near the Thai border, small rice-hulling machinery purchased by the Thai farmers has the internationally significant result of placing the control of the agricultural economy in Thai hands.

My Thai friend tells me, however, that he has great difficulty in persuading the Thai to repair this machinery properly when it fails to operate. Advice concerning correct procedure seems to be of little use. He has concluded that the only advice is to tell them under such circumstances to leave the machine entirely alone and to call immediately for him. This counsel, however, they rarely take seriously. Instead what frequently happens is the following. The rice-hulling machine is operated by an engine with two radiators for keeping the engine cool. Pipes run from the top of one radiator to the bottom of the other. Often when anything goes wrong the natives release these two pipes and cut them off, running them straight across from the top of one radiator to the top of the other and from the bottom of one radiator to the bottom of the other. Inevitably the engine overheats and is often ruined. When asked why they do this, the reply is that it is [intuitively] simpler. In other words the supposition is that everything necessary to understand the engine is given in the intuitive image by naive observation.

Some who have been engaged in introducing Western medical methods into Asian villages report a similar experience. Western doctors have been able to take a village with a health condition the lowest of any in the world and in three years raise the health of this village near to that of the modern West. It is not unknown to find, however, after training a native health officer over a period of several years to carry on after the Western doctor leaves that, with the departure of the Western adviser, the village reverts to or discouragingly near, its original condition. The specific Western practices are still carried on even meticulously but other things occur which destroy what the meticulous practices accomplish. It does little good, for example, to pasteurize milk if the boy who delivers the bottles sticks his dirty thumb through the paper cap, or if the cook pours the milk into a wet dish in which uncooked vegetables fertilized with night soil have been soaking.

This does not mean that Asian leaders and communities cannot become proficient in Western ways. It does mean, however, that the task is much more difficult than that of setting up a model of a Western program in an Asian community under expert Western supervisors and then supposing that after Asians look at, or are trained to operate, or copy it that it will then spread like an epidemic over vast areas. One never knows even for the single successful model whether it has taken root, until after the Western advisers leave.

This does not mean that the Asian mind is physically or neurologically incapable of thinking in Western ways. There are countless Chinese, Japanese, Indian and Egyptian scientists and technologists who can not merely apply Western technology, but also think in the abstract, scientific, formal, technical ways necessary to create the new theories of mathematical natural science from which the technology derives. The point instead is that there are at least two major types of concepts of nature (there are, of course, many others as well) which men have used to conceptualize the raw data of their experience and the native Asian has been trained in only one of the two types. With proper teaching he can master the other type as well.

The predominant traditional Asian type derives from what Chiang Monlin has called the naive observation of nature, the other type derives from the deductively formulated scientific theories of nature which require every fact to be seen as an instance of a determinate universal law. Asians are used to concepts of the former type. So long as they approach Western know-how with merely these concepts, they will never understand this know-how or use it properly. Westerners have mastered, since the time of the ancient Greeks, the other type of concept as well.

Chiang Monlin affirms that only as Asians grasp this more abstract, theoretical mode of knowing nature will they be able to understand and apply Western know-how effectively. Only by mastering also this basically Western scientific and philosophical way of conceptualizing nature in terms of laws and concepts which are universals will they understand and apply effectively the Western type of political constitution, economic system and legal processes. For only through this form of knowledge is it possible for men to find the values transcending family loyalty necessary to make these Western social forms effective.

This is the reason why Chiang Monlin, while Vice Chancellor of Peking National University, came to the conclusion that the traditional way of introducing Western science and technology into China was erroneous. Chinese leaders supposed that gadgets and the know-how alone were sufficient, and that the Western abstract, scientific theory and attendant mechanical mindedness upon which the machinery and the know-how depend for their existence can be dispensed with. The result, however, was the failure to take proper care of even the most elementary Western machinery. When it broke down it was patched instead of repaired, and then the patch was patched. Such experiences convinced him that the introduction of Western know-how into China will not be effective until the Chinese learn to look at the novel Western science and its technology from the more theoretical, conceptual standpoint of the underlying Western philosophy of that science. Otherwise the Chinese people look upon the new Western ways with the only philosophical concepts for understanding them which they possess, namely the Confucian ones. Then the new Western instruments and processes are misconceived, carelessly operated and ineffectively repaired, if not ruined. As Chiang Monlin puts the matter, "the Chinese rule-of-thumb ways which are an enemy to accurate calculations" persist.[35] It is not an uncommon experience in Asia to see new Western machinery sitting in the fields rusting itself away because the Asians who assembled the parts put the gears together in the wrong way and stripped them the first moment the machines were operated.

This does not mean that every craftsman or peasant in an Asian village must understand Western electromagnetic theory and quantum mechanics and the Western philosophical way of conceptualizing man and nature in terms of deductively formulated theory in which individual facts and events are understood as instances of formal relations or law. But it *is* necessary, however, for the teachers of these humble village folk and for the directors of the research laboratories and engineering schools in the main national centers of Asia. It is necessary, moreover, that the millions in the villages be taken out of the habit of supposing that any modern scientific process or instrument which is handed to them can be understood in terms of the intuitive images of it given in naive observation. To accomplish this in a way that will insure the effective continuation of the practical project after the Western or expert native adviser leaves it is necessary to accompany the training of eyes and muscles required to operate the new machine or process with an elementary education in the new way of thinking necessary to understand what one is doing.

The Modern Review of Calcutta concludes a recent article on the "Mechanisation of Agriculture" with the words:

The main obstacles are under-employment in agriculture, low average income, low technical efficiency of imported machinery, high capital cost and running expenditure, absence of quick repair service, absence of trained men and absence of mechanical-mindedness amongst the general mass.[36]

Chiang Monlin was never able to convince his Chinese political friends and colleagues of the necessity of attacking the problem of introducing Western know-how into Asia at the basic cultural, theoretical and philosophical level. Only Sun Yat-sen of the Chinese political leaders was aware of the necessity of this fundamental theoretical and philosophical approach. Chiang Monlin tells us that Sun Yat-sen saw the need of teaching the Chinese to become "used to handling abstractions and generalizations." [37] The capturing of the minds of men is as necessary for effective economic aid as it is for other matters. The prevalent assumption that the problem is a purely practical economic one is quite fallacious.

Western advisers who regard themselves as practical are often as unaware of the need of paying attention to the mentality and cultural background of the Asian people as are many superficially Westernized Asians such as Chiang Kai-shek. These Westerners frequently suppose that all one needs to do is to set up a model farm village or health program in the Western manner taking no account whatever of the indigenous native cultural background and mentality or of the basic way of thinking which is second nature to the West yet essential for understanding the new Western ways that are introduced. It is precisely this lack of awareness of the role of the indigenous native cultural mentality or of the basically novel way of thinking of Western mentality which is the explanation of the reversion of initially successful Western projects back to the old state of affairs, after the Western advisers leave.

So crucial is this point that it will be well to follow in detail what Chiang Monlin has to say about the difference between the Asian intuitive scientific and philosophical approach to nature and the Greek Western approach by way of abstractly formulated and theoretically constructed universal concepts and laws. He writes:

As I read more books on Greek life and culture it became more clear and convincing to me that some such striking contrast did exist between ancient Chinese and Greek thought and . . . this was probably the main [reason] for the divergence in development of Eastern and Western civilizations. . . . The intellectual quality of the Hellenic genius was to seek the *general truth* in these [the previous Asian, Babylonian and Egyptian] sciences by generalizing and formulating their principles, a process which paved the way for the discovery of natural law.

For the Greeks there were two worlds: the world of the senses and the world of reason.[38]

This distinction has been misunderstood by most Western philosophers. It is precisely Chiang Monlin's distinction between nature as understood in terms of intuitive images given by naive observation and the events and individual things of nature understood in terms of abstract, general scientific concepts, laws and theory. Nature in the latter meaning is not sensed. Otherwise the basic laws of Newton's, Einstein's or Schrödinger's physics could be verified directly by mere inspection, and Western scientific knowledge would be absolutely and finally certain. The fact, however, is that this Western type of empirical knowledge is verified only indirectly by way of the deduced consequences of its basic laws and hence has to be held tentatively, subject to change with new information.

Referring now to his own countrymen, Chiang Monlin continues:

We did not, like the Greeks, try to venture into generalization [of the Western type]; nor, like modern Europeans, did we try to get universal laws from particular discoveries—a trait inherited from the Hellenic world. . . . I do not mean to say that the Chinese do not think logically. But their minds were not aided by systematic mental gymnastics. This defect has been reflected in Chinese philosophy, political and social organization, and daily life. It has become more glaring as the rest of the world came to live under the light of modern science in an industrialized society. . . . I constantly [therefore] tried to drive home in the minds of my people the importance of the development of the intellect. I gave it up as a bad job and changed my tactics to preaching the study of natural science. Instead of leading people to the source of the current, I reversed the process by letting them see the current first.[39]

His main point, however, is that Asians will never be able to direct the current effectively unless they have first grasped the type of mentality necessary to comprehend its source.

If this be true, as the foregoing analysis of non-Aryan Hindu, Buddhist, Taoist and Confucian Asian mentality indicates it is, an interesting question arises. How is it that the Asian Japanese attained an effective use of Western ways so quickly?

American observers who were in Japan after the occupation tell us that the Japanese were by no means completely successful in preventing their Asian mentality from rendering useless some Western ways which they attempted. Things were again and again copied rather than understood, with the result that when new circumstances arose for which the old, copied instrument was in part but not fully appropriate, the most grotesque Rube Goldbergian apparatus appeared. Some post-war observers conclude also that the Japanese leaders who declared the war quite overestimated the degree to which they possessed and had mastered Western instruments and were later quite shocked by the losses sustained.[40]

Nevertheless, the degree to which they succeeded compared to the Chinese requires an explanation. This explanation is to be found in certain factors in Japanese culture which are peculiar to it in addition to the mentality, values and institutions common to Asia generally. One of these unique factors is Shintoism. Japanese culture is not purely Asian in the sense in which we have been using this word. It is instead a combination of Hindu-Buddhist-Taoist-Confucianism with Shintoism. This synthesis is called by the Japanese, Bushido. Bushido exists only in Japan.

By 1850, however, the Shinto component had been pushed into the background. Following upon Admiral Perry's arrival in Japan in the middle nineteenth century, Japanese Shintoism was, most significantly, not merely revived but put in the center of the cultural picture. Admiral Perry confronted the Japanese leaders with Western nationalism and the power of modern Western military weapons. Western nationalism requires, as its name suggests, primary loyalty to the nation rather than to the Asian joint family. Shintoism contributed exactly this. For it is of the essence of Shintoism that the Japanese people are the descendants of a sun goddess. Furthermore no other people on this earth are descendants of this sun goddess. This led the Japanese to regard themselves as a divinely chosen people with a divinely inspired culture. The Emperor moreover, is, according to the Shinto tradition, a direct royal descendant of the sun goddess and her official representative on earth. Thus, according to Shintoism, the primary religious and political loyalty on earth is to the Emperor. Thus the usual Asian primary loyalty of the individual to the joint family is bypassed in the interests of a higher loyalty to the nation. This is the key to the warlike spirit of the Japanese during recent years, a spirit so contrary to the aforementioned peace-loving spirit of Confucianism, Taoism, Buddhism and the non-dualistic, non-Aryan Vedanta Hinduism of which Mahatma Gandhi is the most recent illustration. This is also the key to the suicide attacks made by individual Japanese in the recent war. According to the Shinto faith there is no higher virtue than giving one's all for the Emperor and the Japanese people and nation.

There is a second factor coming also from the Shinto tradition. Between the Emperor at the top of the social hierarchy and the many joint families of the peasants at the bottom there is a feudal aristocracy with more and more special privileges the higher up the hierarchy one proceeds. It was only necessary, following upon Admiral Perry's visit, to put the economic, industrial development of Japan in the hands of a few of the uppermost hereditary aristocratic families to have the Zaibatsu (i.e., "financial clique") which Mr. Pauley in his report to the United States government immediately after the war described as

. . . the comparatively small group of persons, closely integrated both as families and in their corporate organizations, who throughout the modern history of Japan have controlled not only finance, industry and commerce, but also the government.[41]

Having done the same with the army and navy, Japan had the unified and directed organization from top to bottom necessary to operate a militaristic nationalistic state. In short, Shintoism provided Japan with the middle officialdom which most Asian peoples lack.

Her remaining problem was to learn how to operate a Western theoretically grounded scientific industrial and military technology efficiently.

At this point the Shinto conception of divinity as a determinate Goddess rather than merely as the indeterminate Buddhist, Nirvana formlessness undoubtedly helped. Furthermore, the sun goddess is not given in naive observation either as a transitory quality coming and going within the continuum of immediacy or as the continuum of immediacy itself apart from its transitory differentiations. Thus again Shintoism perhaps prepares the Japanese for an understanding of the things one sees in terms of objects which are not immediately experienced. This is of the essence of Western scientific understanding and explanation.

It is likely, however, that the more basic reason for the capacity of the Japanese to master Western know-how so quickly is to be found in a linguistic factor in their culture. The typically Asian, Buddhist-Taoist-Confucian component of Japanese culture entered in the seventh century A.D. from China. This culture gave to Japan the written symbolism of the present Japanese language. Putting aside for the moment certain additions made by the Japanese to the Chinese written symbolism, it may be described as follows. The Chinese symbolism is basically pictographic. There is no alphabet. Each particular factor in experience tends to have its own corresponding unique symbol. This at least is the nature of the symbolism in its original elements. It is to be emphasized that such a pictographic symbolism is ideal for the kind of knowledge given by naive observation. To each particular image given through the senses there is a corresponding symbol which in some cases is similar to the sensed image it denotes. Thus, for example, the symbol for man is an inverted y in which the bottom portion represents the man's two legs and the top portion represents his trunk. Similarly the pictographic Chinese symbol for house is two short vertical parallel lines with an inverted v over them representing the roof. If knowledge is that given by naive observation and, as we noted previously, naive observation is always only knowledge of individual particulars, then a pictographic symbolism is the ideal type of language. The essential point about such symbolism is that syntax and grammar, that is, the relation of one symbol to another in an expression, has very little to do with the meaning of the individual symbols. Thus the inverted y standing all by itself conveys the full meaning as given in the sensed image.

Now clearly a mind built only of such meanings rooted in such an atomistic, pictographic symbolism simply cannot understand Western science. For as Chiang Monlin and our foregoing analysis have revealed, it is of the essence of Western scientific thought and knowledge that a particular individual fact and the concept designating it are never understood apart from the proposition or law in which the symbol for this fact stands as a term. This is but another way of saying that in Western scientific knowledge following the ancient Greeks, no particular image or fact given inductively is understood unless the general law of which it is an instance is given. Now a general law requires a sentence with a structure, a grammar, a syntax for its expression. It follows, therefore, that if one is to learn to think scientifically in the Western sense of this word about scientific objects or technological instruments and processes, one must learn to think relationally rather than in terms of atomistic images. For this one needs a symbolism which is syntactical and primarily grammatical rather than merely pictographic and atomistic in character. And in such a syntactical, grammatical relational symbolism the individual elementary symbols a, b, c, d, e, etc. by themselves mean nothing. Thus it is that a symbolism that is essentially syntactical has a meaningless alphabet and the pictographic symbolism of the Chinese does not.

Now it happens that the Japanese possessed a vocal language before the Chinese-Buddhist-Taoist-Confucianism culture with

its pictographic, written symbolism came to Japan in the
seventh century A.D. Furthermore, this prior native Japanese
spoken language is strongly syntactical and relational in character. There are reasons to believe, therefore, that it may be the
basic syntactical, relational way of thinking native to the Japanese mentality and of longer standing than the Buddhist-
Taoist-Confucian Chinese component of his culture which ac-
counts for the greater speed, as compared with the Chinese,
with which the Japanese leaders and people learned Western
know-how.

Evidence for this shows even in their present written symbolism. When a Chinese writes his equivalent of our English
sentence, The man goes up the mountain, he writes but three
symbols, one for man, one for ascending and one for mountain.
When the Japanese, using the script brought from China,
writes this same sentence, he uses five symbols. The two additional symbols introduced by the Japanese add syntactical relational meanings.[42] In short the Japanese written symbolism,
even though it derives from the pictographic symbolism of the
Chinese, is a synthesis of the pre-Chinese native Japanese indigenous folklore language with its relational mode of thought
and the Chinese pictographic symbol with its more atomistic,
less syntactical, mode of thought. This type of symbolism and
the mentality of which it is the expression may prepare the
Japanese mind to an extent to which the Chinese mind is not
prepared, when confronted with any Western process or object
to look for the meaning of what is before him, not merely in
the images given by naive observation but also in terms of the
more abstract relations in which particular elements and parts
of the object function as mere terms. This is of the essence of
the Western more abstract mode of thought in which an individual particular event or thing is never understood except as
its unobservable component parts are conceived as instances of
universal formally or syntactically expressed determinate laws
or rules.

If this importance of the linguistic symbolism is correct, then the people of India should find the mastery of Western ways easier than have the Chinese, since the Aryan contribution from the West to ancient Hinduism gave India the Sanskrit language which is syntactical rather than pictographic in character. In this connection it is interesting to note that the Sind Valley civilization of India excavated in this century at Mohen-jodaro and Harappa, which is dated as roughly 3000 B.C., long before the coming of the Aryans to India, is pictographic in character. This pictographic symbolism, however, seems to be connected with that of ancient Sumeria. If so, when its meanings are fully deciphered, it will be found to differ in important ways from that of China.

The linguistic factor is not without its importance for our basic problem of the ways to peace. We have already found that Gandhi's non-Aryan Hinduism, Buddhism and Confucianism regard laws and codes as the immoral way to settle disputes and something to be used only as a last resort. The Aryan values of Aryan Hinduism, however, which appear especially in its second caste, who are the Aryan rulers and conquerors of the pre-Aryan purely Asian Indians, is exactly the opposite of this. They settled disputes by appeal to codes. There are, moreover, different codes for the different castes in the case of the same dispute. Here the ethical criterion clearly is not that of the mediator but that of a person who believes that justice is rendered when conduct is measured against specific rules.

If no particular fact is understood unless the grammar of the sentence in which it is described is grasped, it follows that justice is not to be given by intuition and feeling and the softening down of rights and differences, but is to be given instead by bringing the individual person and the individual dispute under the grammatical proposition or rule apart from which individuals are devoid of their meaning. This suggests, therefore, that the Aryan conqueror's use of codes to settle disputes in ancient Aryan Hindu India and the Aryans' contribution of the syntactical Sanskrit language are essentially connected.

There is, nonetheless, a fundamental difference between the

type of codes which the Western Aryans introduced into Aryan Hindu India and the type of codes which arose when the Greek scientific way of knowing nature passed over through Greek philosophy and Roman Stoicism into the creation of Stoic Roman and later Western law. This difference becomes clear if one compares the codes of Manu of the Aryan Hindus with any post-Stoic Roman Western type of code, ancient or modern. The Aryan Hindu codes are expressed in terms of particular natural objects and social groups. In short, the terminology is not abstract or technical. It is that of an inductively given natural history description of human relations in terms of the syntax of Aryan grammar. The terminology of Western law, following the Stoic Romans, is quite different from this. It is technical in character after the manner of the technical concepts of Greek deductively formulated mathematical physics and modern Western science. This more technical legal terminology of the West permits a large number of different codes in Aryan Hindu law to be expressed as one single, technically formulated abstract code.

The difference may be summarized as follows. The codes of Aryan Hinduism are those of a purely Aryan linguistic grammar referring to common-sense objects, persons, castes and things. The codes of Western law, following the Stoic Romans, have the grammar of a deductively formulated theory with an abstract technical terminology. The difference in short is that between the linguistic grammar of natural history scientific knowledge and the more technical formalism of deductively formulated abstract scientific theory.

It is the step from the former type of grammar to the latter which the Aryan Indian must make if he is to connect Western know-how with indigenous native Indian mentality effectively. The problem of choosing a national language for India should be made with this type of consideration in mind. By their study of the law of British India and of Free India's constitution many Indians have of course made this step. The problem is to achieve it with the masses.

Another crucial factor involved in the introduction of Western ways into a resurgent Asian culture should now be evident. Not only is it necessary to go beneath the Western instruments and processes to the Western basic mode of thinking out of which they arise, but it is also necessary in doing this to use as far as possible the native indigenous cultural factors. Only if one revives the native culture and uses it as far as it is compatible with what one is after can there be a resurgent Asia. An Asia which merely takes a constitution, technology and ways from the West will be at heart as much a product of Western cultural imperialism, even though it be operated entirely by Asians, as would be an Asia made in the Western image by Westerners. Moreover, it is utterly impossible for Asians, even if they wanted to do it, to slip out of their unconscious linguistic conventions and all of the cultural habits that they have built into their emotions and their affections by centuries upon centuries of oral and written tradition. Before anything vital and lasting from outside can be brought in, the healthy, vigorous living plant capable of standing the operation involved in a foreign graft must be present. One cannot impose a foreign graft, no matter how necessary it may be in Asia or how vital it may be in the West, upon a dead or inhibited native plant.

This is one of the mistakes that Westernized Asians tend to make. Becoming enthusiastic about the obvious need of Western scientific and technological ways and their political and legal forms, the easy temptation arises to negate or even repudiate one's own Asian culture. The result is the inevitable lack of enthusiasm which characterized contemporary India in 1950. The masses simply do not comprehend what is going on. This is one difficulty which Prime Minister Nehru's secular state faces. To both the Hindu and the Muslim natives it seems to mean the destruction of both the Hindu and Muslim indigenous values. Neither a Hindu nor a Muslim understands a separation of life into two components—the one religious, reserved for a Sunday morning, and the other secular concerned with all the important affairs of life for the remainder of the week. This is why the contemporary leaders of the Socialist party in India are convinced, notwithstanding the Western origin of their social theory, that the true policy for India is not a secular state but a pluralistic religious one, rooted in national federalism combined with a state's rights, religious culturalism. It is interesting to note that this was Iqbal's (the founder of Pakistan) initial proposal for India. Had this proposal been followed, as Iqbal, Jinnah and the British wanted to follow it, Iqbal and Jinnah would have kept the Muslim communities of India within India and partition would not have been necessary. Return to this suggestion is the ideal solution of the problem of Kashmir. Again we see how essential attention to the indigenous cultural factor is for wisdom with respect to politics and economic technology.

We should now be able to understand also why all previous attempts to merge Asian and Western ways have failed. Few Asian or Western leaders, previous to Chiang Monlin, have appreciated the difficulty, or the cultural and ideational roots, of the problem.

Any foreign policy for the United States which does not take these difficulties and their cultural, ideational basis into account is doomed to failure. It is because the Communists in Asia more than anyone else are now doing this that they are having their present success there. The truth is that President Mao of China not merely understands Communist doctrine to the minutest detail in the most technical way; he also understands and has made a deep study of traditional Chinese Asian mentality. He is not merely aware of symbols and folksongs of ancient China to an extent which causes his armies to make use of them, he is also aware, as President Chiang Kai-shek was not, that the Confucian doctrine of the primacy of family loyalty is incompatible with a nationalist China and the interfamily financial integrity and loyalty necessary to run a modern technological society. The British anthropologist who saw Mao's troops march singing into Peking informs me that Mao is acquainted with this incompatibility between the traditional family loyalty and the loyalty to the community which is necessary to improve the people's lot and is telling them honestly that they must choose. Whether this be the full story about what is going on in China need not concern us. The point is that it is the wise and only way to proceed when one is trying to combine foreign ideas and ways with those of a native culture.

One must be clear about the mentality and values of the indigenous native culture. One must be clear also about the instruments from the West which are necessary to improve the native lot and one must face the conflicts and the choices that are necessary in gaining the more basic Western mentality and values necessary to make the Western instruments effective.

The task of doing this should be easier in the case of an Asian leader using liberal democratic Western ways and values than it is in the case of a Communist Asian like President Mao. A liberally educated, scientifically informed democracy, with its ancient Western religious, scientific and philosophical roots, permits the Asian to get the needed Western ways with the minimum alteration in his own great culture. This is the case because liberal Western democratic norms, values and processes with the more laissez faire individual endeavor and enterprise upon the part of farmers, industrialists, educators and creative artists, permit the understanding and achievement of the Western know-how with less repudiation of the religious, family and individual values of Asian culture than is the case in a Communist society which makes every phase of human experience subject to the dictates of the state as defined by a mid-nineteenth century German philosophy. To make this point clear to all Asians should be the basic aim of the foreign policy of the American people when they place their know-how at the Asian's disposal.

When a Western adviser goes to Asia, his first concern should not be to set up a pilot's scheme in a native village on the Western model. It should be to determine the full range of cultural values, habits, beliefs and mentality of the native people. If one does not first understand the culture and mentality of the Asian community into which Western know-how is being introduced, one cannot introduce it effectively. Having determined the indigenous culture and its mentality and potentialities, one's next task should be that of reinforcing every native factor which will sustain the Western know-how with the minimum alterations in the native mentality and ways. After having tapped Asian values and symbols sufficiently to call forth the confidence and enthusiasm of the masses, then one can incorporate the foreign way, confident it will be a permanently living thing, even when the foreign adviser has left.

The wisest expenditure of Western funds and advice will be made if it is restricted initially as far as possible to the village level. Not only is this where the people are; this is also where the native values abide, waiting to burst forth into flaming brilliance as a living, indigenous resurgence. The simple process of merely organizing local men within the Asian village community of elders to clean out the tanks so that more water can be caught in the monsoons and to clean out the ditches so that more water from the tanks can get to the fields will raise the productivity of the present cultivated land of many Asian areas to a remarkable degree. If into this situation one adds improved seeds, the fostering of the native social system of the village elders and the introduction of what Acharya J. B. Kripalani and the Indian Socialists, Jaiprakash Narayan and Asoka Mehta, call a capital-saving economy with its very simple improved instruments capable of being made by the artisans in the villages, one will not merely give the natives confidence in themselves and go a considerable way toward the goal of sufficient food, but, what is equally important, one will have nurtured and nourished the indigenous social and religious traditions which, once they come aflame, will provide an unbreakable dyke against the advance of the antireligious materialism which is Communism.

While this is going on, the middle officialdom can be trained in high centers in the ways of democratic control from the top down by free democratic study, committee meetings, discus-

sions and debate. With this achieved, the larger projects introduced nationally at the top can be connected, without the dead
touch of neo-Brahman verbalism and middle level corruption,
with the mass movements and resurgent, indigenous culture
flaming up from the bottom. Then Gandhiji's India and Prime
Minister Nehru's India can become one, and Iqbal's vision
can be in Islam. Even Chiang Monlin's wisdom can bear fruit,
by the spiritual force of its truthfulness alone, in the hearts of
his Confucian brothers on China's mainland, when they become
increasingly disillusioned, as they will, with a Communist
ideologically directed leadership which, after appealing to Chinese values initially, piece by piece destroys them as it must if it
is to remain Communistic. Also Princess Poon's beautiful Buddhist Thailand of the peasants' hearts can merge with Bangkok's Western ways to the mutual gain of both.

But if this is to occur, the secular leaders of the world must
believe in and act upon the principle that nation as well as man
does not live by bread alone. If the bodies of men are to be fed
by a native effort of resurgence, however implemented by foreign ways, their minds and spirits must also be united by a
common mentality, and this mentality must be such as to generate and sustain both the native resurgence from within and
the foreign ways from without. Also, statesman, swami, preacher,
Pope and Mufti must face the fact that no religion or culture
in the world has the monopoly on either the spiritual values
or the moral indignation of mankind. Western technology and
peace-making by law have spiritual roots different from those
of the philosophies and religions of Asia. Similarly, Asian peace-
making by mediation has spiritual sources other than those of
the philosophy and religion of the West. The successful merging of Asian resurgence and Western ways requires the union
of both types of mentality and spiritual value.

8

THE RESURGENCE OF ISLAM

To turn from the literature of Hindu-Buddhist-Taoist-Confucian Asia to that of Islam is, to a Westerner, like moving from a low hanging humid, all-embracing haze into an upper region of fresh, clear air. There is a realistic, explicitly expressed definiteness and directness about the Quran and its Islam which permits one of the West to breath more easily and to see things more clearly, as if one were at home in the clime to which one's physiology is adapted. From the outset also there is an emphasis upon the moral as the determinately lawful. Allah is a God of justice and his creatures are going to be judged.

Nor is this reaction difficult to understand. The intuition of the inexpressible Brahman, Nirvana, Tao or *jen* is foreign to the general outlook and mentality of the West, however immediate in one's experience one finds it to be the moment one takes one's attention off the objects and the subject in the focus and the focusing of attention, to become the all-embracing formlessness evident in the periphery of attention within which one's transitory self as subject and the transitory objects come and go. Islam, on the other hand, derives from the same Greek science with its emphasis upon true knowledge as definite lawful knowledge and from the same Hebrew Christian tradition as does the West. In fact, Islam gave to the West through its Arabian universities in Spain much of the source material and the enlightenment which made the West what it now is.

Judaism, Christianity and Islam in their historical development derive from common roots even though each adds unique elements. There is the underlying solidarity of the Greco-Hebrew Christian Islamic world as well as the solidarity of Asia. Thus, for a Westerner to move from the Asian Far East into Islam is, for all the novelty, in a very real and fundamental sense, to be coming home.

This passage into a more familiar world exhibits itself in the introduction to the two poems, *Complaint* and *Answer* by the Indian Muslim poet, philosopher, lawyer and statesman, Iqbal, who perhaps more than anyone else was the author of Pakistan. Altaf Husain's introduction begins as follows:

> Rabindranath Tagore and Muhammad Iqbal reigned contemporaneously for many years on the twin peaks of the Indian Parnassus. Each represented the genius of the people amidst whom he rose. . . .[1]

Both were Indians under British rule. Both, moreover, conceived the main task of their lives to be the synthesis of their respective religious beliefs and cultures with the beliefs, thought and practice of the West. Tagore was a Hindu Indian whose province was Bengal. Iqbal was a Muslim Indian whose home was Lahore in the Punjab.

Nevertheless, Altaf Husain is forced to add:

> There is little common ground on which the genius of Tagore may meet the genius of Iqbal, because there was a fundamental difference between the two. Iqbal was very much more than a poet or a philosopher. He was an interpreter of those immutable Laws, which, in their operation, bring about the rise and fall of nations. His poetry is born of a lifetime of serious thinking and study of those laws.[2]

Already we are on Western ground. From the soil of India, this Muslim is speaking to us in Western terms. To understand either nations or poetry one must see each particular phenomenon as an instance of a determinate law.

Altaf Husain continues:

In this [study] his teacher was the glorious Quran. . . . The Quran is unlike any other revealed book in existence. . . . It contains nothing out of harmony with the progress of scientific thought. The smallest particle in this universe, as well as the highly complicated system of the stars, are governed by definite Law. Nor is man left out of its governance. But Man alone has been endowed by his Creator with will. His submission to Law must therefore be conscious, not mechanical.[3]

This role of conscious, free choice and acceptance by the individual person is the basic assumption of the whole of Iqbal's religious and political thought. At this point also he strikes a warm note in the heart of the Protestant liberal democratic West. In short, in his emphasis upon law he is classically Greek and Roman. And in his equal emphasis upon human, personal, individual, free choice not merely in the acceptance of this law but also in the reform of its traditional outworn specifications to bring its spirit into accord with contemporary needs and practices, Iqbal is Protestant, liberal and modern.

Nor is this an accident, for Iqbal has done far more than live and breathe the Quran and write a classic work on the development of Islamic metaphysical thought in Persia. He has also been a pupil in his youth of the British philosopher, McTaggart. In fact, McTaggart's emphasis upon the primacy of the individual human spirit has its influence throughout the whole of Iqbal's poetry, philosophy, political thinking and action. Moreover, Iqbal has read, understood and incorporated into his synthesis of Islamic and Western values the major philosophers of the West from the Greeks to the present including even the difference between Whitehead's and Einstein's interpretation of the theory of relativity. Here was a man living his life under British rule in the heart of India's Punjab, thinking and writing in technical Western as well as religiously and philosophically inspired Islamic terms. The final philosophy comes to expression in his *Reconstruction of Religious Thought in Islam,* which quotes as freely from the American Professor Hocking as it does from European and Islamic thinkers and writers.

The resurgence of Islam in our time had at its head not merely Kemal Atatürk of Turkey, but also in Pakistan, the largest Islamic nation, a thinker, lawyer and statesman of the stature of Iqbal. We will do well, therefore, to understand him and to pass step by step through the thoughts which led his Indian Muslim colleagues and followers, such as Jinnah, to the creation of Pakistan and to the conception of the role of Islam in the contemporary world which Iqbal envisaged. The best approach is through the two poems, *The Complaint* and *The Answer*, with which the aforementioned introductory remarks of Altaf Husain have been concerned.

The first poem is somewhat shocking, for it is nothing less than a complaint against God. The background of the poem may be put as follows: Iqbal sits in his study in Muslim Lahore. Near and afar are Hindus worshiping the images and their thousands of gods. He is a devout believer in the Quran which he has devoured and studied until it is of the very essence of his own self and spirit. He has been also to Europe. Outside his study are the mosques and the forts similar to the great monuments he has seen at Delhi, at Agra, at Hyderabad and even to the East in Bengal—monuments which mark the triumph in India of four of the greatest emperors perhaps any dynasty in any civilization in the world has ever possessed. These former rulers of India, the great Moguls, brought to fruition a rich, prodigiously creative and beautiful Indo-Muslim culture of which these forts and mosques and the unparalleled Taj Mahal are but a partial expression and beside which the culture of British India looks not merely secular and unartistic but also verbally legal and commercially crude, for all the gold braid of the British viceroys. Yet under this British rule Muslims move about like slaves asking the British masters for the privilege to do this or that, or even to own their own Islamic souls.

Iqbal recalls also his studies and travels in Europe. He has read all of the best in science, philosophy and religion that the Hebrew, Christian and modern liberal West has to offer. He has thought it all through. He has digested it. He has come to terms with it. He has also found it wanting—wanting as compared with the insight, depth and equal scientific and philosophical profundity of the true Islam.

And why is it wanting? He tells us in his *Reconstruction of Religious Thought in Islam:*

Humanity needs three things to-day—a spiritual interpretation of the universe, spiritual emancipation of the individual, and basic principles of a universal import directing the evolution of human society on a spiritual basis. . . . The idealism of Europe never became a living factor in her life, and the result is a perverted ego seeking itself through mutually intolerant democracies. . . . Believe me, Europe to-day is the greatest hindrance in the way of man's ethical advancement.[4]

The cause he locates at bottom is too great a separation in Christianity between ideals and daily life. This shows especially in Luther's Protestantism but it is true also of Catholicism.

. . . the lesson which the rise and outcome of Luther's movement teaches should not be lost on us. A careful reading of history shows that the Reformation was essentially a political movement, and the net result of it in Europe was a gradual displacement of the universal ethics of Christianity [i.e., the definition of the good in terms of universal principles holding for all men irrespective of race, creed or nation] by systems of national ethics . . . the modern man has ceased to live soulfully, i.e., from within. In the domain of thought he is living in open conflict with himself; and in the domain of economics and political life he is living in open conflict with others.[5]

In his travels in Europe Iqbal went to Spain where he saw at Cordova the university which transmitted to Europe much of the technical Greek scientific and philosophical thought brought there by the Islamic Arabs after being held in custody by them following upon the decline of Athens. From these reveries in his study in Lahore, there must have arisen the perplexing question in the mind of every Muslim in British India: Why is it that we Muslims, who have in considerable part helped to make these Greco-Christian Westerners what they are, why are we now their subjects?

All these architectural monuments and cultural achievements, from the Pyrenees of Spanish Europe to the Bay of Bengal, the followers of Allah have created for Allah. Yet, as their reward, Muslims everywhere are in disrepute, ruled as here in Lahore by the British Christians. Why does Allah, after all that Muslims have done to spread His glory here on earth, thus let his followers down? This is Iqbal's *Complaint*. These are some of his words:

> Before we came, how strange a sight
> Was this most beauteous world of Thine!
> For here to stones men bowed their heads,
> And there in trees did "gods" enshrine! . . .
>
> And canst Thou say that even once
> One of these did Thy name recite?
> It was the might of Muslim arms
> Fulfilled Thy task and gave them Light. . . .
>
> We made our Azan's call [the Muslims call to prayer]
>   resound
> Beneath proud spires in Western lands,
> And made that magic melody
> Thrill over Afric's burning sands. . . .
>
> Whose was the fateful wrath which made
> All idols shrink in terror just?
> "There is no god but God," they cried,
> As crumbling down they kissed the dust. . . .
>
> Yet see how still Thy bounties rain
> On roofs of unbelieving clans,
> While strikes Thy thunder-bolt the homes
> Of all-forebearing Mussalmans! . . .
>
> So be it then, so let us pass,
> Let other nations hold the sway—
> When we are gone, reproach us not
> That Tauhid [the unity of God] too has passed away! [6]

Such is the contemporary Muslim's complaint to Allah. In Iqbal's *Answer* comes Allah's reply. It begins with the angels' comment upon this complaint which rises to Heaven from a speck on earth.

"That they alone are blest with speech
    How proud these humans be,
Yet, ignorant, they lack the art
    To use it gracefully."

Then spake a Voice Compassionate:
    "Thy tale enkindles pain,
Thy cup is brimming full with tears
    Which thou couldst not contain;

Even High Heaven itself is moved
    By these impassioned cries;
How wild the heart which taught thy lips
    Such savage melodies! . . .

On him who merits well, I set
    The brightest diadem,
And those who truly questing come,
    A new world waits for them.

Apostate hearts and palsied hands
    Your earthly lives debase,
You all, to your great Prophet, are
    Bringers of deep disgrace; . . .

The Tulip of the wilds once reigned
    The Queen of blossom-time:
In this once lay the quintessence
    Of Loveliness sublime." 7

Truly Allah has not forgotten the Muslims who planted the
beauty which is the Alhambra, the Taj Mahal, the Fort and
the world's largest mosque at Delhi. But

Unto a nation Faith is Life,
    You lost your Faith and fell,
When gravitation fails, must cease
    Concourse celestial.

You love your homes the least among
    The nations of the earth,
You are the most incompetent
    In knowledge and in worth; . . .

These were your great progenitors;
    You lack their brain and brawn;
You sit and wait in slothful ease
    For every morrow's dawn.

And did you say, for Muslims I
    Mere promises dispense?
Unjust laments at least should show
    Some spark of commonsense.

Eternal is the Law of God
    And Justice is its name,
Should infidels like Muslims live
    The meed shall be the same. . . .

And one your Kaaba, One your God,
    And one your great Quran;
Yet, still, divided each from each,
    Lives every Mussalman.

You split yourselves in countless sects,
    In classes high and low;
Think you the world its gifts will still
    On such as you bestow? . . .

It is the humble and the poor
    Who still my name esteem,
Theirs is the word, theirs is the deed,
    Yours the shame they redeem.

The rich are drunk with wine of wealth,
    Their God they hardly know,
It is because the poor yet live
    That wells of Faith still flow. . . .

When sons, lacking their fathers' worth,
    Are neither skilled nor sage,
With what deserving can they claim
    Their fathers' heritage? . . .

Aspiring for the Pleiades,
    How simple it all seems!
But let there first be hearts like theirs,
    To justify such dreams. . . .

Upon your nation's sky you rose
    Like stars of brilliant hue,
The lure of India's idols made
    Even Brahmans out of you; [8]

Earlier in his life the intuition of the all-embracing formlessness of the Hindu's Brahman almost made an Asian mystic out
of Iqbal.

"Enlightenment" ensnared you all,
    And all your "fetters" fell,
The land of Kaaba [the sanctuary at Mecca]
        you forsook,
    In idol-land to dwell! . . .

Yet, let the gardener not be sad
    To see the garden's plight,
For soon its branches will be gay
    With buds, like stars of light;

The withered leaves and weeds will pass,
    And all its sweepings old;
For there, again, will martyr-blood
    In roses red unfold.[9]

Here enters Iqbal's emphasis on the role of the individual's free
will.

On thee relies the bark of God,
    Adrift beyond the bar,
The new-born age is dark as night,
    And thou its dim pole-star. . . .

Beneath thy foes if chargers neigh,
    Why tremblest thou in fright?
For never, never, shall their breath
    Extinguish Heaven's light.

Not yet have other nations seen
    What thou art truly worth,
The realm of Being has need of thee
    For perfecting this earth.

If aught yet keeps world alive,
    'Tis thine impetuous zeal,
And thou shalt rise its ruling star,
    And thou shalt shape its weal. . . .

Thou art like fragrance in the bud,
    Diffuse thyself: be free.
Perfume the garden breeze, and fill
    The earth with scent of thee.

From dusty speck, do thou increase
    To trackless desert-main.
From a faint breeze, a tempest grow,
    Become a hurricane! [10]

Thus it is that Muslim passion merges with Islamic power and resurgence. One understands also why Iqbal opens his introduction to his *Reconstruction of Religious Thought in Islam* with the words, "The Quran is a book which emphasises 'deed' rather than 'idea'."

But Iqbal was more than a professionally trained philosopher who earned his doctorate at Cambridge University and the University of Munich and a poet of such stature that upon his death on April 21, 1938, Rabindranath Tagore wrote, "India has lost a poet whose work has a great universal appeal." [11] He was also a lawyer professionally trained in England who was called to the Bar by Lincoln's Inn in 1908. So great was his stature both as a lawyer and as a statesman that he was knighted by Great Britain's King, notwithstanding the fact that he was one of the leaders of Muslim India in the Indians' movement for independence from the British Raj.

On August 15, 1947, Pakistan and India attained their separate political independence. As early as 1930, Iqbal led the movement for this independence and specified for the Muslim community the principle governing the terms upon which the Muslims could accept it. Previous to this he had established himself with them as one of their most respected councilors and leaders. From 1925 to 1928 he was a member of the Punjab legislature. On December 29, 1930, he delivered the Presidential Address of the All-India Muslim League which met at Allahabad. This League, like the Congress Party led by Gandhi and Nehru, was dedicated to the independence of India. But whereas the Congress Party aimed at an independent India built on a monistic theory of political sovereignty rooted in a single cultural ideology—either that of the democratic secular state of the West as in the case of Nehru, or that of the intuitive, non-Aryan more purely Asian Hinduism as in the case of the Mahatma—the Muslims were as yet not quite clear concerning what the positive political form and living law culture roots of the new India were to be. Iqbal was the first to see the very serious situation which the Muslim community and its Muslim Indian culture faced.

What he saw was that a secular state in independent India, after the model of the liberal modern democratic West, might very well have the effect of destroying the living law habits, beliefs and faith of the Muslim community entirely, since in an independent India operating on a monistic theory of political sovereignty the Hindus would control the situation, outnumbering the Muslims at least two to one. Iqbal realized also that while the Gandhian, more indigenously rooted Hindu basis for the new India is very effective because of its method of noncooperation in removing the British Raj from India, this political philosophy of intuitive, non-cooperative man-to-manness is likely to be inadequate for building a modern Indian national state. In fact because of the key place of the joint family in Hindu Indian society, Iqbal saw that it is not at all clear that a Gandhian Hindu India can find the grounds for communal loyalty beyond the Asian family and the village which are necessary to build a modern nation. More than this, actual Hinduism has in it not merely the positive man-to-manness of its purely Asian Gandhian component, but also the Aryan factor with its caste system and its pluralistic, monarchic theory of government with its power politics ethics as represented in the five-hundred-odd Indian princely states. Consequently, how a modern India sensitive to the democratic mass movements of the world could be built on the cultural foundations of modern Western democracy when there is an overwhelming Hindu majority was also not clear. Whether, therefore, the new India followed the Congress line either of Pandit Nehru's secular state or of Gandhi's intuitive Bhagavadgita religious state, the result, Iqbal believed, would be a failure of the Islamic culture of one hundred and twenty million Muslim Indians to play the role in the new India which it merits.

He concluded, therefore, that the Muslim community in India was facing a crucial problem, not yet appreciated by its members, the answer to which would determine its life or death. Thus in his Presidential Address to the Muslim League in 1930, he said:

Do not think that the problem I am indicating is a purely theoretical one. It is a very living and practical problem calculated to affect the very fabric of Islam as a system of life and conduct. On a proper solution of it alone depends your future as a distinct cultural unit in India. Never in our history has Islam had to stand a greater trial than the one which confronts it today. It is open to a people to modify, reinterpret or reject the foundational principles of their social structure, but it is absolutely necessary for them to see clearly what they are doing before they undertake to try a fresh experiment.[12]

After saying that he has "given the best part of . . . [his] life to a careful study of Islam, its law and polity, its culture, its history and its literature" and that this "constant contact with the spirit of Islam, as it unfolds itself in time, has . . . given . . . [him] a kind of insight into its significance as a world-fact," he adds: "I propose not to guide you in your decisions but to [present] . . . the main principle which, in my opinion, should determine the general character of these decisions." [13]

The basic principle is one generally accepted by contemporary American legal science. The principle is that positive law in any society will never be effective unless it corresponds to the underlying living law of that society. What this means, put more concretely, is that any constitutional form of government with its particular political and ideological theory, such as that then being considered for the forthcoming free and independent India, will not be effective or good unless it takes into account and draws upon the underlying cultural habits, beliefs and values of the four hundred million Indians to which it refers.

Once the problem of the constitutional forms for the new India is faced in this way, the inadequacy of either the Nehru or the Gandhian proposal of the Congress Party becomes evident, according to Iqbal. Both of these proposals introduce a monistic theory of national sovereignty. They require, therefore, for their justification and effectiveness a living law in India which is also monistic (single, or culturally homogeneous) in character. The living law of India is, however, pluralistic in character, containing Hindu, Muslim, Sikh and many other communities. Also the secular state is foreign to the mentality both of the Hindu community and of the Muslim community. It rests, Iqbal believed, on a false bifurcation of man made by Greek and modern Western philosophy when it divides man into spirit and matter as with Plato and Aristotle or into material substances and mental substances as with Descartes and Locke or into natural science and moral science as with Kant and subsequent humanists.

Islam [Iqbal adds in his Presidential Address] does not bifurcate the unity of man into an irreconcilable duality of spirit and matter. In Islam God and the universe, spirit and matter, church and state, are organic to each other. Man is not the citizen of a profane world to be renounced in the interest of a world of spirit situated elsewhere. To Islam matter is spirit realising itself in space and time.[14]

For Iqbal, therefore, as for Gandhiji, an Indian politics which is secular and consequently does not flow out of India's religions is not true, or realistic politics. Iqbal, therefore, put the following question:

Is it possible to retain Islam as an ethical ideal and to reject it as a polity in favour of national polities, in which religious attitude is not permitted to play any part? This question becomes of special importance in India where the Muslims happen to be in a minority. The proposition that religion is a private individual experience is not surprising on the lips of a European. . . . The nature of the Prophet's religious experience, as disclosed in the Quran, however, is wholly different. It is not mere experience . . . happening inside the experient and necessitating no reactions on his social environment. It is individual experience creative of a social order. Its immediate outcome is the fundamentals of a polity with implicit legal concepts whose civic significance cannot be belittled merely because their origin is revelational. The religious ideal of Islam, therefore, is organically related to the social order which it has created. The rejection of the one will eventually involve the rejection of the other. Therefore the construction of a polity on national lines, if it means a displacement of the Islamic principle of solidarity, is simply unthinkable to a Muslim.[15]

Iqbal does not mean, however, that the Muslim community must become an independent nation, withdrawing from India after the manner of present Pakistan. What it meant for him instead was that the new constitution for India must be built on a pluralistic rather than a monistic principle of national sovereignty. In other words, the new constitution must be a federal one based on the principle of cultural living law pluralism, not on the monistic theory of sovereignty of the Congress Party in either its Nehru Western secular state version or its Gandhian Buddhist Hindu Gita religious version. The reason for this is that the living law of India is not that of a single community with the same religious, social, political habits, beliefs and norms. It is that of two major communities—the Muslim and the Hindu—with their radically different religious, political, legal and other cultural values, and of other communities as well. It is possible, as Iqbal noted in his address, for four hundred million people if they choose to do so together to create a single community of habits, beliefs and values. But this, he added,

. . . involves the long and arduous process of practically remaking men and furnishing them with a fresh emotional equipment. It might have been a fact in India if the teaching of Kabir and the Divine Faith of Akbar had seized the imagination of the masses of this country. Experience, however, shows that the various caste-units and religious units in India have shown no inclination to sink their respective individualities in a larger whole. Each group is intensely jealous of its collective existence. The formation of the kind of moral consciousness which constitutes the essence of a nation [rooted in a monistic theory of political sovereignty] . . . demands a price which the peoples of India are not prepared to pay. The unity of an Indian nation, therefore, must be sought, not in the negation but in the mutual harmony and co-operation of the many.[16]

In other words, the constitution for the new India must be based on a religious living law pluralism. It must be a federal constitution with communal religious or secular states' rights as each particular state may choose.

True statesmanship [Iqbal adds] cannot ignore facts, however unpleasant they may be. The only practical course is not to assume the existence of a state of things which does not exist, but to recognise facts as they are. . . . And it is on the discovery of Indian unity in this direction that the fate of India as well as Asia really depends.[17]

With prophetic insight, he notes that this is as important for the future fate of Asia as it is for the preservation of the unity of Muslim and Hindu India. For

India is Asia in miniature. Part of her people have cultural affinities with nations in the east and part with nations in the middle and west of Asia. If an effective principle of cooperation is discovered in India, it will bring peace and mutual good-will to this ancient land. . . . And it will at the same time solve the entire political problem of Asia.[18]

Thus India can remain one nation, Iqbal added, provided

. . . we are . . . [willing] to recognise that each group has a right to free development according to its own cultural traditions. . . . I love the communal group, which is the source of my life and behaviour and which has formed me what I am, by giving me its religion, its literature, its thought, its culture and thereby recreating its whole past as a living operative factor in my present consciousness.[19]

Yet

. . . as far as I have been able to read the Muslim mind, I have no hesitation in declaring that if the principle that the Indian Muslim is entitled to full and free development on the lines of his own culture and tradition in his own Indian homelands is recognised as the basis of a permanent communal settlement, he will be ready to stake his all for the freedom of India.[20]

This problem of the different cultural norms of the Hindu and Muslim communities of India still remains after partition, in the present India of New Delhi. There are still forty million Muslims within the latter nation. Except for the few leaders who have stayed with the Congress Party, their lot is not a happy one as anyone who has been to Osmania University in Hyderabad knows and as the leaders of India's Socialist Party, who by birth are Hindus and hardly to be accused of prejudice in this matter, clearly recognize. In fact the Socialist Party's solution of the present Hindu-Muslim communal problem in partitioned India is exactly the one which Iqbal proposed in 1930 for India as a whole. It was in fact Asoka Mehta, the Secretary-General of the Socialist Party, who first called the writer's attention to the key importance of Iqbal in the creation of Pakistan and for an understanding of the Kashmir problem, the tension between Pakistan and India and the unsolved communal problem within present Free India.

But how is Iqbal's responsibility for the creation of Pakistan to be reconciled with his desire that the Muslim community remain in an undivided free India? The answer to this question appears also in his Presidential Address of 1930. The answer is that if the leaders of the Congress Party persist in their policy of demanding an Indian constitution built on the monistic principle of national sovereignty of either the secular state or Gandhiji's Buddhist Gita Hinduism, then the Muslim community will have no alternative but to set itself up in the world as an independent nation on Islamic religiously political principles. Furthermore, Iqbal told his fellow Muslims that, at the Round Table Conference in London convened to work out the basis upon which India would receive her independence and to which both he and Mahatma Gandhi were India's delegates,

Mahatma Gandhi . . . gave the Muslim delegation to understand that he would personally agree to Muslim demands and would try to persuade the Congress, the Hindus and the Sikhs to agree to them, provided the Muslims agree to three things: (i) adult suffrage; (ii) no special representation for the Untouchables; and (iii) Congress demand for complete independence. The Mahatma de-

clined to refer the matter to the Congress and failed in his efforts
to get the Hindus and the Sikhs to agree to this arrangement.[21]

In any event when, for whatever may have been the reasons,
this form of constitution and government for an independent
India was not accepted by the Congress Party leaders, the fateful choice put before the Muslim Indians by Iqbal in 1930 was
made in the 1940's and an independent Pakistan became the
fact on August 15, 1947. It is to be noted that in 1937 Liaquat
Ali Khan, later Premier of Pakistan, drafted the following independence resolution which was passed by the All-India
Muslim League as late as 1937:

> Resolved that the object of the All-India Muslim League shall
> be the establishment in India of full independence in the form of
> a federation of free democratic states in which the rights and inter-
> ests of the Mussalmans and other minorities are adequately and ef-
> fectively safeguarded in the constitution.[22]

What this constitution for a national India based on a
pluralistic theory of living law sovereignty would have meant
in practice was also specified by Iqbal in his Presidential Address of 1930. "I would like to see the Punjab, North-West
Frontier Province, Sind and Baluchistan amalgamated into a
single state." [23] In other words, what are now West Pakistan
and East Pakistan would have been two independent states
with complete cultural autonomy in a single federal India composed also of similar Hindu states with their complete cultural
autonomy and such other states as preferred to be secular in
character. It is precisely this type of federalism which exists today in Canada.

In this connection, Iqbal said:

> The principle of European democracy cannot be applied to India
> without recognising the fact of communal groups. The Muslim de-
> mand for the creation of a Muslim India within India is, therefore,
> perfectly justified. . . . [It is] inspired by this noble ideal of a
> harmonious whole which instead of stifling the respective individ-
> ualities of its component wholes, affords them chances of fully
> working out the possibilities that may be latent in them. . . . To

my mind a unitary form of government is simply unthinkable in a self-governing India. What is called "residuary powers" must be left entirely to self-governing states, the Central Federal State exercising only those powers which are expressly vested in it by the free consent of federal states.[24]

He adds that "if a federal government is established, [any] Muslim federal state will willingly agree, for purposes of India's defence, to the creation of neutral Indian military and naval forces." [25]

Such is the importance not merely of the resurgence of Islam which Iqbal, Pakistan and Turkey illustrate, but also of cultural pluralism as a principle for solving the domestic as well as the international problems of the contemporary world. This principle will become increasingly important in the sequel.

What is it in the faith of Islam that makes a monistic communion with Hindu, and one may add, Buddhist, Taoist and Confucian Asia, so difficult. The basic difficulty centers in the radically different concepts of the nature of the moral, political and religious individual in these two cultures. As has become clear already, the true self in Confucianism, Taoism, Buddhism and the non-Aryan component of Hinduism is the one, intuitively given vastness or all-embracing ocean of immediacy which is the Confucian man-to-manness described by Chiang Monlin, the Tao of Taoism, the Nirvana of Buddhism and the non-dualistic Vedanta of Hinduism. It is to this which Gandhi appealed when he carried his Indian masses with him. It is this which sustained the Sufism which Iqbal first followed and from which later, because of his deep philosophical study of Islam and the West, he turned away. It is this concept of the true moral person also which generates the intuitive, mediational method of settling disputes rather than the code method of the second caste Aryan Hindus and of Islam and the West. In this Far Eastern more purely Asian theory of the self, the way to peace and to the fullest realization of one's true self is by the softening down and even the denial of the part of one's self which makes one different from anyone or anything else.

Gandhi, writing of what it means to become a votary of the Gita, says, "And yet, if one is to become a zero, this is precisely what one desiring perfection has to become." [26] To this no Semitic theist whether he be Hebrew, Christian or Muslim can subscribe as the whole truth about the moral, political and religious nature of man; nor can any modern Western secular humanist. For secular and religious Islamic and Western man alike, the definite personality of the self, its unique definite form or λόγος is ultimate, real, moral and divine. Value, virtue, goodness and spiritual fulfillment come by expressing that which makes one different from anyone or anything else.

This is Iqbal's thesis in his great, stirring and influential poem, "The Secrets of the Self," and also in his *Persian Psalms* of which the following are samples:

> If but one atom I must give
> Of this the fabric that I live,
> Too great a price were that, for me
> To purchase immortality.
>
> Give me the heart whose rapture fine
> Flames from a draught of its own wine,
> And take the heart that, self-effaced,
> By alien fancy is embraced.[27]

Compare this with Tagore,

That I should make much of myself and turn it on all sides, thus casting coloured shadows on thy radiance—such is thy *maya* [i.e., the creation by the formless Brahman of something other than himself as mere transitory appearance].

Thou settest a barrier in thine own being and then callest thy severed self in myriad notes. This thy self-separation has taken body in me.

The poignant song is echoed through all the sky in many-coloured tears and smiles, alarms and hopes; waves rise up and sink again, dreams break and form. In me is thy own defeat of self.

This screen that thou hast raised is painted with innumerable figures with the brush of the night and the day. Behind it thy seat is woven in wondrous mysteries of curves, casting away all barren lines of straightness.

The great pageant of thee and me has overspread the sky. With

the tune of thee and me all the air is vibrant, and all ages pass with
the hiding and seeking of thee and me.[28]
I dive down into the depth of the ocean of forms, hoping to gain
the perfect pearl of the formless . . .
And now I am eager to die into the deathless. . . .[29]

Of this Hindu concept of the self, Iqbal says in *The Tulip
of Sinai:*

> The Brahman spake on Resurrection's day
> To God: "Life's lustre was a spark at play:
>   But, if I may so speak without offence,
> The Idol lasted more than Adam's clay." . . .
>
> Moslems! I have a word within my heart
>   More radiant than the soul of Gabriel;
> I keep it hidden from the Sons of Fire,
>   It is a secret Abraham knew well. . . .
>
> Enquirest thou, what is this Heart of thine?
>   The Heart was born, when Fire consumed the Brain:
> The joy of Agitation formed the Heart,
>   And when this ceased, it turned to Clay again. . . .
>
> A beggar thou didst stand on Sinai,
>   For of itself thy soul is unaware;
> Stride boldly forth; be searching for a Man;
>   In that enquiry God Himself doth share.[30]

To find out, however, what Iqbal means by the soul and self,
one must go to his more philosophical writings. In the English
introduction to his poetic volume, *The Secrets of the Self,*
which "took by storm the younger generation of Indian Muslims," [31] he states the Islamic and Western doctrine,

To my mind, this inexplicable finite centre of experience is the
fundamental fact of the universe. All life is individual; there is no
such thing as universal life. God Himself is an individual: He is
the most unique individual. The universe, as Dr. McTaggart says,
is an association of individuals; but we must add that the orderliness and adjustment which we find in this association is not eternally
achieved and complete in itself. It is the result of instinctive or
conscious effort. We are gradually travelling from chaos to cosmos
and are helpers in this achievement. Nor are the members of the
association fixed; new members are ever coming to birth to co-

operate in the great task.   Thus the universe is not a completed act: it is still in the course of formation. There can be no complete truth about the universe, for the universe has not yet become "whole." The process of creation is still going on, and man too takes his share in it, inasmuch as he helps to bring order into at least a portion of the chaos.[32]

Here Bergson and Whitehead as well as McTaggart and the great Semitic Christian religious tradition have had their influence on Iqbal.

Contrast this conception of perfection and divinity as an ideal, never fully realized form or λόγος with Stella Kramrisch's definition of Hindu architecture: Hindu architecture is a formal method of binding the "nameless formlessness" which is the Hindu divinity to material existence.[33] Iqbal emphasizes that "The Koran indicates the possibility of other creators than God." At this point Iqbal drops the following footnote: "Koran, ch. 23, v. 14: 'Blessed is God, the best of those who create.' "[34]

Iqbal adds:

Obviously, this view of man and the universe is opposed to that of the English Neo-Hegelians as well as to all forms of pantheistic Sufism which regard absorption in a universal life or soul as the final aim and salvation of man. The moral and religious ideal of man is not self-negation but self-affirmation, and he attains to this ideal by becoming more and more individual, more and more unique. The Prophet said, . . . "Create in yourselves the attributes of God." Thus man becomes unique by becoming more and more like the most unique Individual. . . . The greater his distance from God, the less his individuality. He who comes nearest to God is the completest person. Not that he is finally absorbed in God.[35]

In another part of the poem [*The Secrets of the Self,* Iqbal continues,] I have hinted at the general principles of Moslem ethics and have tried to reveal their meaning in connexion with the idea of personality. The Ego in its movement towards uniqueness has to pass through three stages:

(a) Obedience to the Law.
(b) Self-control, which is the highest form of self-consciousness of Ego-hood.
(c) Divine Vicegerency.[36]

Again we see how good, moral, religious and political conduct is measured in terms of determinate principles or laws.

Vicegerency occurs when, by true knowledge,

. . . the discord of our mental life becomes a harmony. . . . Thus the Kingdom of God on earth means the democracy of more or less unique individuals, presided over by the most unique individual possible on this earth. Nietzsche had a glimpse of this ideal race, but his atheism and aristocratic prejudices marred his whole conception.[37]

Iqbal affirmed the basis for an international democracy. In an essay on "Muslim Democracy" published in *The New Era* in 1916, he wrote:

The Democracy of Europe . . . originated mainly in the economic regeneration of European societies. Nietzsche, however, abhors this "rule of the herd." . . . But is the plebeian so absolutely hopeless? The Democracy of Islam did not grow out of the extension of economic opportunity; it is a spiritual principle based on the assumption that every human being is a centre of latent power, the possibilities of which can be developed by cultivating a certain type of character. . . . Is not, then, the Democracy of early Islam an experimental refutation of the ideas of Nietzsche? [38]

In the *Letters of Iqbal to Jinnah,* he gives a hint concerning what this Islamic Democracy means when related to the contemporary mood of the masses. With them,

The problem of bread is becoming more and more acute. . . . Happily there is a solution in the enforcement of the Law of Islam and its further development in the light of modern ideas.[39]

It is to be noted that for Iqbal Islamic law is not something finished to the minutest detail and God-given in the ancient past. It has to be reformulated continuously. Only its basic creative philosophy and spirit is given by the past. This persisting spirit must, therefore, be given a fresh expression in the light of modern knowledge, conditions and needs.

After a long and careful study of Islamic Law [he adds,] I have come to the conclusion that if this system of Law is properly understood and applied, at last the right to subsistence is secured to everybody.[40]

What is there in the basic philosophy and spirit of Islamic law expressed in the Quran which insures such consequences? Foremost is its basic affirmation that before God all men are equal. From this the leaders of contemporary Islam conclude that the creation of many of the caliphates with their monarchical dictatorships and gulf between ruler and people is a corruption of the spirit of Islam. Also, the direct relation and responsibility of each individual to God entails the rejection of the Asiatic patriarchal joint family with its inheritance only of sons and the control of the property always in the hands of the eldest surviving son. The laws of Islam when properly applied, therefore, prevent large accumulations of wealth. The Muslim, Justice Doctor Mir Siadat Ali Khan, of Hyderabad State, gave me an instance. He had just come from the settling of an estate. Islamic law, as he correctly applied it that afternoon, had the effect of dividing an estate of some $53,000 between seventy heirs.

He pointed out also that Islamic democracy in practice brings people of every walk of life together in prayer. Even scavengers can sit with, worship with and marry other Moslems. In Islam also there is no class consciousness. Islam also is something bigger than any nation. It is Turkish, Persian, Indonesian and Indian, not merely Arabian. The traditional identification of Islam with historical Arabian military imperialism is also a perversion of Islam, the modern Muslims of Pakistan and India maintain.

Vital, living Islam they affirm is always freshly creative. It does not merely transport an old form of itself. In western and central India, for example, Islam gave birth to a new language —Urdu. At the present moment Islam, carrying out the spirit of democratic economic equality, is introducing an income tax at the national level in Pakistan. But instead of giving it its Western name, they call it by the Urdu word *zakah*. The reason for this is that in the Quran Muhammad affirms that every true believer will give a portion of his means to the community. The Urdu word for this gift is *zakah*. This is the manner in which a resurgent Islam is grafting Western ways into its indigenous Muslim Indian culture.

All modern Muslims do not, however, believe with Iqbal in an Islamic religious state. Those of Turkey have introduced a secular state on the modern Western model. The same position is taken by many Indian Muslims who have remained in free India, such as A. A. A. Fyzee and Maulana Abul Kalam Azad, India's present Minister of Education and Natural Resources and Scientific Research. In the case of the latter, at least, this is made easier by the fact that he is a Sufi Muslim heavily under Gandhiji's influence. Again we see how contemporary Islam is shedding its traditional militaristically imperialistic associations.

Clearly there are other political and cultural beliefs in the world than those of the liberal democratic West for providing the foundations of a truly economic and peaceful world democracy. Buddhism, Gandhi's non-dualistic Bhagavadgita Hinduism, Taoism and Confucianism, as well as Islam, are such other ways. A wise foreign policy for the democratic United States will welcome and encourage these other ways and cooperate with them. As Iqbal has said: "The flame of life cannot be borrowed from others; it must be kindled in the temple of one's own soul." [41]

9

HOW CAN WE DEFEND
FREE CULTURE?

In considering this question, it is necessary first to determine what other people think about it. The European attitude is well known. What is the attitude of Asia and of Islam?

Most Asian and Islamic nations are recovering from rule by Western powers. The resentment of the West which this has engendered still persists. Asians feel that not merely their European rulers but also the United States have used Asian economic resources to feed the industrial machines of the West without regard for the best interest of Asia and the Middle East. They believe also that in this process Western values, ways and institutions quite foreign often to those of their own indigenous culture were imposed upon them. Western codified law, missionary and educational institutions and the necessity of mastering Western languages are examples.

Moreover Westerners justified their presence on Asian soil usually in two ways. Either they were protecting the native people from worse rulers or they were bringing a superior culture and "know-how." To many, these explanations merely added insult to injury; they amounted to the assertion that the native people were inferior both physically and culturally.

This background must be kept in mind if we are to understand the recent failures to win full cooperation for the defense of the free world and if we are to learn how to avoid these failures. The failures show in two ways. First, there is the neutral and even negative official reaction of India and many other Asian peoples to the presence of American troops in Korea even when their presence there is an officially ordered police action of the United Nations. Second, there is the same neutrality and even criticism of American efforts exhibited unofficially by Asian scholars at the Pacific Relations Conference at Lucknow in 1950 and at the Conference for Cultural Freedom at Bombay in 1951.

These negative reactions become in part at least understandable when one notes that both the United Nations' police action and the scholar's conferences had two emphases. One emphasis was upon the imperialistic, dictatorial nature of Communism and the necessity of a policy of military containment including the securing of American air force bases throughout Europe, North Africa, the Middle East and Asia in order to protect Asians and ourselves against this Communist threat. The other emphasis was upon the superiority of the American way of life and the contribution of American "know-how," as implemented by what some Senators have termed "a hard-hitting Voice of America and Information Service." The anti-Communist approach of the military police action and the professor's conferences tend to impress Asians as American hysteria with respect to Communism and but another instance of the traditional Westerner's practice of having reasons convincing to himself for stationing Western troops on Asian soil. The cultural and economic program with its stress on the American way of life and "know-how" tends similarly to strike Asians as another instance of the Westerner's assumption of cultural superiority.

The crucial question now arises, Can anything be done to correct this situation? If the previous methods of enlisting others in the joint enterprise of protecting the free world have backfired in this manner, what other methods can we pursue which have a chance of succeeding?

It has become popular recently to suggest increased economic aid as the sole answer. That this aid is necessary, the annual famines of India and many other countries make evident. That it is wise to give it, if Communism with its claims of economic well-being is to be countered with something constructive, is obvious. But what guarantee is there that this increased economic aid will not be taken as but another instance of Western economic imperialism and of the Westerner's sense of superiority to be used as an entering wedge for imposing an economic and political imperialism?

If nothing else but the economic aid is provided, there is no such guarantee. In fact the chances are likely that even if our economic program succeeds, we will accomplish little more than turn over to the Communists a more economically efficient Asia rather than the present famine-ridden, more poverty-stricken one.

Why such a pessimistic conclusion concerning the effectiveness of intensified economic aid alone? The answer to this question becomes evident if one asks another question: Have the Russian Communists, who won China and the five per cent of the Indian population who voted Communist in the recent Indian election, been taxing the Russian people in order to pour economic aid into China or India? It is hardly necessary to add that the answer is No. The Russians have drawn manpower and food from China, instead of giving aid. The best that Moscow and Peking have done in India is to promise an occasional 50,000 bushels of wheat or rice which have never arrived. The Communists have achieved their present success in China and South Asia partly by picturing an Asian economic utopia, but mainly by winning the minds and deeds of young Chinese, Indian and other Asians to the Marxist-Communist ideology. Instead of spending countless sums of money to send in military equipment, armies or economic aid and thereby running the risk of suggesting to Asians, as other Westerners have done, that they are imperialists, the Russian Communists have exported ideas. By winning local native Asian leaders to the Communist political and economic philosophy, the Soviet Union has placed itself in the enviable position of sitting comfortably and peacefully at home, not guilty of dispatching its army even under the United Nations into Asian territory, while the native Asian leaders do the Communist fighting for them, always in the name of throwing out the American and other Western "imperialists" now so patently on Asian soil. With the native Asian leaders thus converted to Communism, the Communist Asians finance Asia's program of economic reconstruction themselves. Russian military and economic aid comes in only afterward at the request of the Communist Asians. These considerations make it clear that it will do little good to introduce even prodigious economic aid into non-Communist Asia or the Middle East in the quantity necessary to lift the Asian masses out of their present poverty if, during this process, we allow the Communists to continue their present program of capturing the leadership of the masses with the Marxist-Stalin-Mao ideology.

Consider also the native people themselves. Are they likely to use the increased economic aid with the care necessary to make it effective if the aforementioned suspicion of our motives continues? The introduction of Western aid, advice and ways into an Asian culture is difficult under the best of circumstances as a previous chapter has shown. Our aid to Chiang Kai-shek's regime, which ended all too often in the hands of the Communists with huge private profits in the pockets of the Generalissimo's friends, is a powerful reminder. How much greater will the likelihood of failure be if the present masses of under-privileged people do not regard us as trustworthy fellow free men?

The crucial question, therefore, must be faced: What is necessary to create the sense of mutual trust without which no joint United Nations' action to deter, or police, aggression and no program of economic aid can be effective? To answer this question it is necessary to shift our attention from what Muslims and Asians think about us to what they think about themselves.

It has been the fashion recently to describe them as intensely nationalistic. The spirit of nationalism has set India and the rest of the non-European world aflame, we are told. So far as the Westernized leaders and the many Asian students with a superficial smattering of Western learning are concerned, this is true, or at least this is the way in which most of them like to think of themselves. It is also an effective argument for them to use with Westerners.

But how far down into the masses does this spirit of nationalism descend? Merely to ask this question is to realize that it cannot go very deep. For nationalism, as we understand it, is the creation of the Protestant Reformation and the liberal political thought of the modern West. About all this the masses of Asians know next to nothing.

In a recent article in the magazine section of *The New York Times,* Philip Toynbee, writing from Iran in the midst of the oil dispute, noted that one completely misunderstands what is happening there if one regards it as the rise of nationalism in the Westerner's meaning of this word. Instead, he noted, one must look to the indigenous Islamic culture for an understanding of what current events mean to the masses. They are aware of the departure or decline of Western imperialism. To them this means not the arrival of modern Western liberal democratic nationalism, but the departure of barbarism and the resurgence of Islamic civilization.

Let us shift the scene from Teheran to Peking. The occasion is the arrival of President Mao's Communist armies as they take over North China. The marching Communist troops were watched by fascinated crowds of tens upon tens of thousands of Chinese. Their fascination arose from the fact that the Communist troops were singing old Chinese folk songs. Thereby, the Communists were giving the Chinese the feeling that in rejecting Chiang Kai-shek with his American political associations and forms, they were throwing off something that was foreign and artifical and returning to their own selves and the vital rebirth of their own indigenous cultural traditions.

In similar fashion throughout the Islamic world from North Africa, through the Middle East, Pakistan, Indonesia to the

Philippines and throughout the Buddhist, Hindu and Confucian world of Indo-China, Thailand, Ceylon, Burma and India the Communists have kept alive the native Asian's image of America, Britain, France and Holland as imperialists, and through native leaders have identified themselves with the resurgence of the indigenous cultural traditions.

Recently *The New York Times* carried a dispatch from Karachi, Pakistan, dated March 20, 1952, reporting that Burmese Buddhists near the Burma border of East Pakistan "have turned Communist" and attacked Burmese Muslims, driving them over the border into East Pakistan. So great is the appeal of the native culture, even when allied with Communism, to the rank and file, that when the Burmese Government sent its army to put down the disturbance, "instead of fighting the Buddhists the army troops sold their guns to them and walked off back home." Truly, it is not nationalism but the resurgence of indigenous culturalism that is sweeping the world.

The secret of the Communists' success is that the Russians are aware of this development and have allied themselves with it everywhere. The key to our aforementioned failures is that we are still operating within, and from the standpoint of the provincialism of, a Westerner's world. The Communists have been winning leaders in Asia and influencing the masses in the Islamic world every day because they have given them the impression that Communism is on the side of the revival of the indigenous culture. We, conversely, have been losing all too often because our approach has been that of merely attacking Communism or of suggesting that cooperation with us entails recognizing the superiority of our particular way of life. These approaches have little appeal in Asia because the masses of Asians know neither what Communism is nor what our way of life means. But an appeal to their folk songs, symbols, sages, values and centuries-old ways of life—these things, the masses of Asians do understand. Moreover, as Gandhi demonstrated for India and Iqbal and Jinnah showed for Pakistan, to such an appeal they respond by the hundreds upon hundreds of millions.

We know, to be sure, that the final aim of the Communists is the complete antithesis of the preservation of the native culture. No Western ideology or way of life is so completely antithetical to Asian values, traditions and habits as is Communism. This makes their approach all the more significant for our problem.

Suppose that we identified ourselves with this resurgence of Islam and of Confucian, Taoist, Hindu and Buddhist Asia, not hypocritically and merely in the initial stage of contact as do the Communists, but sincerely and always as a matter of permanent principle. Suppose that we not merely urge the Asians to preserve their particular cultural values and traditions for mankind but emphasize in addition that we value and prize them. Suppose also that we point out the danger to them of copying our ways or those of any one else. And let no one make any mistake on this point. The danger of importing ways from the Western world, whether they be American or Russian, is real. The risk is that the Asians become alienated from their own culture, thereby ceasing to be themselves while at the same time not becoming thoroughly grounded in the scientific, philosophical, religious and other cultural roots of the West necessary to understand and apply its ways effectively. The result then is a falling between two stools. The people become so superficially Eastern and so superficially Western that they are nothing. Then so-called governments run by a sequence of military coups take over, if some foreign invader does not.

To put the matter even more concretely, suppose that there came from the official statesmen of the United States, official pronouncements backing the revival of Islam, of Hindu, Buddhist, Taoist and Confucian Asia coupled with the affirmation of the wisdom of the Asian peoples building their political institutions in the light of their own revitalized cultural traditions and values.

Consider what would happen were this done. Instantly the Asian's image of us as a people continuously suggesting the inferiority of his particular culture would be broken. Broken also would be their conception of us as a people putting forward reasons convincing from our cultural standpoint for placing our troops on Asian soil. In short, would we not have the solution of our problem? Is not the key to the protecting of the free world the revival of Asian, Continental European, African and Latin American values, not the attack upon Communism or the high-pressure selling of our own values?

Such a resurgence can do more than set the masses of Asians aflame. Were the Chinese today to recall their own great Confucian culture, they would become acutely aware of its basic doctrine of filial piety. The incompatibility of this with Communism which replaces not merely family loyalty but every phase of one's personal life with a nineteenth century made-in-Germany Marxist loyalty to the nation dictated by Mao and spelled out by Lenin and Stalin would be too patent to need anyone else's commentary. Similarly, the more the other Asian people return to their own Hindu, Buddhist or Islamic roots, the more they become aware of the inescapably religious core of their life and institutions. Once this occurs they themselves will know and decide what to do with materialistic atheistic Communism.

Since the foregoing was written, *The New York Times* of May 3, 1952, carried an article from Rangoon, Burma, by its expert Asian correspondent, Tillman Durdin. This article said:

The Burmese Government is reaching back into traditions of the centuries before British rule in its efforts to build a new national consciousness and a new cultural unity in Burma. The restoration of Buddhism to the vital position it once held in Burmese life is the most prominent aspect of the Government's efforts.

A genuine Buddhist revival is in progress in Burma today, assisted by official measures and by the leadership of devout Buddhists among Government members. Buddhist shrines are now more crowded than ever before; new pagodas are being erected and old ones burnished with new coatings of gold leaf. The teaching of

Buddhism is being intensified, and the Buddhist priesthood is steadily assuming more importance.

The new Burmese Government, organized in March, includes a Ministry of Religion. . . . An attempt is being made to select the most learned and most worthy monks for prominent positions, . . . The teaching of Buddhism in Government schools has been reinstituted. . . .

Government leaders say frankly that one reason why they are encouraging a Buddhist revival is that they feel a philosophic resistance to communism must be created in Burma. Genuine Buddhism and communism are regarded as incompatible and Burmese leaders propose to encourage the people of Burma in a faith that can challenge the appeals of Communist ideology.

The article adds that Prime Minister Nehru has recently sent Buddhist relics to Premier U Nu as a gift from India to Burma and that in the previous year the same thing was done by Ceylon. The gifts were exhibited throughout the country and the populace came "by the thousands" to see them at each place. Again we see the solidarity of Asia which philosophical and cultural unity provides.

Consider also the likely change in the Asian's attitude toward us. Initially the policy upon our part of supporting the native culture will give us little advantage relative to the Communists since we will be doing later what they initiated. But very soon the merely short-term character of the Communists' identification with native values will become evident as their longer-term aim of completely replacing Asian ways with Marxist Western ones begins to take its toll of one thing after another that the Confucian, the Taoist, the Buddhist, the Hindu and the Muslim cherishes. Then our permanent policy of backing indigenous values as a matter of principle and practice will begin to tell.

At this point may not our Asian good neighbors respond as follows: "A free United States which is big enough to respect my civilization and its values in this way is worthy of my hearty respect. For the protection of this way of looking at freedom we can be comrades. From such a United States I can accept economic aid temporarily and some of the Western technological, political and philosophical ways and beliefs necessary to make it effective, while at the same time preserving my self-respect. And should we both find it to be necessary, I can even permit the presence of his troops beside mine on our sacred Islamic and Asian soil without any fear of the loss of my own cherished spiritual and cultural values or of my political freedom at his hands. Certainly a United States which stands on the permanent principle of encouraging any people to be themselves, to build their institutions in the light of their own native traditions and values and to draw from outside only as they choose after the native plant is vibrant and thriving—such a free people I can trust."

Is not such an Asian image of us the true United States of America? Is not this our way to the preservation of the free world?

One final caution remains. Pronouncements of principle will not suffice. Was it not our own Emerson who said, "What you do speaks so loud I cannot hear what you say." If our deeds do not correspond to our words, the peoples of the Middle East and Asia will not hear what we say.

This means that if our stand for their cultural resurgence is to be heard by them, we must align ourselves against imperialism everywhere. This will raise momentary difficulties perhaps with some of our European allies and friends, but these difficulties must be put on the table and faced and met with the correct answer. Nor will this harm our European friends. Great Britain has today the friendship of India because she accepted Indian independence before it was too late. John Bull is our friend and we are his because he respects the moral and political doctrines of John Locke to which we appealed in gaining our independence, and we respect John Bull for giving us those principles through the wisdom of one of his seventeenth century sons. A stand upon the principles of political independence of people anywhere, builds friends; it does not destroy friendship.

More than this, the people of Great Britain and France are not likely to trust and support the United States, however much some of their politicians in power may try to persuade us to the contrary, unless we do stand for native self-government everywhere. The British-owned press throughout Asia and Africa is the quickest to publish any bit of news about the United States which suggests it to be for imperialism. The British and French public back home are instantly nervous and critical whenever there is a suggestion from the United States that its leaders are going to take things into their own hands and go all-out in China or anywhere else to put things there the way a few uninformed hot-heads think they ought to be. The majority opinion of the British and French public itself probably does not believe in imperialism, even though they may not know quite how to withdraw from it gracefully in present circumstances. The people who at Bunker Hill fired the shot heard round the world simply cannot be more imperialistic than the British and French public and be themselves. Police action under the United Nations, Yes! Taking the law into one's own hands to go all-out in a military campaign to make some Asian or Islamic people think and do what some unrepresentative and irresponsible politician hungry for publicity thinks they ought to do, No!

What about backing the French in Indo-China and Tunisia? With respect to the latter there does not seem to be any problem concerning what the answer should be. To give these Muslims independence does not mean practically putting them under a Communist dictatorship and imperialism far worse than the French status they now have. The philosophy of political independence in which we believe must, therefore, be the basis for our deeds and words in this matter. We should help the French to save the friendship of Islam before it is too late.

In Indo-China the situation is not so simple. Where we must stand in principle is quite clear. But it would be a sorry stand for principle which in practice results in its opposite. And this is what leaving the Indo-Chinese to themselves backed with nothing but high words about our stand for their rights to build their political institutions by themselves would mean. Then one's deeds of non-action would turn Indo-China, and probably the whole of South and East Asia, over to a dictatorial Communist imperialistic rule. Deeds again would speak so loud our words in support of political independence for the Indo-Chinese and their fellow free Asians could not be heard.

The moral policy for this situation is the honest facing of the facts of the situation. These facts are that the people of the United States stand for the right of the Indo-Chinese to build their political and cultural institutions in their own free way. We hope that they will find a way to do this within free, independent and friendly relations with France. But if they think not, that is their own business, not ours. The second fact in the situation is the presence of vast armies of Chinese Communists north of the Indo-Chinese border in numbers too large to be interpreted as merely defensive forces to protect China from an attack by Indo-China. Third is the fact of the Communist aggression in Korea and the Chinese Communists' and Soviet Russia's support of that aggression at Lake Success and with volunteers and jet aircraft in the field. Fourth and even more important is the nature of the ideology which Stalin's and Mao's Communists affirm, teach and act upon. This ideology, as the sequel will show, is unequivocally imperialistic, militaristic and committed to world revolution and conquest. To leave the Indo-Chinese and the rest of Asia helpless before these facts is hardly, therefore, to match our words concerning their right to independence with deeds that make these words real.

In such a situation there are but two morally justifiable courses. Either one pursues Gandhiji's pacifistic non-Aryan Asian moral way to peace or one pursues the way to peace by world law backed with the police force necessary to make it effective. To go with the French in Indo-China on a purely power politics basis will be to make our stand for political independence a sham in the minds of the masses of mankind throughout the world. It will be practically to underwrite with our deeds all the charges of power politics' imperialism that the Communists hurl against us. It will in short be practically to hand the masses of the world to the Communists upon a silver platter made of the shiny dollars of the United States taxpayers' money.

To leave the Indo-Chinese to Gandhiji's way to peace will produce the same result, not perhaps because Gandhiji's way would not succeed if all people practiced it, but because, even if all Westerners withdrew from Indo-China, the Asians themselves would not follow his method. We have already seen that, notwithstanding Gandhiji's influence, Pandit Nehru and his Congress Party were not able to practice it in India. They found it necessary to choose the way to order and peace by law backed not merely with police but with an army. The Indo-Chinese would do the same were every Westerner to withdraw from Indo-China's soil.

Clearly, therefore, the moral way in Indo-China is by law backed with police power. But this law must not be French-made or United States-made. It must be made and policed in the name and by the decisions of the world community. The task of a wise statesmanship upon the part of the United States is that of persuading, by an honest, objective presentation of the aforementioned facts, the majority members of the United Nations and our Asian friends in Indo-China, Japan, Indonesia, Thailand, Ceylon, India and Islam of the wisdom of this course. There are spiritual resources and moral principles capable of resolving the problem of the contemporary world if we will but use them.

10

THE SPIRITUAL FOUNDATIONS
OF WESTERN CIVILIZATION

In building a sound foreign policy it is not sufficient to know the mind of the rest of the world. We must also know our own mind and what we stand for. Here we shall consider only those values which Australia, Canada, Ibero-America, New Zealand and the United States have in common with the other nations of the West. The unique values of the United States will be specified in the last Chapter.

The classical spiritual values of the West are two in number: (1) Greco-Roman science and philosophy with their unique concept of law, and (2) the Hebrew-Christian religion.

The former of these two spiritual roots grew first, since Europeans were Greeks and Romans before they became Christians. In fact Stoic Roman law with its technical terminology, which is now a commonplace in every law school in the West, was created before Europe became Christianized. Moreover, Christianity itself is as much Greek and Roman as it is Hebrew. Were it not such a synthesis it would never have encompassed Western civilization. The Hebrew component, of course, paralleled the creation and development of Greek science and philosophy. It provides a natural transition to Greece and Rome.

In many respects the Hebrew society of the Old Testament is identical with the Asian societies of the Far East. The social unit was the patriarchal family. Only sons inherited and the share of the eldest son was double that of the others. Also upon him rested the greater responsibilities.

Even so there is one marked basic difference between the patriarchal family of the Hebrew and that of a non-Aryan Hindu, Buddhist, Taoist or Confucian society. In the latter, as we have noted, the use of law as a method for settling disputes is regarded as something to be avoided. Individuals are not measured against determinate rules, but are instead encouraged to cover up their transitory, relativistic rights and differences and to cultivate, through mediation, the all-embracing formlessness common to all things—human and inorganic objects alike. In the Old Testament, however, from beginning to end the emphasis is upon law: "Receive, I pray thee, the law from his mouth, and lay up his words in thine heart," is the injunction given in the Book of Job.[1] Exodus 13:9 and 10 say,

And it shall be for a sign unto thee upon thine hand, and for a memorial between thine eyes, that the Lord's law may be in thy mouth: for with a strong hand hath the Lord brought thee out of Egypt.

Thou shall therefore keep this ordinance in his season from year to year.

There are, of course, the Ten Commandments.

Now these are the commandments, the statutes, and the judgments, which the Lord your God commanded to teach you, that ye might do them in the land whither ye go to possess it:

That thou mightest fear the Lord thy God, to keep all his statutes and his commandments, which I command thee, thou, and thy son, and thy son's son, all the days of thy life; and that thy days may be prolonged.[2]

Clearly this is not a code of good behavior tailored to each person, time and circumstance. Deuteronomy 1:16 and 17 enjoin:

And I charged your judges at that time, saying, Hear the causes between your brethren, and judge righteously between every man and his brother, and the stranger that is with him.

Ye shall not respect persons in judgment; . . .

Obviously each person and each dispute is not unique. All men are equal before the law.

More than this, law transforms men into moral beings. "The law of the Lord is perfect, converting the soul. . . ." [3] Verse 10 adds: "More to be desired are they than gold, yea, than much fine gold: sweeter also than honey and the honeycomb." Proverbs 13:13 affirms that: "Whoso despiseth the word shall be destroyed: but he that feareth the commandment shall be rewarded." Clearly the good is not to be found in the cultivation of inexpressible common feeling and intuition but by means of definite words and explicitly expressed rules and commandments.

Isaiah, Chapter 2, tells us that instead of generating litigation and discord, law is the way to peace. After saying in verse 3 that "for out of Zion shall go forth the law," there follows verse 4 with its famous description of the consequences: ". . . and they shall beat their swords into plowshares, and their spears into pruninghooks: nation shall not lift up sword against nation, neither shall they learn war any more." Such are the moral values and power of determinate statutes and law as conceived by the Jews of the Old Testament.

The New Testament continues in the same vein. Jesus is reported in The Gospel According to St. Matthew, Chapter 23, verse 23, as saying:

Woe unto you, scribes and Pharisees, hypocrites! for ye pay tithe of mint and anise and cummin, and have omitted the weightier matters of the law, judgment, mercy, and faith: these ought ye to have done, and not to leave the other undone.

The Gospel According to St. Luke, Chapter 16, verses 16 and 17, add:

The law and the prophets were until John: since that time the kingdom of God is preached, and every man presseth into it.

And it is easier for heaven and earth to pass, than one tittle of the law to fail.

St. Paul in his Epistle to the Romans, Chapter 2, verse 11, says: ". . . there is no respect of persons with God." He adds also in Chapter 3, verse 20, that "by the law is the knowledge of sin." In verses 12 and 14 of Chapter 7, he tells us, "the law is holy," and "the law is spiritual."

There is a radical difference, however, between the concept of law in the New Testament and that in the Old. We have come upon it before in connection with Christ's saying that He comes to break up the joint family.[4] This revolutionary difference occurs because between the time of the Old Testament and the New Testament the Stoic Romans created a unique type of law due to the impact upon Roman society of Greek natural science and philosophy. The spiritual foundations of Western civilization are the product of this synthesis in Christianized Rome of Judaism and Greek scientific natural philosophy.

This is why the spirit of the Christian West is as Greek as it is Hebrew in its roots, as the Protestant Dean W. R. Inge has emphasized.[5] In certain very important respects, it is if anything more Greek than Hebrew. The great achievement of the West as compared with Asia is its capacity to achieve political unity over social groups and geographical areas extending far beyond the Hebrew or Asian joint families or tribes, a political union, moreover, the moral communal roots of which have nothing to do with family, tribe, status or inductively given station. The concept of such a society was first envisaged by the Stoic philosophers who created Western law. This new, more universal concept of law and political organization the Roman Stoics derived from Greek natural science and philosophy. It did not come from the Hebrew tradition, as the type of social organization exhibited in the Old Testament and the failure of the Jews to preserve their political organization through Western history clearly demonstrate.

This unique genius of the West with respect to political organization has been clearly seen by the contemporary Indian, N. C. Chaudhuri. In his analysis of Indian culture and its history,[6] he points out that insofar as Indian society has ever in its history achieved a political organization beyond the typical

Asian joint family village elders system by moral norms and controls, in which the King is largely a mere model for the local families, the achievement has been due to a synthesis of Asian values with Western ones. Indian civilization in its fullness is, he says, a sequence of three such syntheses: (1) The Indo-Aryan synthesis which began at about 1500 B.C. and ended in A.D. 1192 with the conquest of India by the Muslims; (2) The Indo-Muslim synthesis which began in A.D. 1192 and ended in 1757 with the conquest of Muslim India by the British; (3) The Indo-British synthesis which began in 1757 and ended on the 15th of August, 1947, when India achieved her present independence.

Chaudhuri notes that there is a decrease in the rich diversity of culture with the sequence of the three epochs, but that there is an increase in the achievement of political organization and unity. Indo-Aryan India is the least mature politically. Islamic India is much more advanced politically. British India with its unique Western type of law achieves the most mature political organization of India's entire history.

This becomes intelligible when the following facts are revealed. The Aryans brought to India the natural history type of political codes expressed in commonsense terms which the relational type of thinking implicit in their Sanskrit language made possible for them. The Muslims brought to India the still greater mentality for political unity which the Islamic tradition that derives from its less developed synthesis of the Greek and the Hebrew-Christian biblical tradition provides. Whereas the British brought to India the genius for political organization transcending the family-village and even the princely states and provinces which Greek science, coming to moral fruition through Roman law, gave to the Western world. The essence of the spiritual roots of this Western political genius, as we shall see, is the previously noted thesis of Greek science that any truly known thing or event is an instance of a theoretically conceived determinate law.

If we are going to know, therefore, what we stand for in the foreign policy of the United States when we support the spiritual values of Western civilization, it is essential that we examine Roman law more in detail in its relation through Greek philosophy to Greek natural science. The heart of the matter has already been hinted at in connection with Chiang Monlin's designation of the difference between Far Eastern Asian and Greek Western mentality. The key notion is that in Greek science nature ceased to be described merely in terms of the way we feel it immediately when we, through naive observation, become aware of ourselves as immersed in its continuum of impressionistic aesthetic immediacy. Instead nature is conceived as something inferred from this naively felt and observed nature but not immediately inspected in it.

An obvious example of nature as known in this Western way, first discovered by the ancient Greeks, is nature as known in Einstein's general theory of relativity or in the electromagnetic theory of Lorentz. In Einstein's theory, nature is conceived as a four-dimensional continuum having a metrical structure with the formal properties described by the mathematical formula which is Einstein's tensor equation for gravitation. This formula is very precisely mathematical, yet neither it nor the metrical structure of space-time which it describes is directly observable. It and its natural object can be thought formally, but cannot be seen. This is what Chiang Monlin means by the rationalistic character of Western mentality. Its way of knowing nature is illustrated again in the contemporary theory of electricity and magnetism in which entities called electrons move according to certain mathematical laws with respect to other entities called protons. Neither any one of these scientific objects, individually, nor the system of them as a whole is directly observable. Moreover, the entity designated by the word "electron" has no meaning by itself. The only scientific meaning this entity has is the meaning given to it by the relations in which it stands to other entities like it or different from it. These relations are not sensed. They are merely intellectually and formally knowable as given in the formula of mathematical physics. Put in slightly more technical language, scientific objects, as conceived since the time of the Greek scientists, are entities satisfying the postulates or laws of some explicit, deductively formulated scientific theory. Since the time of the Greek mathematical physicists to be a scientifically known individual is to obey certain definite universal laws. Apart from the laws or postulates of the theory, any scientific concept is a meaningless term. An electron in other words is a term in a relatedness, the grammar of which is that of mathematics rather than, say that of Sanskrit or of ordinary English prose.

But what, it may be asked, can all this have to do with ethics and law and the political genius of the West? The answer should already be evident. If good conduct is conduct which proceeds from true knowledge about what conduct has to relate, namely man and his fellow men and nature, and if knowledge of man and nature reveals man and other entities in nature to be the instances of determinate laws with a syntax or grammar not derived from inductively given family, village or tribal relations, then the moral basis for political organization becomes free from such limitations. To be a moral man means to be a citizen not of one's family or one's tribe or of any particular geographical area, but to be a citizen of a community of theoretically constructed, technically conceptualized relations. Thus large numbers of men living too far apart for intuitively felt contact can achieve a common bond of unity by the free individual acceptance of a common constitutional contract which has nothing to do with inductively observed family, caste or tribal status.

As Zeno the Stoic and Socrates the Platonist among many others put the matter, "I am a citizen of the universe." Φύσει (nature) as revealed in experimentally verified, logically constructed theory rather than observed social convention (θέσει) becomes the model for just, peaceful and divine political, economic and social organization. One becomes saved by the word. As the distinguished student of ancient law, Sir Henry Maine, has put the matter, the shift is made "from status to contract." [7]

The reason why this shift from a merely inductive intuitive

approach to man and nature to an indirectly verified, logically formulated, theoretically constructed one makes possible the larger and more universally applicable political forms should now be obvious. To make such a system work, it is not necessary to have the moral citizen in an intimate, warmly felt, inductively given contact in an Asian joint family or village of elders or in an ancient Roman paterfamilias or its slightly enlarged city-state. Nor is it necessary, in order to achieve bonds of unity over a wider area, to take men out of their attachment to inductively given social commitments and forms by a process of non-attachment and pacifistic non-cooperation into the Confucian's all-embracing vastness or the non-dualistic formlessness of Nirvana, Tao and Brahman after the recent manner of Mahatma Gandhi. Instead, men thousands of miles apart, widely separated in time, can enter into bonds of unity merely by accepting a common theoretically constructed doctrine for the ordering of their economic and social life together. Intimate, warm feeling and mediational contact are not necessary.

The Pax Romana initiated in the vital fullness of Roman philosophical Stoicism is the first instance of this. As one contemporary English scholar, Lawrence Waddy, has shown, these Romans "were the people who came nearer than any others in any age to the peaceful government of the civilized world." [8] The later, rich, theoretical development and formulation of Islamic law and the single order brought into Spain, the Middle East and even India by Islam is a second instance.

This conception of scientifically known, theoretically conceived man and nature was called the λόγος (logos) in the philosophical and religious tradition of the West. But this logos was more than scientifically verified theory of the true for nature and for natural man as a part of nature. It was also at the same time the criterion of the divine for religion as the first verse of the Fourth Gospel tells us.

Not only did it result in the creation of Stoic Roman Western legal science with its technical formulation, but also, following upon the decline of the vision and influence of Augustus, it

passed to the early church fathers, into the Christian Roman
Church itself and the Holy Roman Empire and through St.
Thomas, Suárez and Grotius into the West's first formulation
of international law. Out of it also arose something completely
foreign to the mentality of Gandhiji's non-Aryan more purely
Asian Asia—the moral concept of a just war. As a contemporary
student of Western law has written, "The invention of the 'just
war' doctrine constitutes the foremost Roman contribution to
the history of international law." [9]

Even in modern times France, as is well known, with its
continental code, uses the logical method of bringing the concrete case and its assignment to a legal category treated as a
minor premise, together with a major premise which is the
universal legal proposition, to decide the case in a logical syllo-
gistic manner. In short the logos operates not merely in the
systematic formulation of the law as a body of determinate
universal propositions but also in the logic of the application of
the law to the concrete case in the judge's decision.

Modern Anglo-American law also, for all its initial emphasis
upon the concrete cases, proceeds in a similar manner, preserving the technical terminology of Roman legal science and
applying the Roman ideal of appeal to inductively determined
universal propositions for the settlement of disputes. The
United States is even more Roman than Great Britain, for by
means of an appeal to its written constitution the Supreme
Court can overrule an act passed by Congress. Even in those
areas where collective bargaining is used, the method is not
the Gandhian, Buddhist, Hindu, Confucian one of cultivating
an intuitive warm feeling of man-to-manness. Such a description
hardly characterizes the spiritual nature of John L. Lewis when
he negotiates a contract for his miners with the United States
Steel Corporation. The method of negotiation, instead, is that
of hard bargaining ending in a determinate and precisely
worded contract. Moreover, even in wage negotiations and recourse to boards of mediation an appeal is often made to the
law and the constitution. Witness the recent decision by Judge

Pine in the appeal by the steel companies to the propositions of the constitution following upon their refusal to accept the recommendation of the board of mediation.

This Anglo-American application of law and its logos as the proper method for bringing order and peace in society and settling disputes has been given new content by modern French rationalistic and British empirical philosophy. This alone distinguishes modern law from medieval law. Countries accepting this modern version of Roman law extend from the Scandinavian nations through Great Britain, the United States and Canada to Australia, New Zealand and even on to Prime Minister Nehru's secular India.

Communist Russia, with its theoretically constructed doctrine made in Germany and based in major part upon Hegel's rationalistic dialectic and the laws and technical concepts of early English economic science, presents another example of the same approach to social organization by recourse to abstract propositions and technical theory rather than warm-hearted intuition or the family, caste and tribal relations observed inductively. It is in fact only by the imposition of this single Marxist Communist doctrine upon the entire world that Soviet Russia believes peace can be achieved.

Truly an event of momentous importance occurred on the surface of this earth when Greek mathematical scientists, using logical and mathematical construction and deduction as well as observation and experimentation, found a new way of knowing and thinking about man and nature. This way of thought passed over through every school of Greek philosophy to create the Roman technically conceptualized science of law and to transform the Hebrew culture and religion into Christianity as it came to expression in the Gospels and St. Paul's Epistles, the Church Fathers, the Greek Orthodox Church Oecumenical and the Roman Christian Church Universal.

Clearly Greek science and philosophy and Roman Stoicism as well as Christ's fulfillment of the Hebrew Old Testament tradition made Christianity and Western civilization what it is. With the locus of the model of justice in theoretically conceived nature rather than in the intuitively felt continuum of immediacy or in the patriarchal family relationship and the ethnological species given inductively by natural history science, fathers were, as Jesus said, put against son, mother against daughter and daughter-in-law against mother-in-law. Forthwith belief in a determinately expressed doctrine rather than loyalty to one's parents, ancestors, caste or ethnological group determined the morally good and just men. And with respect to a particular determinate, theoretically expressed doctrine which is believed, father and son, daughter-in-law and mother-in-law, nation and nation, and even man-to-manness can differ without any moral sense of failure of loyalty to family or tribe or God. A British peer can belong to the Tory Party; his son to the Socialist Labor Party. An American father can be a New Deal Democrat, whereas his son votes Republican. The reason for the absence of any sense of lack of loyalty is that in the West, after ancient Greek mathematical physics, Zenonian, Platonic and Aristotelian philosophy and Stoic Roman law, theoretically formulated doctrine rather than inductively given family feeling and piety defines the morally good father, son, daughter or mother-in-law.

Moreover, the different theoretically formulated doctrines may be logically incompatible. Then something occurs which is foreign to Asian Asia. Moral and religious differences arise which are not (as the Vice President of India, the Hindu philosopher, Professor Radhakrishnan suggests) [10] merely different ways of approaching or saying the same thing. Real, not merely verbal conflict is present in both the religious and the moral sphere. Moreover, such conflict arises not as Professor Radhakrishnan suggests because of intolerance and a failure to understand the other person's or nation's theoretically formulated doctrine, but because of a careful reading and understanding. In other words, the relation between moral men and doctrinally guided nations becomes dialectical rather than merely that of seeing, approaching or expressing the same moral goal and object in diverse ways.

That this is the case with Russian Communism is shown by its name. It calls itself not merely materialism, but dialectical materialism. The word "dialectical" expresses its conviction that the relation of its theoretically formulated ideals and program to those of any other people, culture or nation is that of logical contradiction. The acceptance of the one is incompatible with the toleration or acceptance of the other. This is especially true in the case of Russian Communism because it affirms that its theoretically formulated doctrine is not merely morally and legally obligatory upon those people, such as the Russians, who believe it, but also upon everyone else whether they accept it or not. This will become evident when we examine Premier Stalin's description of the theory and practice of Communism.

When two countries governed by dialectically related (i.e., logically incompatible) ideals, such as North and South Korea, or the U.S.S.R. and the traditional democracies, face an international dispute, the dispute is completely misunderstood and falsely conceived if it is described as a difference merely of ways to a common goal. A goal is meaningless except as it is specified by a given ideology or the factors in knowledge which that ideology designates. Hence, when the ideologies are incompatible, the goals are also. Being in its essence dialectical, justice with respect to such a dispute simply cannot consist in the mediational, pacifistic Gandhian purely Asian technique of softening down or covering up the determinately expressed doctrinal differences as if they were of secondary importance and merely verbal.

To ask a people or nation with a theoretically formulated morality to compromise the basic principles of that morality is, from the standpoint of the spiritual foundations of Western civilization here outlined, to ask them to stop being moral men. Clearly until Western peoples and nations give up their

own science, philosophy, religion, ethics and law to become non-
dualistic Vedanta Hindus, pacifistic, intuitive Buddhists or
mediational followers of Confucius, such a way to peace when
dealing with Western nations or with Asian nations introducing and pursuing a Western political ideology or economic
program simply will not work. More than this it is to ask the
Western believer, or the Asians who accept a Western constitutional form of government, to be false to their own beliefs,
ideals and values.

To become clear upon this dialectical character of the relation between theoretically constructed ideologies of the Western type is exceedingly important at the present time. One of
the major nations in the world is guided by Marxist Communist
doctrine. This ideology is also that of the North Korean aggressors and their Chinese as well as Russian supporters. It
explicitly asserts itself to be dialectically related to all non-
Communist ideologies and societies. Put more precisely this
means, as they themselves make clear, that their way of life and
goal is logically and in practice incompatible with that of any
non-Communist people.

This would not be too dangerous for peace were they content
to restrict their dialectical ideology to themselves. Unfortunately, however, as Chapter XI will show, Premier Stalin
demonstrates that no Communist can be a true believer in this
dialectical ideology unless he engages in revolutionary activity
by resort to force to negate and destroy all societies in the world
which are built on other ideologies.

To suppose, therefore, that nations frankly governed by
Marxist Stalinist Communist doctrine have the same goal as
the rest of mankind is to ignore what Communists call their
doctrine, namely dialectical and historical materialism, and to
pay no attention to what they say it requires them to do. It is
to fail to realize also that in the West where social, religious,
legal and other norms are obtained by theoretical contractual
construction rather than by natural history description of traditional status, different doctrines are not, as is the case with

Brahman, Nirvana and Tao, merely verbally different ways of saying the same thing, but may be, and in the twentieth century actually are, both logically and in practice, incompatible.

But if the Gandhian (more purely Asian) way to peace is neither a moral nor a practicable way to resolve disputes between nations governed by different Western dialectically related ideologies, how then are we to proceed? There are two answers to this question. The first will concern us in Chapter XII. The second calls for an investigation of the basic problem to which the self-contradictory Western ideological doctrines are different answers to determine which is correct. This will be done in the final chapter.

It remains here to indicate the way in which the Greek scientific knowledge of nature as something theoretically constructed and expressed in terms of logically formulated laws, called a logos, has worked itself out as a norm in other fields than that of politics and law. Religion ceases to be thought of as the immediate immersion of oneself in the all-embracing formlessness which is the non-Aryan Brahman, Nirvana or the Confucian vastness. Nor will it be thought of as harmony with naively observed nature with its cycles and rhythms after the manner of the Confucian Chinese or the Hindu's communion with natural phenomena at dawn and dusk. Instead the heart of the religious and good life will be regarded as the imposing of an ideal, theoretically conceived pattern, λόγος or polity called the Kingdom of Heaven or the City of God upon the directly observed confusion, filth, evil, chaos and tendency to formlessness of the immediately experienced world.

This is why the Son of this Fatherly Divine λόγος had to come into this naively observed world to teach men there the prayer, "Thy will be done on Earth as it is in Heaven." This is why Plato, before Jesus, saw that the spirit of the Western world is the vision of the New Atlantis, and why the distinguished contemporary Mexican poet, scholar and statesman, Alfonso Reyes, has written,

America is a Utopia. . . . It is the name of a human hope. . . .
From time to time the philosophers divert themselves in outlining
the contours of the desired perfect city, and these outlines invoke
Utopias, of which the Constitutional Codices—if I may be permitted
an observation of actuality—are nothing more than the last mani-
festation.[11]

Seneca's *Ultima Thule* echoes the same spiritual theme for the
early empire of Stoic Rome. At the same time the creators of
Christian thought point out that man is saved, not by walking
in the woods beside a cool pool after the manner of Confucius,
but "by the Word." As the ideal order for the community is
not given in direct experience, it can be known only by words,
i.e., by theoretically or ideationally expressed doctrine. It was
natural, therefore, for the Greek Christian Fourth Gospel of the
New Testament to open with the sentence, "In the beginning
was the Word [the original Greek is λόγος], and the Word was
with God, and the Word was God." [12]

Forthwith the love of God is what Spinoza was later to describe as the intellectual love of God. Notwithstanding this
intellectual essence of the Divine love, the Fourth Gospel
is emotionally the most moving portion of the New Testament.

The practical consequences of these new tidings are equally
unique. One treats other men with intellectual love when one
judges them with the same universal, definite legal rules one
uses to judge oneself. Particular man is universal man, an instance of the same universal commandments or laws. Then and
only then does a Western Christian religious man who truly
knows the spiritual foundations of his own faith, do unto others
as he would have them do unto him.

Initially, however, this Greek scientific and intellectual conception of the good and the divine did its beneficent work
in the world by way of the theory of ideas as universals in Greek
and Stoic Roman philosophy and in the creation of the Western
science of law. Only later, when Rome's political leaders failed
to match their ideals with their deeds, did that synthesis of

Greek science and philosophy and the Hebrew religious fulfillment occur in Jesus, St. Paul, the Church Fathers and the
Christian Church Universal which is Christian Western civilization.

It is well to remember that even before this synthesis appeared, Rome created an order within which peace under law
reigned. This order embraced the whole of Europe including
Great Britain and Central Europe, as far east as the present
line between East and West Germany, Greece, Macedonia, Asia
Minor, Syria, Lebanon, Palestine and Egypt. Over this vast area
they established a lawful political stability and an era of peace
which lasted, as Lawrence Waddy has recently written, "for
longer than other Empires." [13] They did this moreover by
solving the problem we today must learn to solve, of putting
"courage in war to a constructive use in peace." [14] The secret
of their success, as this English scholar points out, is their
concept of justice embracing all families, tribes, peoples, villages
and city-states. This concept of justice, according to which any
individual regardless of his inductively given status is an instance of and equal before the same explicitly expressed universal law, they received from Greek physics and philosophy
through Roman Stoicism.

Consider the previous humble beginnings of which this
remarkable achievement initiated in 31 B.C. by Augustus was
the fruition. The earlier story opens in a village, typical in
Europe then and in Asia now. This village is made up of
patriarchal families of farmers. It is located on a hill called the
Palatine beside an Italian river called the Tiber. The time is
around 500 B.C. just after its citizens under the leadership of
their elders had expelled the last Etruscan. From this they grew
to embrace first the other city-states of Italy, then Carthage,
Gaul, Britain and Spain and finally Greece, Macedonia and
the eastern empire. So far, however, there was nothing new.
Countless previous peoples had done this before them. The
novelty came when these Romans found a new way of making
the transition from war to peace a more lasting one.

The key to their success was that one of the peoples whom they brought under their sway were the Greeks. Thereby, they had the good fortune to be conquered by Greek scientific and philosophical ideas. Augustus himself, then known as Gaius Octavius, was studying in Greece when the news of Caesar's death called him back to Rome in 44 B.C. But long before this, Greek logic and physics and its ethics and politics had been brought to Rome by every school of Greek philosophy. In 159 B.C. the Greek Panaetius, a Platonist who taught Aristotle and Theophrastos, visited Rome. Four years later the Greek philosophers Diogenes, Carneades and Critolaus came to acquaint the Romans with every phase of Greek thought from logic and its deductively formulated mathematical physics to ethics and politics. In 129 B.C. the "scientific Panaetius" returned to head the Stoic school in Athens for the next twenty years.[15] Scipio was captured by these Greek scientific and philosophical ideas. An expert student of this period tells us that "round Scipio and his Greek friends Polybius and Panaetius there gathered a society of the noblest and most intelligent men of Rome; and in this circle the Latin language as well as Greek philosophy found a new birth." [16]

The Latin language is formal and syntactical, as countless Western school boys know. Forthwith through the pens of Virgil and many others this Greek formal, logical, scientific, philosophical, moral and legal way of thinking went into the emotional life and thought of even the humblest of Roman citizens. A few years later came "a great astronomer," [17] Posidonius. Arnold in his classic work on Roman Stoicism tells us that Posidonius acquired "a brilliant reputation . . . in . . . Rome [and that] Cicero made his acquaintance at Rhodes in 78 B.C., and refers to him more often than . . . to any other of his instructors." [18] Arnold adds: "In physics and logic alike Posidonius upholds the doctrine of the Logos, and it appears that it passed directly from him to Philo of Alexandria, and so into Judaeo-Christian speculation." [19] Hence it was, as Arnold writes, that for a long time to come Stoic principles were faithfully inculcated in thousands of Roman homes, and young men taught in childhood to model their behaviour upon the example of [such teachers] . . . formed the salt of the Roman world.[20]

The importance of this can hardly be over-emphasized. It means that the transformation in the living law habits, beliefs and emotions of men necessary to sustain the new positive legal and political forms was achieved. These Roman Stoics did not make the mistake of supposing that one can impose new legal and political forms upon a people or culture whose mentality and habits are quite different, without at the same time, through prose and poetry and new moral teaching in the family, transforming the people's beliefs, emotions and habits accordingly.

Such was the intellectual and cultural situation which Augustus inherited when he returned to Rome from his studies in Greece. Let no one suppose, however, that the social and political situation itself corresponded to this vision of a far-reaching political order at peace with itself under a rule of law modeled on the logos of Greek natural science. The situation in fact was quite the reverse. In this first century before Christ, civil war was rampant. Cruelty, slavery and bloodshed were everywhere. One could hardly imagine an intellectually conceived philosophical ideology coming into operation at a more unpropitious time.

Consider Augustus's account of what he did as reported in his diary. He tells us that first he stopped the civil war throughout the empire. Second, he writes, "I restored the Republic to liberty." [21] Then he reduced this free Republic to what he termed "a state of peace." [22] So great was his success that, as Waddy tells us, even the cynical Tacitus, writing a hundred years later, had to admit that Augustus "lulled the world with the opiate of peace." [23]

What did Augustus and these Roman Stoics mean by freedom? They meant something rooted in the method of acquiring Western scientific knowledge, as an examination of what they called "logic" will show. To understand this it is necessary to examine the light which the Greek natural scientists' knowledge of nature threw on the nature of man.

It is usual to suppose that the verified theories of natural science are of use only for technology. What every school of ancient Greek and Roman Stoic philosophy saw was that these theories of natural science reveal also the true nature of man. This happens because they exhibit not merely the laws and structure of nature but also the mind and spirit of man and the type of meanings which make up his mind as a knower of nature.

In other words when one looks at a theory of mathematical physics as these men did, not merely from the standpoint of what it says about nature but also from the standpoint of what it reveals concerning the nature of the scientist's or of man's mind, one learns as much about mental and spiritual man as one does about physical nature. To put the matter more concretely, mental man has to be the kind of natural entity in nature which can discover, formulate, reason logically about and experimentally determine the truth or falsity of the scientific theories of nature.

It is at this point that, for these Greeks and Romans, the spiritual nature of man exhibits itself. Man is not merely a physical body functioning as a term in the logical structure of nature; he is also the kind of creature who, by free inquiry, trial and error and observation, can discover and formulate the abstract technical concepts and theories which, when verified empirically, tell him what nature is. It is in this freedom of inquiry necessary for the discovery of the truth about nature that the spiritual, moral and political freedom of man finds its root meaning. This is the reason why a society which does not permit for its people free inquiry in the quest of knowledge is a society in which its people do not know what freedom is.

Strictly speaking, a society which denies such freedom to its people is logically inconsistent; such a society is self-contradictory. The very words that specify the form of a society that denies the freedom can only come into being as a result of free human inquiry. Thus in denying free inquiry, it denies the very thing that makes its own discovery and formulation possible.

The examination of any theory of natural science with respect to the light that it throws on the nature of man as a knower has an even more pointed implication for morals and the basic root of the moral life. It shows first that moral and political freedom come before rather than out of any theory of the state. Secondly, it makes it clear that the meaning of good and bad and of sin and virtue have their real basis in natural man, not as an objective term in nature, but as a scientific knower of nature.

This should not surprise us. It is as old as the Garden of Eden story of the Book of Genesis. Adam and Eve were innocent, incapable of either sin or virtue, until they tasted of the tree of knowledge. In other words, it is because men are knowers of as well as objects in nature that they escape innocence and become capable of sin and virtue. To know oneself and nature truly and to so act is virtue. To live a lie, that is to act upon the basis of a false conception of nature and one's complete self, is sin.

When, therefore, men know nature in different ways the content of their moral life becomes correspondingly different. This is why the knowing of nature by immediate conformity to its cyclical rhythms and by identification with its Nirvana-Brahman formlessness tends to go with the Buddha's and Gandhi's way to peace. Similarly, it is because the ancient Greeks found a new way of knowing nature and man's mind and spirit as knower, in terms of logically constructed theory only indirectly verified, that moral and spiritual man in the West came to be regarded not merely as a free man possessing the right of freedom of inquiry as antecedent to anything else, but also as one who aims at achieving peace by the free acceptance by free men of a common contractual or theoretically constructed law.

One of the tragedies of Western history is that the creators

of the Roman Catholic Christian Church became more dazzled
by the moral and political power of a universal common law
than by the freedom of the spirit and the freedom of inquiry
which it presupposes. Such theoretically formulated rational
knowledge is not given *in its specific content* either intuitively
through naive observation or as a revelation to Jesus and to
His followers, St. Peter and St. Paul. They can reveal to us that
the Fatherly spirit which is the perfect λόγος exists or they can
exhibit the presence of its Holy Spirit working in us, but they
do not tell us what it is in the detail necessary for specific legal
conduct. This, a Eudoxus, a Plato, an Aristotle, a St. Augustine,
a St. Thomas, a Newton, a Locke, an Einstein, a Whitehead
and a Dewey have to fill in for us in their approximate but
nonetheless mortal, incomplete and imperfect ways.

The Church Fathers made the mistake of following the Stoic
Zeno instead of the Stoic Cicero. Zeno, coming earlier in the
development of the moral implications of Greek scientific
knowledge of nature, affirmed that one knows this knowledge
with absolute intuitive certainty. When Socrates, however, at
the beginning of his life pushed knowledge of natural science
aside as erroneous for ethics and thereby restricted himself to
an intuitive ethics, he found that so far as intuitive knowledge
was concerned he was more impressed by his ignorance than by
his knowledge. Free inquiry into, but not immediate possession
of, true knowledge was the spirit of Socrates. He found, moreover, as did the Asian sages before him, that determinate
knowledge given with immediacy varies from person to person.
As the Sophists of his time showed, it was one thing for one
man and another thing for another. This discovery that determinate, intuitively immediate knowledge leaves one in moral
relativity, therefore, caused Socrates later in his life to return
to the knowledge of speculatively inferred, theoretically constructed and indirectly tested natural science as the basis for
ethics. It is this later Socrates whom Plato describes in the Republic. This Socrates tells us that man can arrive at a determinate idea of the good "only" by passing through the hy-

potheses of "the previous [theoretically and mathematically formulated natural] sciences." [24] Only then does one find determinate laws and knowledge the same for all men, thereby escaping sophistry.

In this statement by Socrates, the word "hypotheses" is of crucial importance. Its presence means that these laws are not given with inductively immediate, intuitive absolute certainty after the manner assumed by the Greek Stoic Zeno. The naively observed world suggests them, as Democritus, Socrates and every Platonist affirm, but does not contain them. This means that their verification is not direct but indirect. Their logical consequences are verified, not the basic assumptions of the hypothesis itself. This is the reason why Plato writes in the *Timaeus* that his account of true knowledge of nature and man is not exactly as he describes it but "something like this." The point is that the formulation of the content of the principles that define a rational moral man and the logos of nature must be held with a certain amount of tentativeness. It is the most probable truth but not absolute truth.

This is precisely what we find Cicero affirming. He distinguishes his more Platonic Roman Stoicism from the Roman Stoicism derived from the Greek Zeno. After pointing out that the theory of nature and of moral man as rational is identical roughly with that of the Zenonian Stoics after they have incorporated into their system Platonic and Aristotelian scientific and philosophical doctrine, he adds, "We say that some things are probable." [25] Put very specifically what he means is that although what is meant by any universal, rationally designated law of nature as verified by natural science is something universal and absolute (the same for all observers or frames of reference) so far as its meaning is concerned, it is knowledge which is merely the most probable so far as the verification or truth of that universal meaning is concerned. This puts the theory in question ahead of other theories and philosophies of nature and of the knowing mind, since its logical consequences have been confirmed by observed facts, whereas the alternative theories fail before the facts. Thus relativism in knowledge and ethics is escaped as much in Cicero's theory as in Zeno's or in that of the later Church Fathers. Cicero adds, therefore, quite justifiably, "We Academicians are not men whose minds wander in uncertainty and never know what principles to adopt." [26]

Nonetheless Cicero and his Platonic Roman Stoics note quite correctly, and here they anticipate modern students of Western scientific method, that the specific scientific principles which their way of knowing tells them to adopt must be held as the most probable theory, not as the absolutely certain, final truth. Why? Because the method by which the principles are discovered shows that the determination of the truth is indirect. The logical consequences of the scientific hypothesis, not its initial basic assumptions, are shown to be true. When such is the case, one must speak merely, as Cicero does, of the greater probability. A given formulation of knowledge is the most probable approximation at the present stage of inquiry to the divine λόγος of nature, thought and moral judgment. It is not the perfect omniscience and goodness itself. This means that freedom to inquire and go beyond traditional formulations of the divine perfection is more truthful and divine than to insist upon the absolute finality of the traditional formulation itself. Again we see how in the spiritual foundations of the Christian Greco-Roman West universal law presupposed freedom of inquiry as much as it requires the operation of the Divine Perfection through the Holy Spirit as the inspiration of human freedom and inquiry.

Whereas the scientific method of knowing nature cannot pick out one theory which is valid in Zeno's sense of being verified absolutely and for always, it can pick out from all present theories the one that is more true than any other. This methodologically correct Ciceronian conception of the nature of Western knowledge of the logos has the merit of making the Greco-Roman Christian's concept of moral man as rational man compatible with and require the concept of moral man as also free man.

When the mortal human Fathers who created the Roman Christian Church Universal followed the less astute Greek Zeno rather than the more informed Socrates, Plato and Cicero they generated the conflict between lawful morality and moral freedom which has riven Western civilization from that day to the present moment. There was no need for this tragedy to have occurred since Democritus, Socrates, Plato and Cicero made it clear that the simple distinction between the absoluteness of what is meant in scientific and philosophical and religious knowledge and the highest probability with respect to the truth of what is meant permits one to reconcile the primacy of moral man as free man with the thesis that moral man is rational universal man—an instance of determinately constructed common-law principles.

It is in this Stoic concept of moral and political man as a freely inquiring knower of the speculatively discovered, theoretically constructed universal logos that Stoic Roman polity rooted the freedom of the citizens in the Republic of Augustus. Similarly, it is in the rationally specified universalism and constitutionalism of the meaning of the logos, when taken as a model for law and polity, that the peacefully ordered Rome and its polity which followed upon Augustus found its universal bond of unity and its far-reaching range of applicability. The Stoic moral freedom enabled the Pax Romana to draw up into itself the free acceptance of peoples of diverse cultures, classes, colors and creeds. It is the concept of the just state as a theoretically constructed constitutionalism valid for all men because of its universalism which gave to the diversity and pluralism which moral freedom generates the unity necessary to bring effective political unity, order and peace. "It was because," as Waddy indicates, "they had [in addition to the notion of moral freedom] a sense of justice, in this true [Western] meaning of the word, that the Romans were on the whole able to put their courage in war to a constructive use in peace." [27]

Because, moreover, his concept of moral freedom caused Augustus to destroy "as little as possible of Roman [and other] tradition; he brought what remained to a new level of fulfilment." [28] By combining "the constitutional settlement" which moral, rationalistic universalism prescribes with the minimum modification of the cultural living law diversity which the moral principle of freedom prescribes he, again to use the words of Waddy, "found the Roman world bleeding and left it healed." [29]

Greek natural science and Roman Stoic philosophy did much more than this, however, for the Roman Western world. The concept of moral freedom and of the moral man as an instance of theoretically constructed, constitutional law made men all equal by nature before the law. Notwithstanding the fact, therefore, that in the first century B.C. Rome and its far-flung community was filled with slaves, the first codifications of Roman law which the Roman Stoic philosophers made in their creation of Western legal science will be found to be concerned with the rules according to which slaves can become Roman citizens. This Roman Stoic conception of natural law as the same for all men was recognized not merely by the legal philosophers but also by a growing public opinion and by an increasing number of statesmen to be incompatible with a society in which some men are slaves and some men are free. To be sure, the process was slow. One cannot change the traditional living law habits of men and societies overnight. But Greek science and Stoic philosophy left the traditional state of affairs forthwith without the sanctions of morality or of just law.

Also, with the rejection of the primacy of the joint family which it entails, it had the immediate effect of branding nepotism as a social evil and of discouraging it. The Gracchan reforms had as their aim, for example, the removal from power of the class to which the leaders of this reform belonged.[30] Also due to Stoic influence the people of Italy revolted, as Gray L. Dorsey has recently reminded us, "not to throw off the yoke of Rome but to receive its mantle of citizenship." [31] Officials, especially the younger men in the Roman civil service, who had been under the influence of Stoicism leaned over backwards to avoid the appointment of relatives or friends to political positions. Arnold informs us also that the Stoics "introduced a new relation between husband and wife based upon equality and comradeship." [32]

Even so after its remarkably long period of order and peace this Roman polity fell. The trouble seems to have been that the later rulers lost the initial vision. They continued to be moral Stoics in word, but failed in deed. The decline began when the "consciences of the young revolted." [33] By this time Christ had made His appearance and had left His impression. The young Stoics, as Arnold tells us,

recognised the Socratic force and example not in the magistrate seated in his curule chair, nor in the rustic priest occupied in his obsolete ritual, but in the teacher on the cross and the martyr on the rack. In ever increasing numbers men, who had from their Stoic education imbibed the principles of the unity of the Deity and the freedom of the will, came over to the new society which professed the one without reservation, and displayed the other without flinching. With them they brought in large measure their philosophic habits of thought and (in far more particulars than is generally recognised) the definite tenets which the Porch had always inculcated. Stoicism began a new history, which is not yet ended, within the Christian church. . . .[34]

Moreover, as Arnold adds, these young men brought into the Christian church "something which the world could not afford to lose." [35]

What Stoicism and its intellectual love of God needed was someone here on earth to give its divine logos human and personal content. In other words, what was needed was the embodiment of the transcendent logos in human flesh. This Jesus' coming as a fulfillment of the law and the prophets provided; thereby the Hebrew religious tradition and the Greco-Roman scientific tradition joined. To the family, tribal and ritualistic law of the Hebrews there had to be added faith as the logos of Roman Stoicism is not given through ordinary observation of conventional social relations. And to the logos of the scientific Greeks and the theoretically constructed law and justice of the Romans there had to be added the warm, intuitively felt meaning of love which is charity.

The synthesis which is Christian Western civilization was

thus a rich and complex one. Jesus' emphasis on faith and love as being beyond the human rationally known law of the family and the tribe gave rise in many minds to the idea that faith in Him alone as a person or even as the divine representative of God on earth was sufficient and that in Him the intellectual love of God expressed in terms of law was unnecessary. This St. Paul had to correct. He did this in the 14th verse of the 7th Chapter of his Epistle to the Romans when he wrote, "For we know that the law is spiritual" and in verse 4 of the 4th Chapter of the Epistle to the Galatians that "when the fulness of time was come, God sent forth his Son . . . made under the law."

But Jesus did something more than merely represent and reveal the divine λόγος known previous to His coming by the Stoic Romans. He offered in addition the spiritual aid necessary to enable this law as known by men's reason under Stoicism to come to fulfillment in human hearts and in the flesh. This is what St. Paul means when he says in Romans, Chapter 8, verses 3 and 4, "For what the law could not do, in that it was weak through the flesh, God sending his own Son in the likeness of sinful flesh, and for sin, condemned sin in the flesh: That the righteousness of law might be fulfilled in us. . . ." In short, Roman Stoicism gave the faith that there is the divine λόγος and probable certainty with respect to its specific content, but it lacked the spiritual dynamic to make this knowledge a lasting, living thing in the lives of men. Christ captured the faithful Roman Stoics because He provided this human emotional dynamic. The Stoics gave the intellectual love of God as a perfect ideal toward which men approximate in more and more probable verified scientific theories of its content. Christ as the human revelation on earth of this intellectual love of the Father gave it the warm, intuitive emotive power as Grace in the hearts of men necessary to make what they want to do come nearer to what they actually do. The Greeks and the Romans gave men the vision of the intellectual love of God in theory. Jesus of Galilee captured the heart of Greco-Roman Western man because in the human simplicity, self-sacrifice and warmth of His life and as the representative on earth of the perfect divine, Fatherly logos He offered to men from God the hope, the power and the Grace which made them feel, as St. Paul witnessed, that what they would that they could do.

11

THE MODERN FRAGMENTATION
OF WESTERN CIVILIZATION

The nationalism which plagues the world at present is in considerable part a product of the modern West. To guide foreign policy correctly and to solve the problem of relating the nations it is necessary that we understand modern Western man.

It is his custom to identify the legal universalism of the Greco-Roman Christian world with absolutism. This we have already found to be a grievous error. Because, however, medieval Christian man, following Zeno rather than Cicero, confused universalism with absolutism is no reason why modern liberals should continue the confusion. Such behavior overlooks the fact that before the Greco-Roman Christian could gain the scientific knowledge of nature in which anything truly known was found to be an instance of universal, determinate laws, he was and had to be free to inquire into nature. In other words his scientific discovery that moral, spiritual and legal man is universal man rested upon his prior realization that moral man is free man.

Only by approaching and partaking of the tree of knowledge could Adam and Eve, Eudoxus and Aristotle, or St. Augustine and St. Thomas taste its fruit. Before Augustus could introduce the justice and the legal universalism necessary to give Rome its unity reaching far beyond the village or city-state and its exceptionally long period of peace, he first, as he himself tells us, had to make the citizens free. In other words, the law which Rome made possible for earthly man had to be first freely discovered and then freely accepted by its subjects. As the American political scientist Charles Howard McIlwain has shown recently: "The fundamental doctrine underlying the Roman state, its true guiding spirit, is constitutionalism, not absolutism." [1] And he adds: "The central political principle of this Roman jurisprudence is not, as has so often been assumed, the absolutism of a prince, but the doctrine that the people is the ultimate source of all legitimate political authority in a state." [2]

It was this Roman concept of law, the same for all men and hence universal, which passed into the institutions of the United States by way of English common law. Not only have the Romans, as Édouard Cuq has said, "fixed for all time the categories of juristic thought," [3] but also, as McIlwain has indicated, English common law "is pretty largely Roman in its derivation." [4] Certainly constitutionalism grounded in the precedents of the past as well as the cases of the present is of its essence.

Greco-Roman Christian constitutionalism not only presupposes freedom; it is also its major guarantee. This is the whole point of the Bill of Rights. It is the point also of the separation of powers which is central to the government of the United States. As Lord Radcliffe has recently said, those of us in the British and American tradition recognize the role of power in Government; but "Our attitude is to be afraid of power . . . . [N]o man or group of men is virtuous enough to hold the privilege of power unchecked." He adds that "if mistrust is the dominant note, then it may be best expressed by such constitutional devices as those of the American Constitution." [5] This is why he said that "the making of the American Constitution was one of the most important events in modern history." [6] Truly the Greco-Roman Christian concept of moral, spiritual and legal man as an instance of universal law protects as well as presupposes liberty.

This idea came to expression in the Middle Ages as much as in modern times. What is the Magna Carta but the thesis that even the King is subject, just like anyone else, to the law? His title to kingship is valid only if he accepts the divine logos as superior to himself. Thus if in the United States and the other American constitutional republics we are very modern, we are also very medieval, classical and Roman. The difference is more one of method—namely a greater emphasis upon the separation of different branches of government than one of kind.

Modern Western man is identical with classical Western man in one other respect. The scientific way of knowing any individual thing in nature as an instance of a theoretically constructed, determinate law is as significant for engineering and technology as it is for politics and law. One major difference between classical and modern Western man is that, whereas the former, because of his attention upon the philosophy of physics, pursued scientific knowledge with respect to its moral, legal and religious implications, his modern descendants pursue scientific knowledge more with respect to its technological applications. Until men like Einstein, Planck, Eddington and Whitehead came upon the modern stage, engineering rather than philosophy was the main concern of modern scientific thinkers. This neglect of the philosophy of physics throughout modern times has had the tragic effect of giving modern man powerful and even devastatingly dangerous scientific instruments without at the same time educating him in the more moral, legal and religious norms necessary to distinguish good from bad uses of those instruments.

The result so far as the foreign policy of the United States is concerned is tragic in two respects. For all the wisdom of the men at the helm, and in recent times this wisdom has been considerable, it tends to leave the American ship of state without a moral rudder, tossed hither and yon by any demagogue who can catch the headlines. It also gives all too often our ambassadors abroad the difficult task of overcoming the Muslim's or the Far Eastern Asian's conviction that the citizens of the United States, because of their apparently excessive emphasis on the gadgets rather than the ends of life, are a people without a culture, guided too much by the whims, enthusiasms and practicalities of the moment.

This situation and attitude rests upon a misconception of the relation of technology to spiritual values of which both contemporary American humanists and our Asian men of culture are guilty. This common misconception is that Western natural science has nothing to do with values or with norms.

The truth of the matter is that Western scientific technology instead of being the evidence for a crass power politics materialism, which our Asian friends and all too many American humanists assert it to be, is an expression and consequence of the moral, legal and religious values at the root of Western civilization. As has been made clear above, the Western concept of moral, legal and spiritual man, as one who is the instance of a determinate law holding alike for all individuals, simply would not be, were it not for Western mathematical physics. It is because Western mathematical physics, first discovered by the Greeks, revealed that there is a way of knowing nature in addition to that of naive observation and immediate intuition and feeling, that the Western type of ethics, law and religion came into existence. For the Western Greek, Roman and Christian, the criterion of the spiritual was the capacity of man to be not merely an inductively given entity in directly observed nature, but also a knower of any event or individual in nature as an instance of a universal law.

Proof for the existence of the spirit, then, consists in the capacity of men to have ideas, concepts and deductively formulated scientific, philosophical, legal and political theories. These things stones do not possess; nor do chimpanzees. Man is like a stone and a chimpanzee in that his body, like theirs, is made of the same kind of chemical and physical elements. Man is in addition a spirit in the basic Western meaning of the word because he has the capacity also to use symbols, combining them by logical construction into propositions in deductively formulated theories, which permit him to know himself and his universe in a new and indirectly tested way. It is not out of man as nothing but so many atoms, but out of the freely inquiring spirit and mind of man with his theoretically constructed, deductively formulated, experimentally verified universal laws of the atoms and their behavior that modern technology flows. Thus the omnipresence and the transforming power of the gadgets of modern man are a testimony not to his materialism and lack of culture, but to his mental, spiritual and moral nature in the Greco-Roman Christian meaning of this word. Both our own Western humanists and our Asian men of culture err when they say, because of our proficiency in natural science and technology, that we are crass materialists who have confused the instruments of existence with its ends, basic spiritual values, norms and goals.

If we in the United States and our neighbors in the modern West are confused morally and have gone astray, it is not because we have pursued our scientific knowledge of nature into technology but because we have neglected the pursuit of it into its philosophy. We have in short lost from our moral consciousness, although not fortunately from our cultural background and unconscious habits, the basic spiritual values which this science of ours exhibits and from which it derives. For everywhere around us, in everything that we think and do, like the oxygen upon which our life depends but of which we are rarely conscious, this Greek Western scientific notion of the individual as a freely inquiring spirit and as an instance of a determinate rule persists and has its sway. It is here even though our contemporary preachers and other humanists, writing ethics off the top of their heads with their hearts and their minds disconnected from science, all too often miss seeing it.

Only in one major phase of our lives does this root Greco-Roman Christian concept of the spiritual as the freely found and accepted lawful universal fail for us moderns in fact to have its sway. This failure appears in the fragmentation of Western civilization into modern political nationalism.

Modern nationalism and constitutional universalism are quite antithetical notions.

It follows [writes Arnold] with equal certainty from the early history of Stoicism, and in particular from the doctrine of Cosmopolis [i.e., that man is a citizen of the cosmos], that differences of class and race were hardly perceived by its founders. . . . There we look in vain for any trace of that instinctive feeling of national difference, that sensitiveness to race and colour, which can easily be recognised in the early history of Greece or Rome, and which has become so acute in the development of modern world-politics.[7]

History itself shows this to be the case. When Greek science first gave earthly man the idea that he could break the norms for binding men together into a single political unit from the immediately felt relations of the joint family and the village elders, the initial movement was not to the present national states but direct to the Western state universal, first in the Roman Empire and later in the Holy Roman Empire. This is consistent legal universalism and constitutionalism.

We have but to put beside this fact the second fact that we are living in an atomic age in desperate need of a universal world law to see where wise foreign policy with respect to Europe and wise statesmanship with respect to Western civilization lies. The task is that of recovering and applying the initial spirit of Greco-Roman-Christian universalism.

How is this recovery to be made? To answer this question we must first determine the causes of modern Western nationalism. Why did the fragmentation of Western civilization occur?

The first reason obviously is the Protestant Reformation. There was no need, however, for this Reformation to take the form of political nationalism. Luther was a follower of the doctrine of the Christian Church Universal. He was merely protesting against the abuses in the application of the doctrine, against the right of certain mortals on earth who applied its truth to be the sole earthly representatives of that truth. There was no reason, therefore, so far as the religious issue was concerned why the principle of universalism could not have been combined with the pluralism of the free, earthly institutions which apply the universal doctrine. In fact, as we have noted, this was the genius of political Rome. It first gave freedom to its citizens and then it gave them universal law. In fact this primacy of freedom is of the essence of the spirit of Judaism and Christianity as it is of Islam. Otherwise the Garden of Eden story has no point. If man is not free first to taste the tree of knowledge, clearly he cannot know its fruits or be guilty of eating those which are false.

Rome, moreover, as we have noted, interfered with the living habits and values of the countless communities of village elders and of city-states which it embraced to the minimum necessary to bring all men under a common law. Thus Gaius at the beginning of his Institutes distinguishes between the *jus civile* which he says varies from community to community and the *jus gentium* which is the universal law common to all the diverse communities. Above this there was, to be sure, the *jus naturale* which gave the new idea of universality and of justice that came through Greek and Roman philosophy from the Greek scientists.[8] Had the Roman Church Universal not confused constitutionalism with absolutism, there would have been no need for Luther's protest to have run its course, generating not merely the right of man to freedom of inquiry and belief, but also the pluralism of constitutionally constructed modern nations, each jealous of its own provincial legal sovereignty. In short, Western man, classical, medieval and modern, could have rejected absolutism without also having to reject the constitutionally unified Europe which we are now painfully trying step by step to recover.

But Luther and the Germans were also responsible for the breakdown of constitutional universalism which the Reformation generated. As Luther himself said about what he did, "I have struck a blow for the German people." In other words, Luther not merely protested against an abuse in the application of the law universal, he also returned the Western European's concept of law to that of the inductively given tribe. Not man as a citizen of the cosmos, but man as a member of the German people is to be the criterion of good European law. This was a blow not merely at the Roman Catholic priest's application of the law universal but at the law universal itself. The fact is that Roman law never established its application east of approximately the present dividing line between West Germany and East Germany. Without keeping these facts in mind, the problem of Germany and of a wise foreign policy with respect to Germany cannot be understood.

It is not an accident that in the concept of law of German thinkers, *Genossenschaft* (the inductively observed fellowship of family, village community and ethnological group or tribe) takes the place of *Gesellschaft* conceived as *Universitas*. Folk and their inductively given status and ways rather than universal man conceived in the light of an ethics derived from the model of a theoretically constructed, lawful natural science more and more absorb the thought and the value system of the Germans as the modern world lengthens.

Only in Kant with his categorical imperative is there an exception to this rule so far as German moral and legal thinking is concerned. In this categorical imperative of Kant, the spiritual roots of the Greco-Roman Christian West make their last appearance in the modern German world. This Imperative is but the repetition of the Greco-Roman scientific concept of the moral as the universal except that the philosophy of natural science has been pushed into the background so that Kant's ethical imperative is an empty one. His categorical imperative asserts that no specific act can be regarded as moral unless it can be generalized into a universal law valid and workable for all men.

But into Kant's ethical thinking there came another element which passed on into modern German culture and its autonomous nationalism. This other factor was the influence of Rousseau. Rousseau's return to nature was in part at least that of a romantic leaving sophisticated society to wander in woods. All society built out of the theoretical constructs of universalized political norms was evil. The intuitive, ordinary common man devoid of theoretical knowledge and sophistication thereby became moral man. Now intuitive man is family man. He is also tribal or folk man. In Germany this means that moral man is German man. Thereby Kant's vacuous, categorical imperative becomes filled in with what is inductively given, rather than a proper theoretically constructed content. Thus universal man in the case of the German became a member of the German folk rather than a citizen of the universe. Thereby all the achievements of Greek science, Greek philosophy, Roman moral and legal universalism and the ancient Christian synthesis were undone. Universal man was corrupted and turned into German tribal man. Inductively given folk rather than theoretically conceived, law-abiding cosmos became the model of the good.

When Germany, following Luther's stroke for the German folk, set the initial fashion, England immediately fell in line. Henry VIII, whose sympathies were with Charles V rather than with Luther, took advantage of Germany's success to shift the universalism of the state and church catholic from a universal Europe to a universal England.

This process of fission thus started, the epidemic of divisions spread with nothing to curb it. Not only did England break from Europe, but the United States broke from England. Even so Roman constitutionalism rooted in liberty persisted. But now the universalism was a provincial one. Geographical boundaries, having nothing to do with the principles that defined its norms, became of the essence.

But between Luther and Bunker Hill there came Galilei and Newton. They brought into being a new mathematical physics. Then not merely the geographical fragmentation of the logos universal but also the theory of its metaphysical, moral, political and legal content underwent a fragmentation. Not universal law as conceived in the philosophy of science of Plato and Aristotle, but universal law as conceived in the differing systems of philosophy of Descartes, Locke, Leibniz, Hume or Kant became the criterion of the idea of the good.

At this point modern Protestant and liberal man put himself over against Roman Catholic medieval and classical man not merely because he had left the Holy Roman Empire but also because he differed concerning the philosophy which defines what the content of the true universal law is. With Henry VIII and even the present Tory Church of England, the content of the logos is for the most part identical with that as conceived by the Church of Rome; only the earthly institution which administers the content is different. But when Locke rather than Hooker or St. Thomas defines the content of the law universal, then a new theory of constitutionalism arises. This marks the difference between the norms of the nationalism of the United States and those of the British parliament which freed itself from Charles I, and the constitutionalism of Henry VIII and his Tudor Tory successors.

When, similarly, Kant came to a different philosophy of Galilei and Newton's physics, than did Locke or his successor Hume, and this Kantian philosophy went into the mentality of both the Germans and the Russians, still another concept of the content of the law universal was at work in modern Western nationalism. When, furthermore, even for German and Russian thought, Kant's theory left problems unanswered which generated Fichte and Hegel; and when in turn Hegel's rationalistic idealistic answer, generated, by its own logic of negation, the antithesis which is Marx's realistic materialism, one more theory of universal law came into the modern world. Its influence under the name of Communism is all too well known to us. Such roughly is the story of the fragmentation of Western civilization in the modern world.

It is important that we summarize its causes. For if, in this atomic age, we are to bring ourselves under the rule of law rather than of war, we must know what these causes are and then remove them. Let it not be overlooked that a pluralism of nations and a pluralism of their national laws mean that between nations there is no law. And without law, when disputes arise, there is, according to Western mentality at least, no recourse but to power and to war.

The basic causes of the fragmentation are three in number. One is the failure of the Roman Christian Church Universal to distinguish its spiritual value of legal universalism from absolutism. This arises, as we have indicated before, because it made the error of following the immature Zeno rather than the more mature and truly Platonic Cicero. In other words, it overlooks the fact that it is really spiritually richer than it supposes. It has within its spirituality not merely the concept of universal law, but also the concept that that universal law presupposes and protects freedom. Providing this error is corrected and practice is brought into accord with the correction, there is no reason why any modern legal thinker or Christian cannot return to the bosom of Mother Church.

The second cause of modern nationalism was Luther's and Rousseau's undoing of the great scientific discovery which created the classical Western concept of the spiritual and the Western Christian civilized world. This occurred when Luther and Rousseau took man back from the theoretically constructed, logically formulated, indirectly tested way of knowing man and nature, to intuitively given, naively observed family and tribal man and nature as the model of the good and the criterion of citizenship. Thereby, the identification of the extent of law with the extent of a given people, German or English or American, arose. Blood or geography rather than universal law became the criterion of the good and the just. Obviously such physiological and geographical distinctions have little to do with universal norms and values. This error brought into the Western world by Luther and Rousseau and others would not have been so bad had its inductive emphasis been followed through to the discovery of the Oriental way to peace which overcomes family or tribal provincialism through the cultivation of the immediately apprehended, all embracing vastness. But this, except for a confused Schopenhauer, these modern German inductive romanticists never did. Thus they lost the universal values of the West while never finding those of the Orient.

The third cause of the fissioning of Western civilization is in the philosophy of modern mathematical physics. We have noted how it gave rise to the differing modern philosophies with their respective differing theories of law and politics and ethics of Descartes, Locke, Hume, Kant, Fichte, Hegel and Marx. It is because differing Western nations are now guided or have been guided in the past by these differing Western philosophies of society and the state that the present Cold War and the ideological conflicts which characterize our world have in considerable part their basis.

Why, we must ask ourselves, did modern science thus generate so many different philosophies of itself, thereby throwing philosophic Marxist Russian culture, Roman Catholic continental European culture and British empirical and pragmatic Anglo-American culture, to mention only a few, so much at odds with one another?

That is a technical question too difficult to handle in the space available here. Suffice it to say that there are reasons for believing that Galilei and Newton wrongly specified the relation between (a) nature as theoretically conceived in their experimentally verified theory and (b) nature as directly observed, and that this erroneous specification upon their part was taken for granted by all subsequent modern philosophers. Once this erroneous assumption is made, the series of different philosophical theories of the modern world result in which each inadequate term in the series generates its equally inadequate successor. Some philosophers and peoples have accepted one of these unsatisfactory modern systems of philosophy as the definition of their legal, political and moral norms, others have accepted another. Hence the present ideological conflict and the corresponding conflict of laws.

When, however, this erroneous assumption made by Galilei

and Newton is corrected, a consistent philosophy not giving rise to difficulties which lead beyond itself comes into being. This philosophy, moreover, has the virtue of requiring for its basic factors in man and nature not only the theoretically given logos of the classical West but also the intuitively given, all-embracing vastness which is Brahman, Tao, Nirvana and the source of the Confucianists' *jen*. Perhaps, therefore, the basis for not merely undoing the modern fragmentation of Western civilization but also for undoing the division between the classical Occident and the classical Orient is at hand. There is, however, one difficulty in the way. This is Russian Communism.

12

THE THEORY AND PRACTICE OF
SOVIET RUSSIAN COMMUNISM

It is the fashion to say that no one knows what is going on behind the Iron Curtain. Even at national conferences of experts on contemporary Russia from many fields of human inquiry it is not unusual to find them in utter confusion after each has presented his particular information, with little idea of how to combine the findings into a single picture. One is often told that integration will not be possible until a Newton of social science appears. The general public similarly supposes that the members of the Kremlin know everything about us but that we know very little about them.

There is little need for this demoralized state of mind. It is largely because many of our contemporary social scientists are so inductively minded in the piecemeal sense of the word that they ignore the necessity of examining the ideology of any society. Inevitably, when this occurs, they find themselves in the position of putting more figures in a column than they can add up to anything. To integrate the facts of any foreign society, one wants not the new integrative concepts of some future Einstein, but the concepts used by the people in the foreign society in question. There is probably no large society in the world today where the integration of life is as much in the hands of its key leader and in which the specific integrative principles for both theory and practice are spelled out in detail as is the case with

Premier Stalin's Soviet Russia. If there is one country in which
we do not need a spy system in order to know what is going on,
or what its future behavior so far as it affects foreign policy
will be, that country is the one ruled from the Kremlin. One
has but to read in order to know. Premier Stalin has put it all
down in writing. As the last paragraph of "The Programme of
the Communist International" tells us:

> The Communists disdain to conceal their views and aims. They
> openly declare that their aims can be attained only by the forcible
> overthrow of all the existing social conditions. Let the ruling class
> tremble at a Communistic revolution. The proletarians have noth-
> ing to lose but their chains. They have a world to win.[1]

It might be said that the foregoing statement represents only
the international Comintern and cannot be taken as representing the aims and integrative principles of the present Soviet
regime. We need have no doubts upon this point either, for in
a book called *Dialectical and Historical Materialism*,[2] Premier
Stalin tells us what his ideology is, and in his lectures to the students of Sverdlov University in April, 1924, entitled *Foundations of Leninism*,[3] he describes not only his aims and those of
all Marxist Leninist Communists, but also the practical strategy
and tactics for implementing them. Since then deeds have filled
in what he writes with concrete detail. Nothing is improvised
so far as either domestic or foreign policy is concerned. This
does not mean that alterations to meet local circumstances are
not made. But such alterations are always relative to a constant,
theoretically specified aim, and even the tactics for altering
one's immediate course and improvising are fixed.

No matter how many retreats and momentary compromises
one may make, one must, as Lenin affirms, "at all costs retain
'moral ascendancy.' "[4] This is done only by keeping one's
ideological aims clearly fixed and uncompromised. To do this
one must, therefore, have an ideologically and theoretically
grounded basis even for the tactics of compromising.

There is no group attacked more vehemently and continuously throughout the 112 pages of Premier Stalin's *Foundations of Leninism* than the opportunists. To be sure that we are getting Communism as the Premier of the U.S.S.R. tells us it should be understood and applied, we shall quote from Lenin or Marx only when the Premier so quotes and approves the quotation. The ideology of Premier Stalin's Communism is not built on the spur of the moment. Nor does it have its roots in mere power politics. The ideology comes first, and power is achieved and directed by means of it—not the reverse. This is why an expert on Russia in the Department of State, Mr. George F. Kennan, now Ambassador to Moscow, found that he was able to anticipate Russian acts only after he had studied the Russian Communist ideology.[5]

Incidentally, this shows, as James Reston has noted,[6] the falsity of the theory of Mr. Kennan that the foreign policy of the United States will be realistic and wise when it is guided and judged largely by power considerations.[7]

Nor is Soviet ideology rooted in merely commonsense, practical considerations. It is instead a technically constructed, philosophical doctrine believed by Communists to be the answer to the basic problems of modern Western scientific and philosophical thought which were noted in the previous chapter. Not every nation in the world has at its head a man who knows the technical philosophical theories of human knowledge of the modern West and who consciously and explicitly roots the aims of his country, both domestic and international, in a particular one of them. This can be said, however, of the Union of the Soviet Socialist Republics.

If we want, therefore, to understand what is going on behind the Iron Curtain, one must be as philosophically exact and technical as is Premier Stalin in his *Dialectical and Historical Materialism*. This work opens as follows:

Dialectical materialism is the world outlook of the Marxist-Leninist party. It is called dialectical materialism because its approach to the phenomena of nature, its method of studying and apprehending them, is *dialectical,* while its interpretation of the phenomena of nature, its conception of these phenomena, its theory, is *materialistic.*

Historical materialism is the extension of the principles of dialectical materialism to the study of . . . society and its history. . . .

Dialectics comes from the Greek *dialego,* to discourse, to debate. In ancient times dialectics was the art of arriving at the truth by disclosing the contradictions in the argument of an opponent and overcoming these contradictions. . . . This dialectical method of thought, later extended to the phenomena of nature, . . . which regards . . . the development of nature as the result of the development of the contradictions in nature, as the result of the interaction of opposed forces in nature.[8]

This establishes the point made in a previous chapter that the ideology of Communist nations is, according to its own basic assumptions, logically incompatible with the ideology of all other nations. Consequently, disputes between Communist and non-Communist nations, such as North and South Korea, cannot be treated as mere differences over means to a common goal which can be resolved by mediation without any betrayal of either disputant's basic moral convictions and principles. The latter possibility is a real one if the ideologies of both nations derive from knowledge of nature which is given by naive observation and immediate intuition of determinate factors which are transitory and secondary to the identification of all men with the all-embracing Brahman formlessness. The Communist ideology of the North Koreans is identical with that of President Mao's Communist China. Fung Yu-lan, as official representative of this China, told his Indian visitors in Peking in 1951 that the philosophy of the New China is dialectical and historical materialism.

According to Premier Stalin and all other dialectical and historical materialists contradictions are inescapable in any knowledge whatever. A contradiction is the name for the relation between things which are incompatible and incapable of reconciliation. When two different things are contradictory, the acceptance of the one necessitates the rejection of the other.

Under such circumstances reconciliation either directly through a meeting of the so-called Big Powers at the higher level or indirectly through a mutual mediator is impossible.

Such would not be the case if Premier Stalin and his fellow dialectical and historical materialists thought of their ideology as merely one thesis against the incompatible antitheses which are the ideologies of all the non-Communist nations of the world. Then the incompatibilities could be reconciled by both parties giving up their particular ideologies to move to a common, single new ideology, called by dialectical thinkers such as Marx, Lenin and Premier Stalin, the synthesis.

Unfortunately, however, such is not the situation. Premier Stalin makes it clear that the giving up of dialectical materialism to pass to a higher synthesis in order to resolve the international disputes arising from the revolutionary and militaristically aggressive attacks of Communist parties and nations upon parliamentary processes and non-Communist nations is unthinkable, for Communism is the final synthesis. There is nothing beyond it—no alternative suggestion—to which the thought of a Communist, a non-Communist or a neutral mediator can go. Nor is there anywhere else that the present or future acts which make history can go. For Communism conceives itself to be not merely the final synthesis but also the empirically verified and materialistically and dialectically inevitable terminus of nature and history. For a mediator, such as Professor Radhakrishnan, therefore, or for President Rhee, Prime Minister Churchill, or the President of the United States, to ask Premier Stalin, President Mao, or the leader of the North Korean Communists to compromise or withdraw from anything they do that is prescribed by their doctrine is, in their opinion, to ask them to make the physical universe and history different from what they are.

Compromise is permissible with respect to tactics in achieving their aim, but not with respect to the ideological aim itself. Thus after specifying that contradiction is of the essence of nature, society and history and that the contradictions in so-

ciety can be met not "by reforms, but only . . . by revolution,"
Premier Stalin adds:

> Hence we must not cover up the contradictions of the capitalist
> system, but disclose and unravel them; we must not try to check
> the class struggle but carry it to its conclusion.
> Hence, in order not to err in policy, one must pursue an uncom-
> promising . . . policy, not a reformist policy of harmony of the
> interests of the proletariat and the bourgeoisie [i.e., any non-Com-
> munist class, society or nation], not a compromisers' policy. . . .[9]

By the proletariat, Premier Stalin means, as the sequel will
show, the urban workers as led by "a single will" with his
specific ideology, or any nation which is so led. By the bourgeoisie, he means the people of any class, society or nation, such as
South Korea, which is not so led.

When, therefore, Premier Stalin informs us that his outlook
is that of dialectical materialism and defines the dialectical as
the logically contradictory, he automatically dooms to failure
Professor Radhakrishnan's trust in mediation as the key to a
wise foreign policy with respect to North Korea, Communist
China and the U.S.S.R., however much he may encourage the
Professor in this hope in order both to gain Asian sympathy and
support and to demoralize the United Nations and its supporters.

This does not mean that there is no hope of a wise foreign
policy with respect to Russia short of war. It does mean, however, that a wise foreign policy must be based in Asia and elsewhere on an objective knowledge of what the Russians think
and are and not on what they would be were they guided by
non-dualistic Hindu Vedanta, Gandhiji's pacifism, Wallacean
liberalism, or some other philosophy than dialectical and historical materialism.

Concerning the Asian mediational way to peace, the 1939
Communist International asserts:

> Tendencies like Gandhism in India, thoroughly imbued with reli-
> gious conceptions . . . [which] see the solution of the social prob-
> lem . . . in a reversion to . . . backward forms, preach passivity

and repudiate the class struggle, . . . must be strongly combated by Communism.[10]

One of the most important tasks [they add] . . . is the task of systematically and unswervingly combating religion—the opium of the people. The proletarian government must . . . ruthlessly suppress the counter-revolutionary activity of the ecclesiastical organisations . . . [And] while granting liberty of worship, . . . carr[y] on anti-religious propaganda with all the means at its command . . . on the basis of scientific materialism.[11]

At this point the second word in Premier Stalin's name for his philosophy becomes important. Whereas by dialectical he means "that internal contradictions are inherent in all things," [12] by materialism, he means

that the multifold phenomena of the world constitute different forms of matter in motion, that interconnection and interdependence of phenomena, as established by the dialectical method, are a law of the development of moving matter, and that the world develops in accordance with the laws of movement of matter and stands in no need of a "universal spirit." [13]

His Marxist philosophical materialism affirms also, he adds, "that the world and its laws are fully knowable." [14] As Lenin put the matter, "Materialism . . . recognizes objectively real being . . . as independent of consciousness, sensation, experience. . . ." [15] Such briefly is dialectical materialism.

If ever there was a self-contradictory philosophy it is this one. That self-contradiction is inherent in nature is scientifically false, but that self-contradiction characterizes Premier Stalin's philosophy of nature there can be no doubt. For the relation of contradiction does not hold between natural facts. It holds only between propositions which purport to refer to the same natural facts. Hence, to affirm that nature contains "inherent contradictions" is to assert scientific nonsense.

Such an affirmation arises from confusing opposing forces or the relation of physical opposition with the logical relation of contradiction. There is nothing logically contradictory in the head-on collision of two cannon balls, since the entire phenomenon is completely understood in terms of Newton's physics and this is a single self-consistent theory. Hence, all the so-called empirical evidence brought forward by Soviet Russia's leader and his fellow Communists to support their scientifically nonsensical dogma that the subject matter of nature contains inherent contradictions and is therefore dialectical, rests on a simple confusion. Only propositions or theories referring to the same facts in nature can contradict one another. The facts of nature may stand in physical opposition to one another but this is not contradiction and without logical contradiction the subject matter of natural science, whether it be colliding stones or hungry animals eating one another, is not dialectical.

No theory of nature is ever regarded as scientific unless it brings the facts of its subject matter together in a logically consistent manner. Any theory would be rejected by any competent scientist instantly if, in its content, it exhibited the self-contradictory. The whole point of the requirement of logical consistency in any deductively formulated theory is to remove contradictions from, not to exhibit them in, nature. Or to put the situation more exactly, there are no contradictions in nature to remove, because, to repeat, contradiction is a relation not between different natural facts but between mutual irreconcilable propositions referring to the same natural facts.

Premier Stalin's uncritical acceptance of Marx and Lenin has completely misguided him also with respect to what science says about universal spirit. As we have shown in the previous chapters, universal spirit is not at all the esoteric, unscientific kind of thing he supposes. It is instead in important part at least, the capacity of man to inquire freely into nature and thereby to arrive at the knowledge of its particular facts as instances of universal laws which must be accepted with probable rather than absolute certainty and with a becoming sense of toleration of alternative, similarly determined theories. Science tells us that the spirit of man is at the least this kind of thing.

Such a conception of the spiritual is by no means a negligible one. Not every premier or people in the world has the privilege of practicing and enjoying it. If, furthermore, as Premier Stalin and his mentor, Marx, maintain, scientific truth about nature and man in nature determines good conduct and good government then, since the knowing of nature is natural to and a unique characteristic of man, and since this knowing presupposes free inquiry and ends in true knowledge as an instance of a theoretically constructed, indirectly verified universal law, it follows that the basic model of the philosophy of the state for a scientifically informed Western man must be that of a freely accepted constitutionalism which presupposes and protects liberty. Just as scientific knowledge reveals the individual human spirit to be freely inquiring man, so it reveals universal spirit in the universal laws and common conclusions freely found and verified by such freely inquiring men. This meaning for universal spirit is not trivial. It insures that no one is above freely found and freely tested universal law. It is the basis also of the doctrine that all men are equal before the law.

Premier Stalin and the Communists' misconception of the relation of logical contradiction to the subject matter of natural science and of the meaning of universal spirit as exhibited in scientific knowledge has important consequences. It leads him and his colleagues not merely to the rejection of a constitutionalism which presupposes and protects free inquiry and moral freedom, but also to the injunction to "smash" it by revolutionary and forceful means. Because of his erroneous notion that the subject matter of scientific knowledge is dialectically related and because he regards a constitutionalism which presupposes and protects freedom as yesterday's state of the subject matter of history which the dialectic of history requires to be negated, it follows from his misconceptions that a constitutionalism which presupposes and protects freedom of inquiry is an evil and that the concept of the spiritual which the previous chapters showed to be the basis of Western civilization is "an opium of the people."

In order to be clear about the ideology behind Russian Communism and the self-contradictory character of this ideology, it is important that we examine in detail the developments in modern philosophy after Kant which led Marx, Lenin and Stalin to their dialectical and historical materialism.

Two philosophical notions, as Premier Stalin has already hinted, provide the key. One is the dialectical theory of every subject matter of knowledge. This theory affirms that the parts of the subject matter of any science are related by the relation of logical contradiction as thesis to antithesis. This idea came to Marx directly from Hegel but derives in fact from Kant, Fichte and Hegel's idealistic theory of how man knows nature. The second philosophical assumption is that this logically self-contradictory subject matter of nature and society is materialistic in character. This derives from the realistic theory of how man knows nature which Marx, Engels, Lenin and Stalin took over from the German theologian Feuerbach.

However, the realistic epistemology of Feuerbach, which is at the root of Premier Stalin's materialism and which enables him to say that science knows objective reality to be independent of the inductively given data of consciousness, is logically inconsistent with the idealistic epistemology of Kant, Fichte and Hegel, which is the source, as the sequel will show, of the dialectical portion of Premier Stalin's philosophy.

The heart of the idealistic theory of knowing nature is that knowledge is a synthesis of data given inductively through the senses and of concepts inherent in the scientist as knower which are brought to the data by the scientist himself. According to this idealistic theory of scientific knowing, there is no subject matter of nature apart from the forms of the knower's thinking. When the Kantian idealist Fichte and his successor Hegel gave reasons for believing that the forms of the knower's thinking, brought by the scientist to the inductive data to constitute the subject matter of any science, are dialectical in character, the subject matter became dialectical also. Logical contradiction then became inherent in anything known.

Thus it is that Premier Stalin, like Hegel, Marx and Lenin before him, landed himself in the thoroughly unscientific position of affirming that the subject matter of nature has contradictions within itself. But what makes this position even more absurd is that Marx and his followers retained this erroneous consequence of the dialectical idealistic theory of knowing anything after they asserted that they had rejected idealism for Feuerbach's realistic theory of how anything is scientifically known.

Had they been truly realistic in their theory of scientific knowing, they would have dropped the notion that the logic of a scientist's thinking about contradictory theories is a necessary form of the empirical content of knowledge. In this case they might have been materialists but they certainly could not have been dialectical materialists. But had they been consistent materialists in the sense of believing in the indirectly verified, scientific objects of deductively formulated Western scientific theory, they would have discovered the concept of spiritual man as one who, when he knows anything with scientific correctness, knows it as an instance of logically consistent (i.e., non-dialectically related), determinate, universal laws which require free inquiry for their discovery and a becoming sense of probability and of toleration of alternative hypotheses, so far as one's sense of their truth is concerned. Then all the nonsense about self-contradictions being inherent in nature would have been escaped and the tragedies of the attack upon free inquiry and upon a constitutional, spiritual universalism which presupposes and protects individual free inquiry would have been avoided.

It remains to specify what these tragic consequences are and how dialectical materialism leads to them. It will be well to proceed, as the Communists do, from the dialectical materialistic philosophy to the conclusions they draw for theory and practice. Premier Stalin tells us that if

. . . the connection between the phenomena of nature and their interdependence are laws of the development of nature, it follows, too, that the connection and interdependence of the phenomena of social life are laws of the development of society. . . . Hence the practical activity of the party of the proletariat must . . . be based

. . . on the laws of development of society and on the study of these laws.[16]

The problem becomes, therefore, that of discovering the factors which by law determine the character of society at a given time and its development through time.

Here the materialism of dialectical materialism gives them what they regard as an absolutely trustworthy clue. They say quite correctly that the character of society is always a function of man's relation to nature. Had they been guided solely by their realistic epistemology, they would have come upon the fact, made evident by the studies of different cultures in this book, that the key to the factor in man's relation to nature which generates his social norms is not any one fact in society or nature, but instead the concepts that he uses to describe and integrate all the facts of nature and himself in his relation to nature. Since the knowledge of nature which generates concepts and theories presupposes free inquiry, the Marxists' philosophical realism would have made free inquiry and moral freedom the very essence of moral and political man and the precondition for the existence of any social science or any ideologically ordered society whatever.

But unfortunately at this point the materialism in dialectical materialism led Marx, Engels, Lenin and Premier Stalin astray. It caused them to single out one of the many inductively given factors in man's relation to nature, namely

the *method of procuring the means of life* necessary for human existence, the *mode of production of material values*—food, clothing, footwear, houses, fuel, instruments of production, etc.—which are indispensable for the life and development of society.[17]

At first sight this seems reasonably plausible. A moment's recollection, however, of what men regard as their needs, as illustrated in the different Asian and Western societies, indicates that it is quite arbitrary to pick out merely material instruments as the sole factor making human societies what they are. In Aryan Hinduism, for example, with its four stages of life for any person, these particular values do become of major, although not of sole, importance in the householder stage of the joint family. The first or studentship stage of man's relation to nature is concerned, however, with the thorough learning of the facts in human experience which give the Hindu his complete conception of experience. In this stage, the concern is with free inquiry and knowledge of man and nature in their fullness in and for itself. In this knowledge of nature, the correctly tutored Hindu under the tutelage of the guru becomes aware of the immediately sensed cyclical sequence of the darkness called night and the brightness called day, with the sequence of the seasons of the earthly human life and also with the all-embracing immediacy which is Brahman out of which and back into which these perishing cyclically successive differentiations come and go. Similarly in the last two stages of the Hindu's life, the concern again is not with the material instruments of production but with the rejection of them and the living upon the minimum of material requirements and the preparation for one's absorption back into the timeless Brahman.

It was quite arbitrary also that Marx and his followers in their Feuerbachian realism did not pick out the cultivation of the warm feeling of children for parents which characterizes every Asian society and every traditional Asian's conception of man in his relation to nature. And so one could go on. But Marx and Premier Stalin's mid-nineteenth century materialism made them think, for some unexplained reason, that they had to pick out as "the force" which makes society what it is only material instruments such as food, clothing, footwear and the tools of production.

They conclude, therefore, that "the clue to the study of the laws of history of society must not be sought in men's minds, in the views and ideas of society, but in the mode of production practised by society in any given historical period." [18]

Having made this arbitrary assumption, implied they think by their materialism, they then distinguish two factors which

they term "the productive forces of society" and "men's relations of production." [19] By the "productive forces of society"
they mean "the *instruments of production* wherewith material
values are produced, [by] the people who operate the[se] instruments of production." [20] By "men's relations of production"
they mean the social relations into which men are thrown when
they operate the instruments of production to produce material
values. From this it follows that the ordering of men in society
is determined solely by the material instruments for producing
material goods. The law of historical development of society
then becomes the law of the change of the instruments of production.

At this point, however, the realistic epistemology of Feuerbach, which has been used to justify materialism and the selection of material instruments of production as the sole cause of
social and cultural relations and values, is dropped and the
idealistic, dialectical theory of knowing of Fichte and Hegel
takes over. Since any scientific subject matter is determined by,
and must conform to, the forms of thinking which are dialectical, the subject matter of present society and its historical
development must be dialectical and hence also contains logical
contradictions. Thus with time, the means of production change
in a way that causes them to negate one another, thereby calling "forth a reconstruction of the whole social and political
order." [21] "Productive forces are therefore the most mobile
and revolutionary element of production." [22] Anything, it is to
be noted, becomes revolutionary, even material tools, when
they become related to one another dialectically. Such are the
absurdities to which the Hegelian dialectical idealistic forms of
knowing can go in constituting the material objects of knowledge even with "realistic materialists."

Nor is this all. Ideas and ideologies are mere afterthoughts
following upon men's relations in production which in turn
are determined by the material instruments of production.
Here the materialism of dialectical materialism has taken over
and Marx is quoted by Premier Stalin as follows:

It is not the consciousness of men that determines their being, but, on the contrary, their social being that determines their consciousness. At a certain stage of their development, the material forces of production in society come in conflict with the existing relations of production. . . . From forms of development of the forces of production these relations turn into their fetters. Then begins an epoch of social revolution. . . . In considering such transformations a distinction should always be made between the material transformation of the economic conditions of production which can be determined with the precision of natural science, and the legal, political, religious, aesthetic or philosophic—in short, ideological forms in which men become conscious of this conflict and fight it out.[23]

The latter statement indicates that Communists have a place for the ideology of others in their thinking and take its relation to their own ideology very seriously, so seriously, as we shall see, and as the word "fight" suggests, that there is no reconciliation between the two. It is to be noted, however, that there is for Premier Stalin and his Communist colleagues one exception to the rule that ideas are determined by the status of men in society as this status in turn is determined by the material instruments of production. The exception is this materialistic, dialectical philosophy itself. It is supposed to be a scientific description of man's relation to nature rather than a social by-product of this relationship itself.

Even so, however, the Communist dialectical materialistic ideology does not determine the character of society; instead the dialectically determined revolutionary changes in the material instruments of production do this. But how material instruments of production can generate other instruments of production which are their logical antithesis is a bit difficult even for a dialectical materialist to comprehend. Premier Stalin finds it necessary, therefore, to immerse these material instruments in a "womb" by recourse to the rather unscientific method of metaphor.

No social order [he writes] ever disappears before all the productive forces for which there is room in it have been developed; and new higher relations of production never appear before the material conditions of their existence have matured in the womb of the old society itself.[24]

At this point the organismal view of society of Hegel's social *Geist* has in truly materialistic fashion degenerated into a social orgasm.

Out of this social womb there is generated by a logical dialectic the successive antithetical "productive forces" with their "revolutionary element." Thereby dialectical materialism generates "historical materialism." In the process five types of production relations with their corresponding societies appear in time: The primitive communal, the slave, the feudal, the capitalist or bourgeoisie and the socialist.[25] That it is very difficult to find these stages in Chinese society or in pre-Western Buddhist Thailand does not appear to bother Marx or Premier Stalin particularly. When anything is "dialectically determined" it, of course, has to be.

But does it? Obviously not. The negation of one thing does not give a unique antithesis. There is more than one way in which the set of propositions which define any given social situation can be negated and replaced by a contradictory set of propositions. Thus not only dialectical materialism but also dialectical historical determinism are a contradiction in terms. If anything is dialectically related, it is not deterministically related.

At the present stage in history, the material womb of society as governed by "dialectical necessity" has generated two logically opposed classes of people in society which the present productive forces of society define. These two classes are composed of those who control the means of production and those who work with the present instruments of production. The name of the latter we must never forget since they are the key to the whole of the Communist social theory and practice. They are called the proletariat. It is important not to confuse the proletariat with the masses. The proletariat is made up merely of those workers who use the modern technological instruments of production of large industry. The hundreds of millions of peasants of Asia and the Middle East who work with their elementary tools are not to be included in the proletariat. They are always called peasants. Their function, as we shall see, is to be "the reserve of the proletariat."

Because of the dialectic the proletariat are related by contradiction to those who control the material tools of production, called the bourgeoisie. There is, therefore, an unavoidable and unmediateable war between these two classes. When the proletariat under their leaders capture control in one nation, thereby removing the bourgeoisie from control of the means of production in that nation, then the inescapable, unmediateable war becomes automatically international since the home nation becomes identical with the class of the proletariat and any and all nations not captured and led by the proletariat compose the class of the bourgeoisie.

Because of the relation of contradiction between the proletariat and the bourgeoisie, whether the two classes be domestic within a single nation or international between proletariat-led and nonproletariat-led nations, the war between them cannot be avoided or settled by democratic parliamentary processes, mediation, collective bargaining, high level conferences or even a democratically voted Socialistic nationalization of industry. Socialistic nationalization gives the control of the means of production to the voting majority of the people, not to the proletariat alone, i.e., the industrial workers, who are always a minority. Consequently, the dialectical determinism of history necessitates that the war must be intensified against all such bourgeoisie until the proletariat, using the peasants as their reserves, smash parliamentary processes and capture for themselves the control of the means of production.

Unless it is realized that this dialectical determinism is the basis upon which Stalinist Communists act, one will not understand their paradoxical treatment of the peasants who work on the land. First, they promise and in fact give them private ownership of the land. This is done for two reasons: First, to liquidate the landlords who are likely to be powerful polit-

ically; second, to secure the support of the peasants as reserves
to smash the parliamentary majority government and give the
minority proletariat the control of the government and society.
Once control is gained the leaders of the proletariat, who
frankly call themselves dictators, liquidate the peasant holdings
and the peasant members in the government. This occurred
with the Peasant's Party in Hungary. Were this not done, the
smaller class of the proletariat and the larger class of peasants
would be the government. Then the control of the means of
production would not be in the hands of the proletariat alone.

Such considerations show how essential it is, if countries like
Soviet Russia, Communist China and Communist North Korea
are to be understood, to pay attention to the ideological factor.
Unless one understands dialectical materialism with precision
and determines precisely how dialectical materialists like Stalin,
Mao and Fung Yu-lan define the proletariat and the bourgeoisie and the relation between them, one will not be prepared for
what they do, know why they do it, or realize what is happening when they confront the world with the Prague coup, the
Berlin blockade, the North Korean invasion of South Korea,
or the concentration of Chinese Communist troops on the
Indo-China border and on the Tibetan borders of India. Without precise ideological knowledge of what dialectical and historical materialism means, statesmen, whether they be Socialistic liberals, Quaker or Gandhian pacificistic neutralists, pub-
licity-hungry fanatical McCarthys, oversmiling or overgrim
generals or power politicians, are like love-sick girls wandering
about blindfold picking petals off daisies in a field of booby
traps fastened to atomic bombs.

The Communists affirm also that every ideology and political
institution but their own is the mere by-product of the dialectically and deterministically outmoded bourgeoisie form of society. Hence, the capturing of the means of production by the
proletariat requires not only the smashing of the bourgeoisie
but also the destruction of liberal constitutional processes and
institutions. In his lectures at Sverdlov University in 1924,

Premier Stalin faced the question raised by the Menshevik Communists in 1917 concerning whether the proletariat should take power before they represented a majority in the country. To this Premier Stalin replied: "No proofs are adduced, for there are no proofs, either theoretical or practical, that can justify this absurd thesis." [26] The practices of these democratic constitutional socialists and liberals are, he adds, "utterly false and utterly putrid. . . ."[27] [*T*]*he dictatorship of the proletariat is the rule—unrestricted by law and based on force—of the proletariat over the bourgeoisie* [and] . . . cannot arise as the result of the peaceful development of bourgeois society and of bourgeois democracy; it can only arise as the result of the smashing of the bourgeois state machine. . . ." [28] Bringing absolute authority to the support of dialectically materialistic reason, Premier Stalin concludes:

> Lenin rightly says that . . . "the era of bourgeois-democratic parliamentarism has come to an end, and a new chapter in world history—the era of proletarian dictatorship—has commenced." [29]

It is quite erroneous, therefore, to suppose that if the traditional democracies will remove their right-wing conservatives and operate with middle-of-the-road liberals or socialists, then Premier Stalin's Communism and liberal democratic constitutionalism can work together. Communists who cooperate with such middle-of-the-road people, whether the latter be conservatives, liberals or socialists, are, if they insist upon liberal democratic constitutionalism, called by Lenin and Premier Stalin "opportunists." For them he reserves his most extreme contempt.

> The theory of "overcoming" opportunist elements by ideological struggle within the Party, the theory of "outliving" these elements within the confines of a single Party, is a rotten and dangerous theory. . . .[30]
> To think that these new tasks can be performed by the old Social-Democratic parties, brought up as they were under the peaceful conditions of parliamentarism, is to doom oneself to hopeless despair and inevitable defeat.[31]

The Party becomes consolidated by purging itself of opportunist elements.[32]

It is well to pause a moment to consider what has happened in the broader development of modern philosophical and social thought to produce this tragic result. The trouble really began with Luther and Rousseau and the attendant German romanticists. When Luther struck his blow for the German people, he shifted man's conception of nature and of the relation of himself to nature from nature as known through the universal laws of deductively formulated scientific theory to nature as given inductively. Moreover the tendency of Protestantism following upon Luther was to go back behind the Roman Catholic Church and its Greco-Roman-Hebrew lawfulness to the sayings of Christ in the New Testament as interpreted intuitively. It is very easy when this is done to by-pass Roman law and Roman Stoicism and thereby miss the concept of moral man as universal man which is as much of the essence of Christian man as is free inquiry and free man. When this occurs both Protestant and modern liberal man tends to achieve the individualistic freedom of Christian ethics at the cost of losing its spiritual constitutionalism and universalism.

In any event with Luther and his Protestant successors the German basis of law was shifted from the concept of man as a citizen of the universe to the concept of political man as the mere citizen of the German folk. Thereby, as the German historian Troeltsch and the English political thinker Sir Ernest Barker have suggested, the great contribution of Greek scientific philosophy and Roman law to the Hebrew Christian Western synthesis tended to be pushed aside in both legal theory and political practice.[33] In its stead arose that legally and morally uncontrollable German nationalism which since 1870 has presented the Western world with the still unsolved German problem. In short the long retreat back from man as universal man, a citizen of nature, through man as family and tribal man to barbarism was initiated by German Romanticism and then achieved at Buchenwald.

With Marx this process went one step beyond the stage reached before Hitler's Germany. The tribe was fractioned into a small, restricted class which was made up of the urban workers using the technological instruments of contemporary modern material production. Thereby moral man was corrupted from being a citizen of the universe, under determinate laws the same for all men, into being the leader of the members of a small class in society guided by a restricted and arbitrary concern with nothing but material clothes, shoes, technological tools and other purely material values.

To this sorry degradation of moral and political man was added its universalization by the Communists for the whole world. This brings us to the inescapable international character not merely of the Comintern but also of Premier Stalin's dialectical materialistic Communism.

Asian pacifists and mediators and all too many Western liberals like to think that Premier Stalin, if the traditional Western democracies would only be "reasonable," would be quite content to reserve his attacks upon liberal constitutionalism for home consumption. Would that it were true. Unfortunately he tells us without any qualifications whatever that such is not the case. In his aforementioned university lectures, the Premier asks whether the Russian Communists can confine their works to "the narrow bounds of the Russian revolution." [34] His answer is,

Of course not. On the contrary, the whole situation, both domestic . . . and foreign . . . , impelled them . , , to transfer the struggle to the international arena, to expose the ulcers of imperialism, . . . to smash social-chauvinism and social-pacifism. . . .[35]

The word "smash" is an interesting word to have applied to social pacifism, permanently in print, by the author of the many recent Stockholm and other peace proposals. Nor does he say this merely once. Speaking of Communist behavior in Russia in 1917 he writes, "It became necessary to overhaul the entire activity of the Second International, its entire method of work, and to drive out all . . . social-pacifism." [36] His first reference to the smashing of social-pacifism is the more significant, however, because it is uttered in the very sentence in which he writes that the Communist revolutionary struggle must be transferred to the international field. More specifically he adds that:

> . . . a coalition between the proletarian revolution in Europe and the colonial revolution in the East in a united world front of revolution against the world front of imperialism is inevitable.[37]

This statement should completely explode the suggestion that a sound foreign policy for the United States and the United Nations can restrict itself to the protection of Europe and Western civilization.

The period of world revolution has commenced, Premier Stalin tells us. Its aim must be "to consolidate the dictatorship of the proletariat in one country, using it as a base for the overthrow of imperialism in all countries." [38] Nor is Communism to be content with supporting the leaders of an Asian people merely to the point of helping them to gain their own independence. Those leaders, if they are to have Communist support, "must fight for the recognition of the whole. . . ." [39] In other words, in return for the aid of Russia in their gaining of freedom from imperialism, the native leaders must fight for the leadership of Moscow. As the 1929 Communist International puts the matter, "The ultimate aim of the Communist International is to replace world capitalist economy by a world system of Communism." [40] It remains to see what recognition "of the whole" by either domestic or foreign leaders means. This brings us to Visiting Lecturer Joseph Stalin, the humorist.

The beginning is, of course, quite sober. The aim is the consolidation of the dictatorship of the proletariat in Russia and the extension of the proletariat revolution throughout the rest of the world. But the practical instruments to this end must be as precisely specified as the theory defining the character of the end itself. We have already learned that the Communist Party is not the party of the masses of the people. It is instead but one small class in the total populace of the state, the class called the proletariat, which is made up largely of the urban workers who handle the modern technological instruments of production. The Communist Party, we are told, is the party of these urban workers, the party of the proletariat.

But, "The Party must be, first of all, the *vanguard* of the working class. . . . [It] cannot be a real party if it limits itself to registering what the masses of the working class feel and think. . . ." [41] The Communist Party is, to be sure, the expression of "the spontaneous movement" [42] of the proletariat which is cast up dialectically from the material womb of society. Being thus the product of dialectical determinism is its virtue. This is its moral credential. So, continues our lecturer, ". . . if it [the Communist Party] is unable to overcome the inertness and the political indifference of the spontaneous movement, . . . If it drags at the tail of the spontaneous movement," [43] it will not be a "real" revolutionary party. Hence, the party cannot even be identified with the restricted class in society which is the proletariat. It must be, instead, the smaller group which is "the vanguard" of the proletariat.

Now, what is to distinguish the vanguard from the spontaneous movement of the proletariat itself? The Professor tells us that "the Party must be armed with revolutionary theory. . . ." [44] It appears, therefore, that the first prerequisite in the practice of Communist leadership is not to provide the masses with food. It is, instead, to arm the vanguard of the proletariat with an ideology. In discussing technical leadership, the Visiting Professor tells his students that the primary principle of practice must be to locate the link which, if grasped, will hold the whole chain of factors in the situation together. Thus it was, he tells us, that:

In the period of the formation of the Party, [in Russia] when the innumerable circles and organizations had not yet been linked together, when amateurishness and the parochial outlook of the circles were corroding the Party from top to bottom, when ideological confusion was a characteristic feature of the internal life of the

Party, the main link and the main task in the chain of links and in the chain of tasks then confronting the Party proved to be the establishment of an all-Russian illegal newspaper. Why? Because only by [this] means . . . was it possible . . . to create a harmonious nucleus of a party, . . . capable of linking up the innumerable circles and organizations into a single organization, to prepare the conditions for ideological and tactical unity, and thus to lay the foundations for the formation of a real Party.[45]

However much the Communists may regard ideological factors as irrelevant by-products and afterthoughts in the case of others, they make it a primary practice for themselves. As Lenin says, "The proletarian vanguard has been ideologically won over. This is the most important thing. Without this, we cannot take even the first step towards victory." [46] Mr. Vishinsky similarly has been reported recently as saying, "We shall win the world with our ideas."

Between the small vanguard with its revolutionary ideology and the non-party members of the proletariat there must, however, be a connection. This connection has been achieved, the lecturer tells his students, by "intangible moral threads." [47] So successful has been this achievement that "recently two hundred thousand new members from the ranks of the workers were admitted to our Party." [48] What a truly "remarkable" achievement! Almost the population of the city of Bridgeport, Connecticut, out of the total Russian population of one hundred fifty million people! "This fact," our lecturer adds, "proves that the broad masses of non-Party workers regard our Party as *their* Party, as a Party *near and dear* to them." [49] His audience at this point must have had difficulty in holding back their tears.

So great is our lecturer's devotion to the removal of all class distinctions that even the fissioning of the Russian people into the vast masses and the proletariat minority class, the division of the proletariat into the non-Party members and the Party, and the division of the Party into its tail-dragging portion and its vanguard is not sufficient. Even the vanguard protected by its revolutionary theory must have a General Staff. Moreover, membership in this General Staff must be very strict. Otherwise, as our Visiting Professor, quoting Lenin in truly scholarly fashion, tells his audience, " 'every striker' can 'declare himself a member of the Party.' . . . [And] the *disorganizing* idea of confusing the class with the Party" [50] is introduced. Moreover, this General Staff of the vanguard of the Party must be organized and disciplined "with practical decisions binding on all members of the Party." [51] Has not Lenin said that,

> *Formerly*, our Party was . . . only the sum of separate groups [held together by] . . . no other relations except those of ideological influence, . . . *Now* we have become an organized Party, and this implies the establishment of authority, . . . the subordination of lower Party bodies to higher Party bodies.[52]

But even this General Staff, separated from the vanguard, which in turn is separated from the proletariat of urban workers, which in their turn are set apart from the masses, is not sufficient to win the revolutionary battle for the removal of all class distinctions. Patiently our scholar's Hegelian quest for unity carries his audience toward the truth. The General Staff cannot have the necessary "solidarity and iron discipline" [53] unless it is the embodiment "of unity of will." [54] The General Staff is "incompatible" [55] with the existence of factions. Lenin tells us that the "Communist Party will be able to perform its duty only if . . . iron discipline bordering on military discipline prevails. . . ." [56] Thus does our scholarly lecturer demonstrate to his university audience what it means to treat society as a science after the manner in which biologists study living organisms. Reason supports the authoritative words of the great Lenin:

> It need hardly be proved that the existence of factions leads to the existence of a number of centers, and the existence of a number of centers connotes the absence of one common center in the Party, the breaking up of the unity of will, the weakening and disintegration of discipline, the weakening and disintegration of the dictatorship.[57]

There must, therefore, be a "purging" from the General Staff of all "opportunist" elements. Lenin tells us that ". . . it may be useful to remove excellent Communists who are liable to waver . . . from all responsible posts." [58]

Only one fact, concerning this required unity of will of the General Staff of the vanguard of the proletariat, did our lecturer fail to make explicit to his audience. But this fact did not need to be put in words to these Russian university students of 1924 since it was present before their very eyes in the flesh.

However, the final touch of their lecturer's sober sense of humor is yet to exhibit itself. The Communists must not only be guided in their vanguard by a revolutionary ideology interpreted and applied with the iron discipline of a single unity of will; the true Party worker must also have a style:

> I am not referring to literary style. What I have in mind is style in work. . . . What are the characteristic features of this style? . . . It has two special features: (a) the Russian revolutionary sweep and (b) American efficiency.[59]

Without Russian revolutionary sweep "no progress is possible." [60] It is "the life-giving force which stimulates thought, impels things forward. . . ." [61] But without American efficiency, it runs the risk of

> . . . degeneration [into] . . . the disease of "revolutionary" improvisation and "revolutionary" plan concocting. . . . American efficiency, [on the other hand,] is that indomitable force which neither knows nor recognizes obstacles; which with its business-like perseverance brushes aside all obstacles; which continues at a task once started until it is finished, even if it is a minor task; and without which serious constructive work is inconceivable." [62]

But without the Russian revolutionary sweep it is liable to disintegrate "into narrow and unprincipled commercialism. . . ." [63]

The tragedy is that Premier Stalin does not have the respect for America's and the Western world's liberal constitutionalism that he has for American efficiency. His respect for American efficiency suggests, however, that the Premier and his disciplined executives who represent the General Staff of the vanguard of the Communist Party of the Russian proletariat are likely to think twice before venturing into any international war in which the United States is on the opposite side.

This does not mean that there is no danger of war initiated by the Soviet Union in a world which includes the United States. Certainly there is little likelihood of an end to the present Cold War. Let it not be forgotten that the basic aim of Soviet policy as specified above by Premier Stalin is the extension to the rest of the world of the revolutionary dictatorship of the proletariat which he has established in Russia. Force is not ruled out in this process. Lenin says that Communist revolutionary democracy

first rallies the proletariat as a revolutionary class . . . and gives it the opportunity to crush, to smash to bits, to wipe off the face of the earth the bourgeois State machinery—even its republican variety . . . ; then it substitutes . . . a State machinery in the shape of armed masses of workers, which becomes transformed into universal participation of the people in the militia.[64]

It is at the latter point that the peasants have the opportunity to express their devotion as reserves of the proletariat.

Premier Stalin is even more explicit when he writes that:

. . . the victorious proletariat of one country . . . should rise against the remaining capitalist world attracting the oppressed classes of other countries, starting revolts . . . in these countries, and, in case of necessity, even sending its military forces against the exploiting classes and their states.[65]

However much Moscow may talk about peace abroad, we can be sure, therefore, of two things. First, its General Staff is enlisting the whole of the masses in a war machine, and, second, the sending of this military machine into other countries is not ruled out. One can hardly expect that a General Staff which repudiates parliamentary procedure and insists that recourse to force is a moral necessity for the salvation of its own people will of a sudden develop moral scruples about the use of force against foreigners.

It appears, therefore, that the ideology and explicitly specified principles of practice of the Soviet Union are such that free parliamentary institutions on this earth can be made safe only by matching the Soviet Communists' internally inconsistent ideology, with its arbitrary identification of moral man with the single will of a General Staff of the vanguard of but one class of people in a community, with an alternative ideology backed with the police power necessary to protect its adherents. This can be achieved if the rest of the world recovers and fosters its own more truly scientifically grounded morality of a legal universalism which presupposes and protects free inquiry and political freedom. Since law is of the essence of such an ideology, this means the construction of an effective international law.

Is an effective international law possible? And if possible, will the Soviet Union accept it?

On the latter point, also, the leaders of the Soviet Union have put their answer in writing. Korovin, one of the authoritative Soviet writers on international law, faces this question of whether the Soviet Union can accept any international law which is compatible with and acceptable by the non-Communist democracies. In answering this question he distinguishes between two groups of interests—the intellectual and the economic. By economic interests he means material needs in the narrow sense of shoes, clothing and tools. Legal, ethical and political principles belong to the group of interests which are of an intellectual character. He then affirms that a single international law for both the Soviet Union and the non-Communist democracies "presupposes some common evaluation, unity of convictions legal, ethical and political. . . ." [66] The question, therefore, as to whether the Soviet Union and the non-Communist democracies can have a common international law for settling their disputes resolves itself into the more specific question as to whether the Soviet Union and the non-Communist democracies have the same norms or ideology.

Premier Stalin has already told us that this is not the case. Mr. Korovin reaches the same conclusion. He concludes, therefore, that *"an intercourse on the basis of intellectual unity*

*(ideological solidarity) between countries of bourgeois and so-
cialist cultures, cannot exist as a rule, and hence the rules of
international law covering this intercourse become pointless."* [67]

In this connection it is very interesting to note that the one
branch of the United Nations into which the Soviet Union
has not permitted its representatives to enter is the United
Nations Educational, Scientific and Cultural Organization. They
will not face and discuss objectively in UNESCO the ideological
differences between the Communist and the free world. Nor
will they collaborate or permit Russian scholars to collaborate
in a scholarly, objective attempt to resolve these ideological
differences.

Notwithstanding their rejection of a common international
law for Communist and non-Communist nations, Soviet students
of international law do regard existing international law as
binding in the case of an aggression committed by a non-Communist nation. Then non-Communist international law has
moral sanction. This international law has no moral or legal
validity, however, when the aggression is that of a Soviet Communist nation. The nations suffering the aggression are not
then entitled to the protection of international law. Instead, as
Korovin makes clear, in the cases of Bulgaria, Rumania, Yugoslavia, Hungary and Poland, they are being "liberated." [68] To
this list must now be added Tibet and the unsuccessful attempt
to "liberate" South Korea.

In fact it appears that in the Soviet Communist theory of
international law there cannot be international law even between Communist nations. At first sight this does not seem to
be true since Article 15 of the Constitution of the U.S.S.R.
confers sovereignty upon every Marxist revolutionary democratic republic. What this seeming overlooks, however, is that
in Article 14 the Constitution lists those matters reserved to the
Soviet Union and hence not within the jurisdiction of the "sovereign autonomous republics." This list, as Mantauts Chakste,
former Justice of the Supreme Court of Latvia, points out,
includes practically all the important state functions.

Nor should this surprise us because Premier Stalin has told us that the many state organs are to be brought under the single will of the General Staff of the vanguard of the party of the urban workers, which directs the world revolution. As one nation after another achieves independence at the hands of this world revolution, its loyalty to local autonomous independence becomes immediately transformed into its duty to unity. Thereby international law between Marxist Communist nations automatically becomes domestic law under the dictatorship of the single will of the General Staff.

It is not to be supposed either that the General Staff must operate subject to laws specified by a legislature which expresses the will of the proletariat. For let it be remembered, non-party members of even the proletariat do not belong to the decision-makers of the Party. Premier Stalin tells us that "the Soviet power is [not merely] the amalgamation and formation of the local Soviets into one common state organization, [but also the] . . . combining [of] the legislative and executive functions." [69]

The Soviet concept of international law and the content of their ideological conception of the moral and legal is such, therefore, that their own norms will not cause them to restrict to their own nation their war against what their ideology tells them is evil. Hence, a world community grounded in determinate legal rules implemented with the force necessary to make military aggression realistically unwise from the Communists' standpoint is absolutely essential.

Does the United Nations provide the required international legal instrument? Unquestionably it does in part. Its application in Korea demonstrates, however, that for all its virtues it has one fatal weakness. To this weakness, as illustrated in Korea, and its removal, we must now turn.

One final caution with respect to the behavior of Soviet Russia must be kept in mind. This caution becomes evident when one notes the Communists' distinction between the principles governing strategy and the principles governing tactics.

Strategy is defined by the basic Communist aim which is that of carrying through the proletarian revolution and establishing the dictatorship of the proletariat over the entire world. With respect to strategy or aim, Premier Stalin tells us that there must be no compromise and that the pursuit must be constant and "undeviating." [70] With respect, however, to tactics which are concerned with minor "ebbs and flows" within the absolute dialectically determined historical movement toward its culmination in the Communist ideal, there can be temporary "retreats" and occasional moments of compromise with the non-Communist world in order to gain time and strength for a resumption of the attack. One of the main instruments in this connection is an appeal to peace and even a temporary conclusion of a peace treaty. One of the objects of such tactics is, Premier Stalin writes, "to demoralize the enemy." [71] The more, therefore, that the world community succeeds in building up a world legal order, with the police forces necessary to restrain Communist aggression, the more one must expect offers of peace and negotiation to the Western world to come through Asian mediators.

It is exceedingly important that we keep in mind precisely what Premier Stalin and other Marxist Communist leaders tell us these peace proposals mean. They must not be allowed for one moment to lure us into the false supposition that the building of a world legal order outlawing aggression with the police power necessary to make the outlawing effective is not necessary.

This should be evident quite apart from what Premier Stalin has told us about the theory and practice of Russian Communism. Even within our own country the settling of disputes by duels and bloodshed is not avoided merely by religious and secular, moral and spiritual education. Legal institutions backed with the police force larger than any likely breakers of the code are also continuously necessary. Even in traditional Asia, for all its intuitive, pacifistic mediational, spiritual values, soldiers and policemen were always recognized

to be required. Gandhi himself would never have lived to become known by the whole of mankind had he not been rescued
and protected upon more than one occasion by policemen in
South Africa and even in India. His assassination came, moreover, when, at his request, effective police protection at his final
prayer meetings was not provided. These considerations make a
concern with the creation of a world law supported by effective
police power all the more evident and urgent.

13

HIROSHIMA, KOREA AND AN
EFFECTIVE WORLD LAW

Korea has obscured Hiroshima. Hiroshima reminds us that we are living in the atomic age. It tells us also that a third world war will be an atomic war.

The full implications of an atomic war have not received the attention in the press or in the public consciousness which they deserve. The facts about this matter are not comfortable ones. This is all the more reason why they need to be objectively faced.

Careful mathematical calculation, based upon information such as that contained in the U. S. Atomic Energy Commission report,[1] suggests that the number of atomic bombs which, if dropped near together in time, will be sufficient because of the accumulative radio activity to destroy all human life on this planet, may be between two hundred and one thousand. It is likely that more than this maximum number of atomic bombs exist at the present moment. It is also likely that should a world war break out this maximum number would be dropped in a brief period.

These facts must be known to the military chiefs of staff and the political leaders of every major country in the contemporary world. One would suppose, therefore, that they would be working day and night to achieve an international organization which would insure and guarantee the settlement of disputes between nations by peaceful means rather than by the present threat of and resort to war.

Roscoe Pound has recently reminded us that history gives no support to those who would achieve a peaceful settlement of disputes by other means than the establishment of legal rules and institutions.[2] This means that the only hope of escape from an atomic world war is the establishment of an effective world law and the police force necessary to enforce this world law.

It was hoped that this was what our world had achieved in the establishment of the United Nations at San Francisco. Korea, however, disillusions us on this point. Events before Korea should also have done so.

In fact, the ink was hardly dry on the signatures to the San Francisco document before the foreign ministers of the major powers which had officially pledged themselves to the establishment of freedom, economic well-being and peace throughout the world met in London to prepare a peace treaty for Germany. Immediately it became evident that vituperation and disagreement rather than peace-making were to be the fruit of their efforts. So bad were the results that a responsible London reporter on the proceedings was forced to write: "[T]he Council of Foreign Ministers . . . was unable to reach agreement, or even a basis for discussion. . . . The meeting has been a complete fiasco."[3] Events since then, within the United Nations and throughout the world, have amply confirmed the correctness of this judgment.

Why, we must ask ourselves, were the practices of the Foreign Ministers in London so different from the signed professions of their respective governments made a few weeks before in San Francisco? One answer to this question is that whereas the United Nations brought almost all the nations of the world under the law of its Charter, it left the major powers outside this law. Or, to put the matter in another way, the United Nations was predicated on the assumption that the major powers could agree. Consequently when the major powers do not agree, as the London meeting first demonstrated and all evidence since then has confirmed, the United Nations seems to fail as a legal institution and as an instrument for the peaceful settlement of international disputes.

This is undoubtedly true, but its truth does not answer the more basic question, Why, in the light of their immediately previous, officially signed professions of a common agreement upon the peaceful purpose of establishing an international legal order for the settling of disputes, did the Foreign Ministers of the major powers immediately proceed to disagree? Why, in short, was San Francisco followed so quickly by the Cold War? Only if we answer these questions will we diagnose the real weakness in the United Nations and be able to prescribe a sound cure. For let it be remembered, in an atomic age, a cure we must have.

The apparent contradiction between the professions of the foreign ministers at San Francisco and their practice in London becomes clear when one notes that the United Nations Charter, to which these and other foreign ministers affixed their signatures, was expressed in terms of abstract nouns such as "peace," "freedom," "economic uplift" and "well-being." This gave a spurious impression of agreement upon the legal norms for settling disputes between nations. It gave an appearance of agreement upon the meaning of these undefined, abstract words. And precisely because these abstract words were undefined, no country and no foreign minister had any difficulty in signing the document with a clear conscience. When Secretary of State Stettinius signed, he undoubtedly read into these words the liberal, democratic meaning which they have in the ideology that defines the economic, political and religious institutions of the United States. When the Foreign Minister of Great Britain's Labour government signed, he undoubtedly read into these words the Socialist, nationalized industrial meanings which freedom and economic uplift have for the British Labour Party. Similarly, when Foreign Minister Molotov signed, he read in his Marxist Communist ideological meanings. This is why there is no difficulty in having international conferences reach apparent agreement upon peaceful procedures and policies providing the conclusions are formulated in sufficiently undefined, abstract nouns.

But before a publicly accepted legal rule can be of any use in deciding a particular, concrete dispute, as any lawyer or judge knows, the terms in that rule must have specific concrete meanings and implications. This, in considerable part the pledged principles of the Charter of the United Nations did not possess.

Consequently, when the foreign ministers, who signed the United Nations Charter at San Francisco, found themselves in London where they were confronted, not with ill-defined abstractions, but with the concrete task of deciding the specific economic and political organization of its institutions and government under which Germany is to be granted peace by the victorious powers, the conflict of the social and legal norms of these signers of the San Francisco document immediately exhibited itself. Instead of a common law, there was a conflict of laws not merely with respect to social norms or substantive law but also with respect to the procedural law necessary to carry on further sober discussion of the problem without vituperation.

The Soviet Union would grant peace to a United Germany only if its economic, political and spiritual life were built on dialectical materialistic principles. The British Socialist Government preferred, although it did not insist upon, the nationalization of Germany's industrial system as a condition for peace. The people of the United States probably preferred a federally regulated free enterprise economy in Germany in which the cartels were broken up and competitive business was introduced. Great Britain, the United States and France would clearly have betrayed their trust at London had they not insisted upon a freely elected, democratic, constitutional government in Germany to which a peace treaty was granted, rather than a dictatorship with its one-party system of elections of either the Nazi or the Communist type. Hence, the impasse and the Soviet Minister's vituperative charges at London, and afterwards, that anyone who did not grant peace to Germany on Communist "democratic," i.e., dialectical materialist, principles was a war-maker and a fascist.

Events inside and outside the United Nations' meetings since then demonstrate that it was not the foreign ministers at London who betrayed the hopes of mankind for peace and misled the world, but the framers of the United Nations Charter at San Francisco. The authors of this world constitution gave the impression to mankind, because of their use of undefined, abstract nouns without specific ideological meaning, that the determinate common legal norms with definite political and economic content, which are necessary for the settlement of any dispute by legal means, had been agreed upon by all who signed this document, when in fact this was not and still is not the case. The specific meanings of the words "freedom," "peaceful settlement" and "economic well-being" to which Foreign Minister Molotov affixed his signature at San Francisco simply are not the same as those of other signatories. In fact, as the previous chapter has shown, his meanings were and remain incompatible with those of any other non-Communist member of the United Nations. London and what has happened since merely brought this incompatibility of moral and legal norms into the open.

Moreover, this incompatibility of cultural, spiritual and legal norms applies as much to the other members of the United Nations as it does to its so-called big powers. The spiritual values of Asia are as incompatible with those of the ideologically understood, atheistic, dialectically materialistic New China of Mao and Fung Yu-lan and Soviet Russia of Stalin as is the liberal constitutionalism of the United States, Great Britain, France and the classical Christian West. Only ideologically uninformed wishful thinking about the New China and the Soviet Union can ever reconcile the dialectically materialistic state of Mao and Fung Yu-lan or Russia's Stalin, who tells Russian university students that even domestic social pacifism must be "smashed," with Gandhiji's and the Buddha's pacifism, or with Prime Minister Nehru's secular democratic state and Five Year Plan in which "pride of place" goes to agriculture rather than to the General Staff of the proletariat.

Similarly within the Asian and Islamic nations there are differences with respect to the spiritual values and norms to be used for settling disputes. Prime Minister Nehru's secular state constitutionalism backed with police power and an army is quite different from Gandhiji's mediational way and his firm stand for the disbandment of India's army. A few days after India gained independence Gandhiji called together the leaders of his Congress Party Government with whom he had gone to jail in the fight for independence. At this meeting he resigned from the Congress Party. When his colleagues protested, his reply was that he knew they would decide to keep and maintain an Indian army and that he could not, in accordance with his principle of no use of force, be a member of a party or a government which did such a thing. Prime Minister Nehru and his ministers admitted that they did intend to have an Indian army, so they had no alternative but to accept Gandhiji's resignation.[4] Even within Free India the norms for preserving peace and order of Gandhiji and of the Congress Party Government are so different that these fellow workers for independence had to part company and go their respective ways once the independence was achieved.

The Islamic nations of the world are likewise interpreting the withdrawal of Western imperialism from the Middle East and Asia as the sign of the rise of Islam and the opportunity to build their economic and political institutions on the ideals of Islam rather than of France, Great Britain, Holland, the United States or Soviet Russia. Pakistan withdrew from India because 80 million Muslims did not trust the norms of Prime Minister Nehru's secular state when interpreted and applied by a government in which Hindus would always have a majority of at least two to one.

These facts show that it is not merely the so-called big powers in the United Nations that read not merely different, but also

logically and practically incompatible content into the words
"freedom," "economic uplift" and "peace" to which they
pledged themselves at San Francisco. Thus the heart of the
weakness of the United Nations is not that it presupposes the
agreement of the big powers, true as this is, but that its undefined terminology suggests that the nations of the world have
a single economic, political and spiritual ideology for the definition of a common world law, when in fact this is not the case.
The world in which we live is in fact one of ideological and
living law pluralism. It is not yet a world of living and common
law monism.

Apparently, therefore, we have been attempting to build
legal institutions for the world without first answering the
question concerning what character any law must have if it is
to be effective. It happens, fortunately, that legal science gives
us an answer to this question. The answer has been formulated
by the great student of legal science, the late Austro-Hungarian
Eugen Ehrlich.[5] He noted in his own province of Bukowina
that laws were often introduced by the different governments
under which this province happened to fall which were utterly
ineffective. This led him to investigate what it is in any society
which determines when newly introduced law is or is not effective. His answer, now generally accepted by legal scholars, is
as follows: Positive law is effective only when it corresponds
to the underlying living law. By positive law Ehrlich meant
the legal constitutions and statutes that are introduced and the
legal institutions which apply and enforce these constitutional
principles and constitutionally legislated statutes. By the living
law, he meant the underlying community habits and embodied
norms of the majority of the people to which the positive law
is applied, quite apart from the positive law itself. What Ehrlich
noted was that positive law can be an effective law in a community even when it does not conform to the underlying living
law habits and ethical beliefs of the people to which it is applied
if the non-conforming living law habits are those of a minority.
Then the living law habits of the majority, to which the positive

law conforms, constitute a public opinion which supports the courts and the police in their application of the positive law to the non-conforming minority. Newly introduced positive law tends to be ineffective and break down when it does not correspond to the living law habits of the majority.

An example of Ehrlich's principle is the failure of the Prohibition Amendment in the United States. This was a duly passed positive law, comparable to the positive world law duly passed and officially signed and confirmed at San Francisco. Prohibition failed, notwithstanding its positive legal status, because the living law habits not only of the vast mass of the people but also of leaders in the community of unquestioned moral integrity and social responsibility, such as President Hadley at Yale, did not conform to it and openly attacked it. Similarly, legal constitutions which are effective in Great Britain and the United States often result in nothing but corruption and government by military cliques and coups when introduced in countries whose living law habits and ideological beliefs are not those of the living law of Great Britain and the United States.

Ehrlich's principle that effective positive law must correspond to the underlying living law of the society to which it is applied now permits us to specify the basic error underlying the attempt of the United Nations to achieve world law. San Francisco built a positive world law suggesting the existence of living law ideological monism when, in fact, the world is characterized by living law pluralism. The United Nations was doomed to fatal weaknesses, therefore, because the monistic thesis of its positive law did not correspond to the pluralism of the world's underlying living laws.

Events following the Korean affair give another illustration of this fatal weakness of the United Nations as an effective legal instrument for settling disputes between nations. To be sure, as we noted in the first chapter, the United Nations can be proud of what it has achieved in Korea. It nipped in the bud the Communist "liberation" of the whole of Asia and thereby prevented the world from being engulfed in World War III in the fall of 1950. This is no mean achievement. It has been accomplished, however, more in spite of the law of the United Nations than because of it. The following considerations will make this clear.

The really discouraging result of the United Nations' success in preventing the North Korean aggression from succeeding is not the more obvious fact of the support of the North Korean aggression in the Security Council by Mr. Jacob Malik and his government and the branding of the United States and the United Nations as the real aggressor. This, of course, is inexcusable and bad enough. But even in domestic disputes under civil law, the lawbreakers often have their friends at court. That North Korea's friends should be the Soviet Union also does not surprise us since these two countries have a common ideology. The mere fact that under law, violators of the law often have friends more interested in saving the violators than in supporting the law does not by itself mean that the settling of international disputes by the legal means embodied in the United Nations is doomed.

The discouraging fact and really mortal blow to the United Nations as a legal instrument for settling international disputes came when the nations not ideologically identified with the aggressor and neutral with respect to the ideology of both North Korea and the major policeman, of necessity the United States, failed not merely to assume their fair share of the policing, but, what is even worse, failed to give their moral support to the policeman. Legal processes can stand up against breakers of the law who have a few friends more interested in supporting the lawbreaker than in supporting the law and its policeman, but legal processes are doomed if members of the community, not ideologically or personally tied to the lawbreaker, do not support the law-declaring body and the policeman. The action most disastrous to the United Nations' program for peace was the neutrality and even the criticism of the ideology of the invaded nation and its leader, and of the major policeman, made by the avowedly law supporting, peace-pursuing nations of the world.

We are again confronted with Ehrlich's principle. Legal institutions can impose their positive norms on a minority in the living law community whose behavior does not conform to those norms. But legal institutions are doomed to failure if the leaders of the living law majority do not rally to the support not merely of the law-making body's decision but also to the law-making body's policeman. Effective world law cannot always count on the lucky circumstance that the few who do assume the difficult responsibility of policing the law happen to have just enough power to balance that of the lawbreaking aggressor. There will not be an effective world law until the policing of the law when violation occurs is clearly recognized as the responsibility of every nation.

It would be a mistake, however, for the leaders of the United States or anyone else to criticize Prime Minister Nehru as *The New York Times* did in its editorial of mid-October of 1950 for reserving unto his countrymen the right of independence of action notwithstanding the decision of the United Nations to brand the North Korean invasion as an aggression and to introduce police action to prevent this aggression from being a success. It is equally erroneous to condemn the Soviet Union for using its veto. For the truth of the matter is that the United States, as well as India and the Soviet Union, reserves this right and would not have sanctioned the entrance of the United States into the United Nations were this right not reserved. To be sure, only the original five major powers in the Security Council have the right of the veto. But if such a right is legally justified for these powers, it is certainly equally legally justified for the Government of India. As our previous analysis has shown, law is not morally justified law unless it is universal law, the same for all. Hence if it is legally right for the United States and the U.S.S.R. to reserve the right to veto a majority decision of the United Nations, it is equally right for Free India to do so.

This fact of the veto has led many people to the conclusion that the United Nations can be turned into an effective legal instrument for settling disputes providing that the veto is abolished or that a majority vote of the members of its Assembly is permitted to override a veto in the Security Council. This, however, is an error.

The error centers in the fact that the United Nations Charter suggests and rests on the positive law thesis that the nations of the world have common norms which can provide the legal rules for the settling of disputes between them, when actually the living laws of the world are many rather than one, and different and even mutually incompatible, instead of identical, in content. The mere removal of the veto would not alter this fatal weakness of the failure of the new positive world law introduced by the United Nations to correspond to the world's underlying, diverse and even conflicting living law beliefs, practices and habits.

The error of introducing no veto is even worse than this. Even if the United States and all the other nations of the world accepted this proposal, they would be wrong in doing so. No nation will ever accept, nor should it ever accept, any positive legal decision by any legal body that violates its own indigenous living law norms. Thus, even if a nation did accept the present United Nations positive law Charter without the veto, it would never accept a later decision from that legal body which violated its own living law norms. Nor should it do so. No people or nation should ever puts its fate in the hands of any legal body unless the positive law norms of that legal body are so specifically defined that the explicit living law norms of the nation in question are protected and guaranteed. It is precisely because of the ambiguity of the positive law norms of the United Nations Charter that no nation can or should accept the jurisdiction of that Charter without the veto. The mere addition of the abolition of the veto to the undefined legal words and institutions which are the United Nations and its present Charter will not, therefore, remove the fatal weakness in the United Nations which subsequent events in London, Korea and New Delhi have revealed.

On the other hand, it is perfectly clear that there is no effective law where the veto exists. What would the law against a murderer amount to if the murderer reserved the right to veto the right of the court to have jurisdiction over his case? Yet it is precisely this kind of situation which a veto in international law and in the United Nations entails.

We seem, therefore, to be in an impossible predicament. We cannot accept the positive law and institutions of the United Nations without a veto, and there is no effective law with a veto. Does this mean that an effective solution of international disputes by legal means is impossible? The answer is unequivocally, No. The possibility of an effective international world order is at hand. Ehrlich's criterion of effective law tells us how it is to be achieved.

Ehrlich's criterion is that law in any field is never effective unless it corresponds to the underlying living law of the people to whom it is applied. The United Nations' law requires the reservation of the veto from anyone who accepts it precisely because it doesn't correspond to the underlying living law of the world. Its positive law norms are written as if the nations and people of the world had a single, common determinate living law norm for defining freedom, peace, economic uplift and well-being in a precise, determinate, unambiguous way. It fails and therefore must have a veto reserved by every one accepting it because its statutes as presently written protect nobody's living law norms. By acting as if every nation has the same determinate norms, it protects and guarantees none. Since no nation or people can predict in any given case what determinate meanings will be read into the ambiguous words of the document, it clearly cannot trust the fate of its ideals, values and living law beliefs and habits to such a law without the reservation of a veto.

But how, if the living law norms of the different nations and people of the world vary from people to people and nation to nation, can any world positive law charter and document be formulated with specific meanings that will fit them all? Clearly no such document can be formulated.

All that this means, however, is that an effective world positive law must give up the traditional erroneous assumption of an existent common ideology for the whole world. It must, in other words, base itself on the living law fact of ideological and living law pluralism instead of on the vacuously verbal and erroneous assumption of living law monism.

Instead of acting as if the many nations of the world possess identical living law values and economic and political norms for the ordering of their respective social institutions, we must honestly face the fact that this is not at present the case and construct the positive world law accordingly.

Put more concretely, what this means is that we must, in world charters, world organizations and the pronouncements of statesmen stop writing and acting as if the different nations, peoples and cultures of the world had common, determinate norms defining what they mean by freedom, peace and economic uplift, and base our world law and our world institutions and the foreign policy of our respective governments on the realistic living law fact that different peoples, nations and cultures of the world embody and act from different living law ideological and cultural premises and assumptions.

The question arises immediately: What more specifically would a world law with its accompanying institutions based on the realistic fact of living law ideological pluralism of the world look like? How would it differ from the present Charter of the United Nations? In the first place, it would guarantee to each ideology and nation of the world protection of its particular norms in its own living law geographical area. For this reason any nation could assign its fate to such an international law without the reservation of a veto since this international law specifically guarantees its particular ideology in its particular domain. To make this guarantee all the more specific and certain, it might be well, after specifying at the beginning of this

world charter its basic principle of ideological living law pluralism, to require also of any member nation the specification of
its specific ideology and living law norms. This would guarantee
to every member nation and make clear to every future judge
of this world law that in any decision each member nation's
specific ideology and living law values must be honored and
protected in its geographical domain until the nation in question itself changes them and so informs the international body.

With the ideology of the United States, for example, or the
Communist ideology of the U.S.S.R. spelled out in its details
and at the same time guaranteed in its geographical area there
would be no possibility of any future judge, due to the ambiguity of the words of the law, failing in his application of
this world law to respect the living law ideology of either the
U.S.S.R. or the United States in their respective areas if both
of these nations submitted *that part of their life which is international in character* to such an international legal institution
without the reservation of a veto. In fact, were any later judge
to give a verdict interfering with the internal living law of say
the United States or the U.S.S.R., veto of this would not be
necessary. The illegality of the judge's decision would be so
clear from the constitution that it would be patently evident to
the world community. International public opinion would then
support the nation in question in not accepting it.

The point of the two foregoing requirements (i.e., the basic
principle of ideological living law pluralism and the inclusion
in the constitution of the specific living law norms of each
country coming under its protection) is to remove any reason
for any nation not accepting such a world law without a veto.
When such a world constitution not only faces the realistic
fact of the differing cultural ideologies of the various nations
but also specifies the ideology of each one to be valid in its
particular geographical area, a veto upon the part of each nation
to insure this is unnecessary.

The prohibitions of such a pluralistically grounded world
law are obvious. To guarantee South Korea in the specific

social norms it has chosen is to prohibit any other nation, such as North Korea, from aggressively invading South Korea to impose its different norms or for any other reason. To protect any nation and its own legally constituted and recognized national order necessitates the outlawing of any interference with that living law by the aggressive, forceful invasion of any other power. Thus what the very simple foregoing provisions of a world law grounded in the realistic fact of the world's living law ideological and cultural pluralism amount to is this: It faces the living law difference in ideologies and cultural norms of the various nations and peoples of the world, guarantees this pluralism and then merely controls it so that the principle of living law pluralism is not violated.

This has the advantage also of not requiring the participants in police action against any violator of the world's law to have the same ideology or to have to pass judgment on the ideology of either the offended or the offending nation. The basis for the police action, for example, against the North Koreans, is not the fact that we do not hold an ideology identical with theirs but that they have violated the principle of living law pluralism by aggressively interfering with the right of the South Koreans to build their social institutions on whatever ideology they choose or circumstances have led them to. Thus to participate in the police action does not force the members of the world community to decide whether they want to be guided by the ideology of one of the biggest policemen in the police force or by the ideology of the aggressor. The legal and moral basis for police action is solely the fact that the aggressor has violated the basic living law fact of national, ideological and cultural pluralism.

There is no such thing as the protection of law without corresponding duties and responsibilities. The Hindu law of Manu and the other ancient Hindu lawmakers in fact spoke rarely if ever of privileges but only of duties. This means that no nation can be admitted to the legally constituted world community to enjoy the protection of its law made effective by police power, without at the same time pledging to assume the responsibility without veto for its share of any police action under that law. In short, community police action under law is everybody's responsibility. If the demands upon a given nation's military forces for domestic purposes are such that it cannot contribute to the international police action, it at the very least has the legal obligation to put its entire moral support behind the legally authorized police action regardless of whether it agrees with the ideology of the offended nation or of some of the policemen. Under a world law based on the fact and principle of living law pluralism, the sole moral and legal consideration in any international dispute is not what the ideologies of the disputants, or of the policemen, are, but that the violator of the law, regardless of what his ideology is, has interfered with the right of the people of another nation to run their domestic political life on any ideology they choose.

There does not seem to be any justifiable reason why any one of the existing nations of the world should not accept the foregoing world law without reservation since it guarantees that particular nation and its ideology in its particular geographical area. Only at one point may difficulty arise. When any nation applies for admission to the world's legal community, its specific ideology must be presented so that no future judge of the world law will be in any doubt about what the ideology is which is to be respected and protected in that particular nation's geographical area. Experts must, however, examine this ideology with respect to its theory of international law. If such an examination shows that the ideology in question is affirmed to be the sole valid norm for judging disputes between nations as well as for judging disputes within the nation in question, this nation, before admission to membership in the legally constituted world community, must be required to duly record in writing the repudiation of its own particular ideology *as the basis for judging international disputes* and take an oath to support, instead, the principle of living law pluralism.

Otherwise the present vituperation which characterizes the

United Nations and international relations generally will continue even under this new world law. The Cold War will not be stopped. Clearly for a member nation to judge other nations from the standpoint of its own ideology is to contradict the principle upon which a world law based on living law pluralism rests. Practically, this would mean that if any foreign minister arose in the world body and proceeded to condemn or judge another nation from the standpoint of his own ideology he would be immediately rapped out of order. The sole question open for discussion before the law would be whether in any dispute the principle of living law pluralism had been violated.

This does not mean that a person, people or nation cannot judge and choose between rival ideologies for themselves and for the settling of their domestic disputes. Quite the contrary. In fact, the principle of living law pluralism presupposes and protects this right. All that is outlawed is the use of a particular nation's ideology for the settling of international disputes. Then only the principle of living law pluralism has international legal status.

But how, it may be asked, can there be any basis at all for judging an international dispute if no specific nation's ideology can be used? The answer to this question is that no dispute falls under the jurisdiction of this world law unless it raises the question of the violation of its basic principle of living law pluralism. Hence this principle alone provides the legal basis for deciding the case. Such a simple basis for decision makes the decision clean cut, unconfused by the appeals by different statesmen to their respective national ideologies. It also makes everyone's responsibility for policing the decision clean cut. The respective ideologies of the statesman have nothing to do with the legal and moral basis for the decision and the legal and moral responsibilities of every nation to police the world court's verdict. So far as the court's decision and the responsibility of everyone for policing that decision is concerned, the principle of living law pluralism alone operates.

This basis for an effective world law accepts realistically the cultural and ideological differences of the nations of the contemporary world. It then merely restricts these differences at the point where they incline to extend themselves to the whole world, thereby preventing vituperation, Cold War, aggression and even hot war being carried on, due to an ambiguous legal terminology, in the name of international law and international morality.

The world is the richer because different peoples and nations have known themselves and nature and thereby described their experience in diverse ways which in turn have led them to various norms for ordering their cultural and national life. All that is required to keep nations holding these different ideologies in their respective places, thereby enriching rather than destroying humanity in an atomic age, is to introduce a world law which guarantees the diverse ideological living law values and which restricts each one to those who want to possess it.

To do this, all that is required is a very brief world constitution which affirms the principle of living law pluralism to be the sole basis for international legal judgment and which backs this single constitutional principle with a police force the automatic moral responsibility of all and so large that any nation will see the folly of violating the legal decision which it enforces.

The making of the police action, once a decision is reached, the automatic moral responsibility of all is as important as the size of the police force itself. For it insures—what was so dishearteningly absent following Korea, namely—that the unanimous moral solidarity of the entire world community is against the legally declared aggressor.

If Hiroshima has made clear to the world the necessity of settling disputes between nations by a world law and if Korea has revealed the tragically disheartening weakness in the world law of the United Nations that we have at present and shown us how to remove this weakness, perhaps the tens of thousands of lives lost in these two places have not been lost in vain.

14

TWO PATHS TO WORLD LAW

Recent developments in the contemporary world indicate that it is moving to an effective world law by two paths. The movement along the first path has been indicated in the previous chapter. It begins with the present excessively large number of nations and in one step attempts to bring them under the rule of law backed with the police power necessary to make this rule of law effective. If this first movement, tried unsuccessfully by the League of Nations and again by the United Nations, is to succeed, a radically amended world law of the United Nations grounded on the basic fact of ideological and cultural pluralism must be introduced. The movement along the second path proceeds toward the goal of effective world law by two steps. This movement, which is occurring before our eyes, consists in starting with the absurdly large number of present national political units and stepping first to a relatively small number of cultural political units. What makes this possible is the fact, upon which we have come again and again, of the decline of nationalism and the rise and resurgence of culturalism.

We came upon this phenomenon first in the solidarity of Asia. The basic cultural, philosophical and religious identities underlying the differences of Buddhist, Taoist, Confucian or non-Aryan Hindu Japan, Korea, China, Indo-China, Indonesia, Thailand, Burma, Bali, Ceylon and India give these nations a common outlook that is already expressing itself in an inclination to political solidarity and unity. Nowhere does this show more dramatically than in the fact that, whereas President Mao is guided by Communist theory and practice and Prime Minister Nehru is drawing upon Anglo-American liberal constitutionalism in the westernization of their respective Asian countries, nevertheless the common bond of unity which is pre-Western, non-Islamic Asian culture not merely binds India in a cultural tie of sympathy to China but also issues in the political sponsoring of Communist China's entrance into the United Nations. Providing the law, morale and police power of the world community can become sufficiently strong to insure the independence of the present non-Communist Asian nations, this tie between them and Communist China will be a good thing. For anything that binds the Asian people to their own religious, philosophical, cultural and moral traditions will be a strong fortification against the further advance of Communism throughout the world. Sooner or later in China there will come a reaction, from the complete Communist westernization of Chinese life, to the living roots of their own Confucian Asian cultural tradition. Any Asian ties which help to keep this common Asian cultural tradition alive until this reaction occurs, are, therefore, to the good.

The resurgence of Islam provides an even more striking instance of the decline of nationalism and the increasing importance of cultural unity as the basis of political unity. There is hardly a day in which the newspapers do not bring a report of the Arab and Islamic nations acting as a single bloc. One day there is the unification of the Arab world behind Egypt against Great Britain's claims on Suez. On another day the Islamic nations protest the action of the French in North Africa, carrying their protest to the United Nations. The freedom loving, lawful universalism, which is the spiritual essence of Islam, that has been rediscovered by Muslim thinkers and statemen such as Iqbal, Maulana Abul Kalam Azad and A. A. A. Fyzee,[1] will more and more exhibit the absurdity of the contrast between the pluralism, impotence and economic backwardness of the many individual Islamic nations and the unity and creative power which the resurgence of the true Islamic spirit makes possible.

Similarly, cultural unity and self-consciousness are beginning to come to expression among the non-Islamic and non-European Africans. Already Great Britain has recognized the independence of the Gold Coast. Here the indigenous cultural resurgence will take much more time before it issues in political unity. But with the mood of the masses of mankind as anti-imperialistic as it now is, we must expect sooner or later to find in Africa a third cultural political unit in our world.

The most notable and spectacular, almost incredible, movement from a pluralism of political nations to a cultural political unit is taking place before our eyes at this very moment on the continent of Europe. As Queen Juliana of the Netherlands said during her recent visit to the United States:

Europe is the only part of the globe where nations are at all seriously negotiating about giving up part of their sovereignty. We [in Holland] feel we can be a reliable pillar of European unity, a unity which is growing by means of the Schuman Plan and other economic and defensive and—perhaps eventually—political integration. Constitutional amendments have been voted lately by the Netherlands Parliament in order to remove some remaining obstacles to our partnership in future supranational organizations.[2]

Writing from Rome on December 18, 1951, immediately following General Eisenhower's visit there, Anne O'Hare McCormick reported:

De Gasperi and the French Foreign Minister, Robert Schuman, are given credit for breaking the deadlock that all but paralyzed progress in Rome and led many observers to conclude that a European army was impossible. Adenauer stood with the French and Italians. . . . The Benelux Ministers shrank from the fateful step of transferring the control of their forces to a common political authority. . . .

De Gasperi admits that this is a revolutionary step. A denationalized army is something new in the world, he says, not to be achieved without a complete reversal of preconceived ideas and sacrifices of sovereignty in the most sensitive areas of national life.

Nevertheless, he is convinced it has to be done. He holds that no European nation can defend itself alone, no matter how strong it becomes, and that a common defense is impossible without an over-all political authority to direct it.

Less than a month later, Anne O'Hare McCormick reported from Bonn, Germany, in *The New York Times* of January 14, 1952, as follows:

Europe is surprised, the French especially are surprised, and a little shaken, that the Bonn Parliament ratified the Schuman plan by the clear-cut majority of eighty-nine votes. This is really a tremendous decision for the West Germans to make. Against the Socialists' impassioned appeals to nationalistic sentiment, all the other parties, with a few individual exceptions, soberly voted to surrender control of their richest national possession to an international authority. . . . [T]he Germans have agreed that the forge of Europe, the forge of former wars, is no longer an all-German preserve, but belongs to the European system. . . . Some observers here predict that in three years the Germans . . . will be in position to control the pool. This thought may have won votes for the Schuman plan. . . .

But this was not the motive for the student demonstrations following the vote in the Bundestag; they were celebrating the promise that the merger will put an end to wars between France and Germany. It was not the note struck by the press comment. . . .

The strength of this feeling is no surprise to a reporter who comes to Germany after a busman's holiday spent . . . outside official circles. . . .

Coming into Germany we crossed three frontiers in a few hours. The formalities were as perfunctory as if the functionaries . . . recognized that the boundaries are fading away. . . . On the highways and byways one senses that the people of Europe are getting tired of the narrow national compartments in which they live. . . .

It is highly significant that the leaders who have managed to survive the political storm of the last few years—men like Schuman, De Gasperi and Adenauer—are men dedicated to the cause of creating a Europe out of its disparate national elements.

Another dispatch to *The New York Times* from Bonn, Germany, dated March 5, added the following information:

Chancellor Konrad Adenauer declared tonight Europe's only salvation was to form a United States of Europe. He said West Germany was ready to join others in drafting a constitution for it.

The cultural factor which has made this development possible has not received the attention it deserves. An examination of the biographies of the men who have led this movement toward the political unification of continental Europe reveals the following facts. Dr. Alcide De Gasperi was educated at the University of Vienna where he received a Doctor of Laws degree. From 1939 to 1943 he was Secretary of the Vatican Library. In addition to being the head of the Italian Government, he is also the leader of its Christian Democrat Party. The cultural background of Dr. De Gasperi and his party is, therefore, classically legal and Roman Catholic. Dr. Konrad Adenauer was educated at the Gymnasium St. Aposteln in Cologne, and at the universities of Freiburg, Munich and Bonn. In addition to being Chancellor of West Germany, he is also the Chairman of the Christian Democratic Union Party. The educational institutions which he attended and the party which he leads are classically legal and Roman Catholic in their cultural emphasis and tradition. Dr. Robert Schuman was born in Luxembourg and educated at the colleges of Luxembourg and Metz and at the universities of Bonn, Munich and Strasbourg from which he received a Doctor of Laws in 1908. When Germany overran France in the last war, he went into the French underground. In World War I his home province was in Germany and he fought in the German Army. His cultural background is clearly that of the secular legal universalism of France and the Roman Catholic Alsace-Lorraine and the West German Rhineland and Bavaria.

It is hardly necessary to point out that France, Italy, Austria, Luxembourg and Belgium are predominantly Roman Catholic cultures. Their legal theory is the continental code which derives from the Stoic Romans. It is not so often realized that the population of Holland is now more than fifty per cent Roman Catholic and that, what is even more important, the division of

Germany between East and West Germany makes the majority of West Germans Roman Catholic also. The Rhineland and South Germany have always been Roman Catholic. West Germany comprises geographically roughly that portion of Germany which was reached and permanently affected by the influence of the ancient Roman Empire. Recently the magazine section of *The New York Sunday Times* carried an article from Geneva by Michael L. Hoffman entitled, "Integration: 1800–1952," with the subheading, "Western Europe's rim is like Charlemagne's."

These two maps speak for themselves. We now see what the three continental European statesmen, De Gasperi, Schuman and Adenauer, mean when they say that the present unification of Europe, notwithstanding all the economic and military con-

siderations which make it such a contemporary necessity, is a
turning back of the clocks of Western history. Literally it is a
turning back behind Luther to the liberal, legal universalism
which is the spiritual essence of Stoic Roman Christian civilization and the repudiation of Luther's identification of moral,
Christian Western man with the German people or any other
tribal, ethnological or provincially geographical group.

Let it not be forgotten also that modern French, Italian and
West German secular leadership even if it be by persons who
are Roman Catholics, has passed through the nurture of modern secular and philosophical liberalism. The spirit of moral
man as free man which Luther initiated as the necessary correc-
tive to the Roman Church's legal absolutism has left its im-
print on the secular leadership of the whole Roman Catholic

continental European world. Every student who passes through
a French lycée is required to take a course in modern philosophy which begins with the liberalizing skepticism of Descartes
and emphasizes modern British empirical philosophical, economic and political thought. No graduate of the aforementioned
universities in Austria, Italy, France or West Germany can
escape the influence of modern philosophical liberalism.

A secularly led Roman Catholic continental European culture, therefore, which throws out the erroneous absolutism of
the early Roman Christian legal universalism and gives expression to the true Stoic Christian legal universalism which presupposes and protects freedom, has a distinct contemporary
possibility of being the living law basis for the unification of
continental Europe and of even the entire West. In any event,
we are now face to face in continental Europe with the fourth
instance of the contemporary world movement from a pluralism of nations to a single political unit grounded in common
cultural traditions and beliefs of long standing.

One of the most revealing facts about this political unification of continental Europe is the refusal of both Great Britain
and the United States to join it. This is the more remarkable
when one recalls that Mr. Winston Churchill was the prime
mover at Strasbourg in the movement toward European union
and that General Eisenhower has been its main efficient cause.
Nor does General Eisenhower fail to represent the American
people in this matter. So great is American pressure from both
the Republican and Democratic parties that Europe unite economically, militarily and politically that continental Europeans
are disturbed by the fear that the United States is overdoing this
pressure. Even Queen Juliana, notwithstanding her warm spontaneous acceptance of continental European unity, felt it necessary to caution the people of the United States against pressing
too fast for European union. Why then this failure of Mr.
Churchill to enter into the European union now that he has become Prime Minister? Why the failure also of the United States
to join? Cooperation with, but not membership in, the United

States of Continental Europe is all to which either Prime Minister Churchill's Great Britain or General Eisenhower and President Truman's United States of America will agree.

In the case of Great Britain the explanation is clear. Great Britain is a member of the British Commonwealth of Nations. This is her primary commitment. This political unit extends from the British Isles through Canada, half way around the world to Australia and New Zealand and then completes the circle via Ceylon, Free India, Pakistan and South Africa. Here is a fifth international political unit that is rooted in a common living law culture. The ideology of this common culture is overwhelmingly Protestant in its religious beliefs and practices, and predominantly British empirical in its liberal economic and political philosophy while at the same time remaining bound to liberal Roman Christian universalism through British law and a common affection for Elizabeth's succession of Queens and Kings born spiritually of Hooker's ecclesiastical polity. When one notes that the culture of the United States is also in major part Protestant in its religious and cultural tradition, British empirical in its political and economic theory, and liberally Roman in its constitutionalism and its common law, its failure to become part of the continental cultural political union also becomes intelligible.

There is, however, a factor in the cultural tradition of the United States which has kept it from being a member of the British Commonwealth of Nations notwithstanding the common religious, economic, political and legal ideals and common defense problems in both Europe and the Pacific. This factor is the origin of this first American Republic in a break from Great Britain and from Europe.

This brings us to the sixth working political union of many nations in the contemporary world, namely Pan America apart from Canada. All the nations in this Pan American Union have come into being because of a political break from Europe. In this process all the younger American republics have introduced legal constitutions and political forms modeled in considerable, if not major, part on those of the first American Republic. This is why the Good Neighbor policy of Pan Americanism works.

To be sure, there is also a divisive cultural factor within this larger Pan America. It stems from the fact that the nations to the south of the United States have broken off from a Europe with Spanish or Portuguese Roman Catholic cultural traditions whereas the United States broke off from those peoples of Europe with predominantly Protestant British empirical religious and philosophical cultural norms and values. Even so, it is only necessary for any Ibero-American to return at the present time to Spain or to Portugal to realize that he is more an American in the sense in which the citizens of the United States are Americans than he is a Portuguese or a Spaniard.

The reason for this realization is that in breaking from Roman Catholic Iberian Europe, these fellow American nations to the south of the Rio Grande broke from the religious absolutism of the Roman Church's universalism as well as from political absolutism. In short they gave, as did the Protestant modern West and the United States, Cicero's rather than Zeno's interpretation to Stoic Christian universalism and legal constitutionalism. This occurred when they repudiated the political authority of the local Roman Catholic ecclesiastical hierarchy as well as that of the foreign emperor. In fact some like Mexico went even further than did the United States and took over the Church's property and secularized all education.[3] In doing this they retained the continental European codified law and added to it the true Greek scientific conception of universal law, namely its presupposition and protection of moral man as free man. Without the latter as well as the former concept in the political and the cultural traditions of the Pan American republics, their independence from Europe would not be what it is.

We find, therefore, that there are seven major cultural political units in the contemporary world: (1) The Asian solidarity of India, Ceylon, Tibet, Burma, Thailand, Indo-China, China, Korea and Japan rooted in the basic philosophical and cultural similarity of non-Aryan Hinduism, Buddhism, Taoism and Confucianism. (2) The Islamic world rooted in the religious and philosophical faith and reconstruction of a resurgent Islam. (3) The non-Islamic, non-European African world rooted in its lesser known culture. (4) The continental European Union grounded in a predominantly Roman Catholic culture with a secular leadership that has passed through the liberalizing influence of modern philosophical thought. (5) The British Commonwealth with its predominantly Protestant British empirical philosophical traditions combined with the bond of unity derived through classical education, English law, the Church of England and its Royal Family from a Stoic Christian Rome that has passed through Hooker, the Tudors and Cromwell's versions of the Protestant Reformation. (6) Pan America rooted in the liberal constitutionalism of the common law of the United States on the one hand and the modern equivalent of Cicero's liberal Stoic Roman legal universalism on the other hand as expressed in governments, and even education, under secular leadership. (7) The Soviet Communistic world comprising the U.S.S.R., her Eastern European satellites, mainland China and North Korea.

This leaves out of account the Scandinavian countries of Norway, Sweden, Denmark and Finland; Ireland, apart from North Ireland; Spain and Portugal; Switzerland; and the future of East Germany, Poland, Yugoslavia, Czechoslovakia and the other Russian satellites.

Ireland is, of course, an untamed maverick. Like Pat himself, if there is a government anywhere, she is "agin it." Sooner or later, however, the meaning of his Roman Catholic faith with its lawful universalism should catch up with even Irish intuition. When this occurs Pat may find it possible to get the regiment into step with himself.

All four of the Scandinavian nations are predominantly Protestant in their religious traditions and British empirical in their liberal parliamentarian economic and political theory. In this respect they belong naturally with the United States and the nations in the British Commonwealth. The North Atlantic Charter and NATO show that this cultural tie has come very close to producing a political bond. To be sure, Finland and Sweden, because of their proximity to Soviet Russia, find it necessary and probably wise to remain neutral in the present rather demoralized world situation when the effectiveness of police action under international law is so uncertain. The moment, however, that international law becomes strong enough, after the manner indicated in the last chapter, the movement to political unity on cultural lines will undoubtedly be so strong that it will embrace these two nations also.

The extent to which Great Britain, Canada and the United States work together politically for all practical purposes in a spontaneous way is equally evident. Any suggestion for the United States and Canada to enter into a treaty guaranteeing that one will not launch a military attack upon the other within the next twenty-five years is so unrealistic as to be absurd. There are no guns from one end to the other of the Canadian border because the people of both Canada and the United States know that the governments of each country are operating from the standpoint of common cultural, moral, political and legal principles. Such spontaneous unity of faith and outlook is worth a thousand written treaties. Already, therefore, we find the contemporary world has taken what may be termed a second step toward world unity and law by binding together two or more of the seven cultural political units indicated above.

The natural place for Portugal and Spain to take is in the continental European Union because of the common Roman Catholic religious and cultural tradition. Already, as the meeting of NATO at Lisbon indicates, Portugal belongs. To be welcomed also, Spain has merely to reform her Stoic Roman Christian constitutional absolutism into the true Greco-Roman Christian universalism which makes constitutionalism presuppose and protect free inquiry and moral freedom.

Even before this occurs, however, Spain should be accepted in the United Nations and extended all diplomatic advantages internationally. In an international world where ideological differences and living law pluralism are facts, a nation must not be outlawed internationally simply because its ideology is not one's own. Certainly if the United Nations can give international status to the absolutism of Soviet Russia with its record of militaristic imperialistic interference in the affairs of other nations, it can give international status to Franco's Spain which at least restricts its absolutism and its militarism to home consumption. The right to freedom includes, ever since Adam ate of the tree of knowledge, the right to err. Franco's Spaniards are not the first people to confuse Greco-Roman universalism with absolutism; nor are they likely to be the last. The Spanish people themselves must find and correct this error. No other people or nation can do it for them. To attempt to do so is merely to add absolutism from without to absolutism within.

NATO and Lisbon remind us that a political union between the British Commonwealth, the continental European Union, the Scandinavian countries and the United States is also already practically in being. A liberalized Roman Catholic Christian legal universalism and liberal Protestant legal universalism can naturally combine. Thereby the spiritual foundations of Western civilization are not merely being rediscovered but embodied in the political life and practice of the Western civilized world. At this point, and only when this point is reached, can Switzerland, with one part of its state Roman Catholic and another part Protestant, join the Western union.

Only the problems of East Germany and the other Eastern European Russian satellites remain. It is likely that once the foregoing unification of continental Western Europe with its predominantly Roman Catholic culture comes to fruition, its magnetic spiritual pull upon those Russian satellites which are predominantly Roman Catholic in their basic living law will be so powerful that the Russian control over them will weaken and crumble. One can go counter to the living law traditions built into people over centuries for a time, but one cannot, as Lincoln said, fool all of the people all of the time.

The same will be true of the drawing power of the cultural
political unification of those nations in the Western world
which are predominantly Protestant. At this point the Communist hold on East Germany and Czechoslovakia is likely to
break also.

But what of the century-old, unsolved problem of Germany?
The basic fact behind the successive wars since 1870 initiated by
the Germans which have shattered the peace of Europe and the
world in each generation is East Prussian junker militarism.
Hitler was merely its demagogic façade, picked from Roman
Catholic Austria and launched in Roman Catholic Bavaria, in
order to bring the Roman Catholic Rhineland and South Germany under the military and political dictatorship of the Protestant East Prussians who were always in the Reich's army and
navy and behind the Hitlerian shoutings and mass meetings.

Since the time of Bismarck the only way the East Prussian
German leadership could make their political and military control work as a source of unity between Protestant Prussia and
the Roman Catholic West and South Germany was by launching
a foreign war. This was Bismarck's frank policy. To cover up
the cultural inclination to division domestically, a common
enemy abroad had to be created. In short, peace and unity at
home were only possible, for culturally artificial modern Germany, by war abroad.

It is important to realize that East Prussian Protestantism is
different from Protestantism elsewhere in the world. East Germany is the part of the Protestant West that Roman Christian
universalism never captured or civilized. The distinguished
German historian Troeltsch has pointed this out in his answer
to his own question concerning why German propaganda with
its emphasis on German Kultur in World War I had no effect
upon the Western Allies.[4]

Protestant East Germany under junker East Prussian military
caste leadership stems not from Luther's freeing of Christian
universalism from absolutism and a corrupt ecclesiastical administration but from Luther's assurance to his folk that he had

struck a blow for the German people. It is the latter type of
Protestantism that came to expression in modern Germany
under Prussian militaristic leadership. A Protestantism which
identified Christian man with the German folk is not Christianity, either Protestant or Catholic. Instead, it is a prostitution
of both Protestantism and Catholicism which reduced each, as
became the case with Goering, von Papen and Hitler, to tribal-
ism and barbarism. It is the Christianity of Christ and the
Church corrupted and turned to at best neutral, and at worst
tribal, militaristic, imperialistic and barbaric ends. This is the
Germany whose revival cannot be permitted again in Europe.

In dividing Bismarck's Germany between East and West Germany on the very line which Rome's civilizing constitutional
universalism reached, the Cold War, helped by the healing
spirit of Western civilization, has perhaps built better than it
knew. In any event, those contemporary individuals who argue
against the rearming and incorporation of West Germany into
the continental European Union overlook the fact that the
German menace from which France and this world has suffered
continuously since 1870 is not that of a liberal secular Roman
Catholic living law cultural leadership, but that of an artifi-
cially unified Germany under an East Prussian junker dictatorship which had to create a "foreign enemy" in order to maintain
its domestic rule.

Also it is not likely that Premier Stalin has allowed many of
these East Prussian aristocratic landlords and imperialistic militarists to survive. East Prussia is now a part of Poland. He knows
very well that a unified Germany under an East German Prussian leadership would immediately demand East Prussia from
Poland and that a united Germany under East Prussian leadership is a far worse menace to Soviet Russia than a rearmed and
politically unified continental Western Europe under liberal,
secular, Roman Catholic cultural leadership within which a
rearmed West Germany is an essential and culturally natural
part.

We can be sure also that however much Premier Stalin as a

matter of tactics, in order to demoralize the West, may talk peace and offer the military and political unification of Germany, there is nothing in his revolutionary, militaristic dialectical materialistic ideology or in his account of proper Communist behavior and practice to indicate that he will ever permit a unification of Germany on anything other than Communistic terms. If he would not permit free elections supervised by the United Nations in North Korea so that little, distant, harmless Korea could be unified, is he likely to do so in East Germany so that big, relatively near Germany can be made one? Even, therefore, if free elections are promised verbally there is little likelihood that the Kremlin's General Staff will permit such elections in practice unless there is a foregone assurance that the result will be a Communist Germany immediately or in the near future.

The problem of Germany resolves itself, therefore, into this: Will continental Western Europe turn back the clock behind Luther's Protestant Reformation and its modern political nationalism to achieve unity on the basis of liberal, secular, Roman constitutionalism and will the people and government of West Germany become an essential and lasting part of this union?

Notwithstanding the understandable desire of the Protestants and Socialists in West Germany for German unity first, so that they may achieve a Bismarckian kind of majority control of German politics and represent something nearer the majority cultural factor in the situation, it is unlikely that their knowledge of what Communism means will cause them in the end to succumb to this superficially tempting Moscow lure. It is notable that even Pastor Niemoeller declined the second invitation to visit Moscow. A West German Protestant informs us concerning what Communism means as described by his East German fellow Protestants who come into the Western Zone:

They come out of a world that is ruled by the idea of communism. An outsider cannot imagine the totalitarian aspects of this regime. Not only are economics and politics dictated, but no choice is al-

lowed in those things usually falling to individual discretion. One
must look at pictures of Marx, Engels, Lenin, and Stalin for they
are everywhere. . . . No avenue of communication is unexploited
in selling the wares of dialectical materialism. Indeed, so compre-
hensive is communism's content and so intense its propaganda that
it is quite proper to call the movement a religion. . . . Modern
communism is a religion—but a religion without God.

Does this totalitarian system leave room for the Church? The
answer is partly yes and mostly no. Religion is recognized as a
"personal affair of the individual" and the Church is allowed to
exist privately for individuals interested in religion. The word of
God may be proclaimed in a church, but never publicly. . . . German public schools have traditionally included Christian education
in their curriculum. Not only has this instruction been removed
from the course of study, but children now read in their textbooks
that Jesus Christ never existed. In high schools and universities, six
hours a week are spent on Gegenwartskunde, i.e., instruction in the
teachings of dialectical materialism, the new religion. Christian
publishing houses still in existence suffer from paper shortages
whereas political propaganda material swamps the land. Printing
presses, of course, are controlled by the state. A Bible society recently published a collection of apostolic passages, but only after the
censor had . . . eliminated . . . I Peter 5:8, "Be sober, be vigilant;
because your adversary the devil, as a roaring lion, walketh about,
seeking whom he may devour . . ." and Ephesians 5:16: "redeem-
ing the time, because the days are evil." [5]

Certainly neither France, Great Britain, the United States,
Italy, Holland, Belgium or Chancellor Adenauer's government
will agree to a United Germany on such terms.

The probabilities, therefore, are that the East German Protestants will have to pay for the past sin of their support of their
East Prussian leaders and that West Germany with its predominantly Roman Catholic culture will be built into the
Continental European Union. This is a far more natural cultural tie than their former dictatorial domination by the imperialistic and militaristic, predominantly Protestant East Prus-
sianism. It is this common cultural bond between liberal Roman
Catholic West Germany and liberal Roman Catholic continental Europe to its West which makes it likely that if the former

is built into the latter in 1952 to form a United States of Continental Europe, the result will be lasting.

Should this occur, the predominantly Protestant East Germans, will have to wait the crumbling of Russia's puppet show of European satellites to gain their freedom. Then they can proceed in one of two ways. Either they can form an Eastern province based on the moral union of Kant's categorical imperative with secular, liberal, Roman constitutionalism and thereby spiritually bind themselves alongside present West Germany into the continental European Union, or they can take their place as a liberal Protestant nation beside the neighboring Scandinavian countries of similar ideology in the liberal Protestant cultural political union which by then may well embrace not merely the Scandinavian peoples but also those of the United States and the British Commonwealth. In either event, the German problem which has destroyed the peace of the world in each generation during the past one hundred years will have been solved.

Such are the successive steps along the second of the two paths from yesterday's excessive number of helpless nations to tomorrow's single world law and government. The steps result in the large number of national political units being gathered up into an increasingly smaller and smaller number of cultural political units.

The advantages of this are manifold. The cultural political unit can protect itself in a way that the small national political unit cannot do. The industry of the Ruhr and the coal and iron of Alsace and Lorraine and the Saar can form a single economic system. Men who are spiritually one can be economically and politically one, thereby healing old military wounds resulting from national animosities that were artificial. Liberal modern man who had cut himself off so much from his classical Christian past that he tended to become superficial can recover the basic spiritual roots of his own civilization and being. Thus again the wounds of the West become healed.

For the United Nations and world law this movement to a

small number of cultural political units is equally important. One of the weaknesses of the League of Nations and the United Nations, noted by many observers, was and is that the majority of the members carry no responsibility for what they say. Being so small, they know that when they talk they will never have to implement what they say if it is finally voted. Politics is like poker. If nothing is at stake, the participants tend to become careless and irresponsible. Moreover, it is a law of life that power always goes to those who assume responsibility for what is done. This means that in practice the League of Nations and the United Nations became the talking and voting place of the majority of the little nations and the responsibility of the small number of big nations who have to execute what is voted.

This state of affairs is bad in two ways. First, the smaller nations resent the injustice of a situation in which the few big nations in fact must decide what is done since they for the most part will have to do it. Second, the few big powers, as in Korea, are with equal injustice forced to take almost the whole of the responsibility for what should be everybody's responsibility. The transition from the many little and big nations of the United Nations to a small number of cultural political units more nearly equal in size has the great advantage of making talking and voting in the world community more commensurate with the capacity and responsibility for executing what is said and voted.

THE CULTURAL BASIS OF
FOREIGN POLICY

The most fashionable theory of foreign policy has been power politics. The practical politician pressed by day to day decisions often finds this theory to be congenial, since it permits him to cover up his mistakes by appeal to transitory nationalistic passions and prejudices while also leaving him with isolationistic independence of action. Its simple-mindedness gives it a wide appeal also among "scholars" who are anxious to hurriedly make a subject out of international relations without the knowledge of the living laws of peoples and the philosophical theories embodied in them which are necessary for an understanding of the nations, their motives and their international policies. To all this must be added the self-awarded sense of realism which the word power suggests to such minds.

Simple-mindedness is not necessarily an evil. A deep-going solution of any problem is at bottom simple. A truly scientific theory of any subject matter contains very few basic assumptions. The principle of parsimony must be satisfied. But both the simple-mindedness and realism of power politics are spurious.

The word power by itself tells one very little. When related to a specific nation it always has to be supplemented. Also there is nothing in the theory of power politics to specify in a given instance what the supplementation must be. Thus it is at once both no theory at all and an unexpressed, very complicated, eclectic theory.

Its realism is equally spurious. As Mr. George F. Kennan found,[1] to face Soviet Russia watching only its power is to be helpless with respect to the estimation of what the Kremlin is most likely to do. And to be thus helpless is to be unable to frame a foreign policy with respect to Russia that is either informed or realistic. Only when Mr. Kennan turned from his power politics theory of international relations to the study of the ideology of Soviet Russia did his theory and practice with respect to the U.S.S.R. become realistic. Thus it is that to watch and to know ideals is at once both the highest idealism and the most down to earth realism. Thus it is also that Mr. Kennan's practice gave the lie to his theory.[2]

Power politics is nonetheless inadequate when it appears under the disguise of historical erudition. Recently one creator of such a disguise has asked for "no annihilation without representation." Representation for Mr. Arnold Toynbee's Great Britain or for any other nation is unlikely to be achieved, however, by an international or intercultural game of "challenge and response." In an atomic age this means suicide for all. An historical induction which extrapolates from the challenges and responses that have produced yesterday's sequence of wars can hardly be made the ethical basis for today's and tomorrow's conduct.

But Arnold Toynbee and in a lesser way the statesman, quickly turned scholar, Mr. Kennan, are not the only ones who have mistaken the proper use to which history can be put. Nor are they the only ones who have disguised an ethics of power politics with the cultural erudition of a student of history. Recent positivistic students of law have done so also,[3] as have all too many professors of international relations who have confused the metaphor "power" with a scientific concept and Geopolitik with social and political science, thereby reaching the conclusion that the wars that were yesterday must go on tomorrow.

If there ever was a weasel word, power, when used other than in the physicist's and engineer's sense, is that word. It is not a scientific concept since, as the late John Dewey has noted, such "Mere general ideas can be argued for or against without the necessity of recourse to observation." [4] This does not mean that capacity to produce steel and the fire power of a nation's military weapons are not important in international relations. But power in these senses is power in the unambiguous non-metaphorical meaning of the physicist and the engineer. To act, however, as if power in this unambiguous sense is the only factor or the decisive factor internationally is not to be realistic, but to live in fairyland as Pearl Harbor showed. It is as if a scientist confronted with a subject matter which contains two or more independent variables acts as if there were only one.

Nor is power in this physicist's and engineer's meaning of the word even an independent variable. For what makes it significant in international relations is not that it exists, but what is done with it. Clearly this depends upon the culture and the spiritual, economic and political norms of the people in whose society it exists. In the hands of Premier Stalin and the Communists it means one thing, as the Premier's lectures on Communist theory, practice, strategy and tactics have already made clear to us. The same amount of military weapons and capacity to produce steel in the hands of Gandhiji would mean quite a different thing. Guided by the spiritual values of the people of the United States it means still a third thing. In the hands of Mr. Toynbee, with his ethics of challenge and response, it would mean a fourth probably not very pleasant experience. Its meaning in the hands of East Prussian militarists is well known. In a world governed by effective law, it could be one of the greatest instruments for the peace and the economic well-being of mankind this world has ever experienced.

Thus power becomes significant in international relations not in itself as a first cause or independent variable, but because of what is done with it, and this depends upon the ideals and ethical, legal and spiritual norms and values of a people. For the United States or any other nation to act, therefore, on the basis of power politics is not merely to betray its own spiritual values but also to be devoid of the most elementary sense of realism and scientific objectivity.

This does not mean that nations and peoples have never been guided by this unrealistic and self-defeating theory of foreign policy. Our study of the mentalities and norms of the major cultures and nations of the world has revealed its presence in many places. We came upon it in Chiang Monlin's description of what happened in the Confucian China of his childhood when Western influences produced effects at the middle level of officialdom which the traditional Confucian ethics of the Emperor in Peking and the council of joint family elders in the villages could not control. Since there were no Confucian norms and social habits to regulate the novel type of middle officialdom made necessary by the Western influences, the power politics of opportunistic, ethically unprincipled war lords appeared.

The foreign policy of the Maharaja rulers of Aryan Hindu India as described in the Laws of Manu is another example. These Aryan conquerors were the rulers. They came from outside India and, therefore, represented a successful imperialism. Sensitivity to the norms and the culture of the conquered people is not the imperialist's normal attitude. Instead, a provincial sense of the superiority of his own norms and people, as representing the sole carriers of "true" culture, predominates. The only rulers permitted must be descendants of the Aryan Manu. Thus the international ethics of the Aryan rulers was one that rested on provincial and even on tribal norms. When such culturally provincial and tribal values define one's norms, power politics follows automatically as a theory of foreign policy.

This is why Mr. Toynbee's making of his own Christian civilization an exception to his inductive rule that all civilizations are born to die is hardly political wisdom in the contemporary world. It amounts to cultural imperialism and leads inevitably, as it did with the Aryan Hindu Maharajas, the Japanese followers of Shinto and the East Prussian militarists, to a foreign policy of power politics. Power politics is nonetheless imperialistic and internationally unethical because the religion and ethics behind it is one's own.

British policy during the past century with respect to the nations on the Continent was another attempt to make power balancing the way to peace. A war each generation in an atomic age will hardly do. This British belief in power derives from the materialism of Hobbes and from Machiavelli by way of Harrington.

The former source reminds us that a materialistic philosophy and a power politics ethics of force tend to go together. Premier Stalin's lectures on the foundations of Leninism do not appear to provide an exception to this rule. Hobbes did, however, see that no peace is possible by the balancing of powers; instead there must be one superior power having absolute sovereignty with respect to the minor powers. Thus even a consistent power politics requires a world law backed with effective police power.

Machiavelli's power politics is an induction from the Italian city-states. When the peace and order under universal law which was the Roman Empire crumbled, then the provincial ethics of the villages with their proper patriarchal families and of their elder brothers, the Italian city-states, took over. Between those states there was, therefore, no law and there were consequently no ethical or legal norms. Where interconnecting norms and law are not present, nothing remains but for power politics to rule.

This is why power politics and wars became the normal thing with the development of Western nationalism. We see again why, if disputes between nations in an atomic age are to be settled without recourse to power politics and war, the nations must be brought under the rule of a single world law and the living law norms capable of calling forth the power from the world community necessary to make that law effective must be found.

The foregoing analysis of some instances of power politics in the world's history shows, therefore, that instead of being a realistically grounded theory of the relations between cultures and nations, it is the sign of the absence of one. Or to put the matter positively, when one's theory of normative conduct embraces only the family with the proper tribal ancestors, the tribe, the city-state, the nation, or the religion of one's own culture, there are no norms for conduct beyond these partial and provincial units.

At any time, and particularly in the contemporary world, what any nation needs for the protection and preservation of its own national, religious and other spiritual values is the confidence of other people in that nation and their willingness to protect its existence and values. If, therefore, in relating oneself to other peoples and nations, one tells them in one's avowed theory of international relations and in one's practice, that might makes right, confidence is hardly won. No people want to lay down their lives for someone else's power.

More than this, one actually drives away cultures and peoples who want to be one's friends and who believe in one's national and cultural ideals as well as in their own. Consider how power politics looks and sounds from the other nation's and people's standpoint. India and Islam then find themselves described as the weak underbelly of Soviet Russia. They find themselves talked about and treated as nothing but pawns in a power politics game. Is it any wonder, under such circumstances, that they go out of their way to be neutral. If there is one sure way for the foreign policy of the United States, or of any other nation, to fail in the contemporary world, this would seem to be it.

A foreign policy of nothing but economic and dollar aid has a similar effect. It strikes nation after nation as an insult to their moral integrity. West Germans, Mexicans and South Americans, Muslims and Asians resent it because it suggests to them that their morals can be bought. Their moral integrity and spiritual pride are insulted.

Again it must be said, nations as well as men do not live by bread alone. True nations and true men live by their spiritual values and their ideals. They will go to jail, starve or die before they will betray these ideals. Nor is the reason difficult to find. Without common norms there is no nation.

The only foreign policy, therefore, which will work is one that wins men and nations by the ideals and spiritual values for which it stands. This does not mean that all men and all nations have or must have the same spiritual values and ideals before they can build an international law and morality and a foreign policy based on ideals. All that is necessary is that there be mutual respect for, and protection under law of, the diverse ideologies and values of the different national and cultural political units of the world when they are restricted to those who want them and not imposed upon other people. This is provided if the aforementioned principle of living law pluralism is made the basis for world law.

The eclectic theory of foreign policy, suggested by Secretary of State Acheson in his article in the Magazine Section of *The New York Times*,[5] has all of the foregoing weaknesses of the power politics theory. At first sight this eclectic theory appears to be most objective, open-minded and reasonable. It asserts that not merely power and economic aid and an information service with its Voice of America and psychological warfare, but also ideologies and ideals should determine the policy of the United States and of other nations.

Unfortunately, however, like any eclecticism, this theory of foreign policy is no theory at all. One does not have a theory of any subject until one has the principle which relates the many factors in its subject matter to one another. It is of the essence of eclecticism that this relation is never specified. Conversely, the moment the relation of the different variables in the subject matter is specified, then it is not the many variables which become the key to foreign policy, but their relationship. Forthwith eclecticism evaporates.

Moreover, this eclectic theory mistakes what an ideology is. Never is it one factor in society. Instead it is the name for the relationship of all the factors. For example, the Aryan Hindu ideology is the theory of the entire organization of Aryan Hindu society from the patriarchal joint families and society of village elders at the bottom to the Maharajas at the top including its power politics in foreign affairs. The Marxist Communist ideology is similarly a theory of the relationship between political, economic, religious and cultural factors within the nation and of the policy governing the relation of such a nation to other nations and ideologies outside the Soviet Union. Ideology is but the name for the all-embracing relation between every factor in human, national and international experience.

These theoretical misunderstandings and weaknesses defeat eclecticism in practice. Its first practical weakness is that one's foreign friends never know which of the four- or five-odd variables is to be used in a given crisis or situation. At one moment their confidence is gained when one makes use of the ideological component and wins their respect for and collaboration in what one is doing. Then they cooperate gladly on ideological and moral grounds and on grounds of international public morality. But at the next instant one shakes an atomic bomb or one's power in the world's face. Instantly all their confidence collapses and Prime Minister Attlee, backed by the full support of the opposition leader, Mr. Winston Churchill, who had been fighting him ruthlessly, is forced to drop everything and rush across the Atlantic to Washington. The next moment it is psychological warfare with some Senator insisting on a hard-hitting Voice of America to sell the American way of life. Then one blasts a loudspeaker at not merely the Russians but also the Asians, the Muslims, the French and the British who want to be our friends. This makes them feel that they are being treated as guinea pigs by a high pressure promoter and advertiser. Again of a sudden, General MacArthur and his political supporters, taking the power politics factor seriously, announce the Western defensive border of the United States to be the line from Vladivostok to Singapore. Nor is this enough. There should be bombing beyond the Yalu together with the launching by Chiang Kai-shek of an invasion of the China mainland which will have as its aim the national state of mind in which four hundred million Chinese embrace the ideology we would like them to have. Forthwith again one's Asian and European friends become jittery.

Since in this eclecticism there is no principle or rule to tell when the power politics or any other factor will or will not be used, one's Asian and European friends, with considerable justification, reach the conclusion that they simply cannot be sure what cooperating with the United States means. Then all the advantages of the ideological position in the defense of free nations under law run the risk of being squandered and the whole long, painstaking task of building up again the faith and confidence of other peoples in the United States and in that for which it stands, has to be begun all over again by our diplomats. Also the spiritual values and the international law and morality in which the majority of the people in the United States and throughout the world believe are kept from being most effective. If the United States has carried the rest of the world with her, as in a sense she has, it is because in spite of the eclecticism, the rest of the world believes that on the whole and in the long run, it is the ideals of this people and their statesmen that will determine what the United States does.

The time has come, therefore, for the people of this country and their leaders to think at least as well of themselves as the majority of leaders and people of the rest of the world do. There is but one way to do this. It is to make the ideals for society and the world community for which the majority of people of the United States stand the sole factor determining her foreign policy and to make everything else secondary to this. Only if this is done will the shoring up of the world with the police power necessary to protect free nations under law, the attempts to alleviate the economic ills of mankind by Marshall Plan and Truman Point Four aid, and the cultural information program or the Voice of America be effective. Only if this be her foreign policy can the young men who are now policing the defense of freedom under law have the assurance that they are not expending their time and their lives in vain.

At a conference of representatives from all the men's and women's colleges of the Eastern United States held under the auspices of the Yale Political Union in the fall of 1951, the following resolution was moved and passed with an overwhelmingly majority:

Resolved, that this House urges the Government of the United States to base its foreign policy upon the ideological principle that each people in the world must be free to build their institutions in the light of their own cultural traditions, drawing upon outside factors only as they deem wise, and that the Government of the United States make its equally necessary military program for policing any power violating this principle, its economic program of Marshall Plan and Point Four Aid and its Information Program concerning the Hebrew-Christian and American way of life secondary to and merely instrumentations of this basic ideological principle.[6]

To this resolution before it was passed there was added an amendment which specified that this foreign policy of the United States should be administered through and in conjunction with the United Nations.

It is to be noted that the foregoing resolution bases the foreign policy of the United States, or of any other nation, upon the fact of the living law pluralism of the contemporary world. The justification for taking this fact concerning what is as the basis for what ought to be was specified in Chapter 1 when we examined the method of the science of international relations. There it was noted, following Ehrlich, that positive legal rules for social policy, whether domestic or foreign, are never effective unless they correspond to the inner order or living law of the societies to which they refer. Since our study of the diverse inner orders of the many nations and cultures of the world have revealed these inner orders to embody different and in certain instances logically incompatible philosophies, it follows that not merely an effective international law but also an effective foreign policy for any nation must be grounded in the living law fact of living law pluralism.

This first principle of effective foreign policy has the merit of being idealistic, since it proceeds from the assumption that no nation is understood unless its ideals are grasped from within. It is also truly realistic since only by knowing the ideology and values of a given nation is one able to know realistically what that nation is and what it is most likely in any given set of circumstances to do.

More than this, one can only truly understand the power of a given people when one comprehends their ideals and values from within. Not only, as we noted in Chapter I, does a given amount of physical power mean one thing in a nation headed by a Gandhi and a different thing in a nation headed by a Hitler or a Stalin, but also the nature of the ideology of a given people or nation gives the only trustworthy clue to the amount of power which that nation is likely to accrue to itself. In the last analysis the only effective power, the only power that can draw physical power to itself, is moral power, and this has its basis in the normative ideals and philosophy of a people which give their society the inner order it enjoys.

It would be a mistake, however, to suppose that the sole advantage of a foreign policy based on the principle of living law pluralism is the amount of physical power which it gives to the nation that pursues it. The greater merit of such a foreign policy was indicated in the chapter on the defense of the free world. In the last analysis the greatest power any single nation in the world can achieve is the confidence, cooperation and support of other nations. Power politics at best makes this potential support neutral, at the worst it drives it away. A foreign policy based on one's own ideology alone has a similar effect upon all nations not holding this particular ideology. Only a foreign policy which, while respecting the ideology of one's own country, similarly respects and supports that of other countries when restricted to their own area, can call forth the confidence, cooperation and support of the overwhelming majority of other nations of the world. A symphony of diverse cultures, the richer because of the diversity, rather than the dull monotony of all the nations fiddling away frantically on one string, is the vision of an idealistically informed and realistically wise foreign policy.

Even so this is not the whole of the story. Already we have noted the movement from the absurd plurality of national political units to the very small number of cultural political units. A wise foreign policy will participate in and support this movement. Again the justification is that only thus is positive action made effective by being kept continuously in accord with the underlying living law of the world. To act as if one's own nation is completely different from any other nation when in fact the basic living law, spiritual beliefs and values of the two nations are one is to act both unrealistically and falsely. There is no true sovereignty except as basic beliefs and principles define it. When, therefore, the principles between nations become one, to that extent the sovereignty must be one also.

Nevertheless the present living movements from nationalism to culturalism still leave one with differences as well as with identities. These differences must be respected. Hence even with the smaller living law pluralism of the seven major cultural political units there must be portions of sovereignty restricted to the component nations and to their component provinces and states. Again a science of international relations which finds the basis for its identities and differences in an objective study of the social elements and compounds themselves can tell specifically where the line between the items assigned to the federal principle of unity and those items reserved to the states' rights principle of plurality is to be drawn. By always taking the living law as the basis for the specification of the properties of the political elements and their relations, domestic and foreign policy is made to stand on firm ground at every step in its formulation after the manner in which a science of chemistry which roots itself in the properties of the chemical elements and their relations moves forward step by step reasonably sure of every move.

What this means, however, is that the major department in the Department of State or the Foreign Office of any government must be not its liaison connection with the Department of Defense, its Information Service or its Program of Economic Aid, but its Division of Cultural Relations. The basis for any foreign policy decision must be an objective understanding of the indigenous culture and philosophy of each and every one of the nations involved in the decision, including one's own, together with a clear knowledge of the relations between these different cultural ideologies. A nation which runs its foreign affairs on any other basis will inevitably be a stupid nation making stupid decisions.

An objectively and scientifically grounded foreign policy must do a third thing. Not only must it root itself in the principle of living law pluralism and in the precise distinction between international federal unity and states' rights plurality which the living movements from nationalism to world law and to culturalism specify, but also it must participate in the movement now starting with the few cultural political units and proceeding toward a single common world ideology.

This common, single world ideology is not yet; it is merely beginning to be in the making. This is why for the present and the immediate future both international law and the foreign policy of any nation must be grounded in the living law fact of living law pluralism.

Nevertheless, each nation and its foreign policy must be participating in and preparing for the increasing diminution of this pluralism. For the unification of the few cultural political units is also a living law fact of the contemporary world. There is to be sure the movement from nationalism to culturalism as illustrated in the resurgence of Islam, the solidarity of Asia, the unification of continental Europe, the British Commonwealth of Nations, Pan America, Africa and the Anglo-American predominantly Protestant liberal world. But each one of these cultural political units is both expressing a traditional culture and reforming it. And in the re-formation, the different cultures of the world are becoming more and more similar. Witness Free India with its Constitution and Five Year Plan and the United States of America.

That this reform of every national and cultural and political unit will go on taking the pluralism of nations and cultures nearer and nearer to a single ideologically homogeneous world community is certain. The certainty arises from the fact that mankind generally has been captured by the vision of the lifting of the economic well-being of men everywhere. The ways of doing this are few in number; in fact an examination of the living laws of the contemporary world shows that at most there are but two and most probably there is but one which is effective in deeds as well as in promises.

The two ways are those of the U.S.S.R. and the U.S.A. The ideology of the former and its practical consequences have already been indicated. To that of the latter we must now turn.

FROM PHILADELPHIA
TO COSMOPOLIS

The United States is a part of the world. It, too, has a culture rooted in empirically grounded philosophical principles and spiritual values which must be understood if statesmanship either at home or abroad is to be informed and wise.

Members of older cultures frequently suppose that no culture is easier to classify and understand than that of the United States. Some, when they are frank, say that the United States has no culture. Many suppose that it can be designated with a mere flip of the hand as a right-wing reactionary Capitalism motivated by an obsession with gadgets and Communists and a lack of sensitivity to spiritual values. The fact that such an overwhelming majority of its citizens already possess the comparatively high satisfaction of their economic needs, which the remainder of the peoples of the world want, is often taken by others as but additional evidence of an overconcern with the mechanics of life and a blindness to its spiritual roots and goals.

These misconceptions arise because those in the older cultures of the world look at the United States through the only conceptual spectacles they possess—namely, those of their own social and cultural forms. These old cultural forms permit anything in the United States which is seen from their standpoint to be assigned only to those convenient pigeonholes which such conceptual spectacles permit. Hence, since the American people are neither Socialists nor Communists nor Muslims nor Hindus nor British Liberals nor Tories, nothing remains for them but to be right-wing Capitalistic reactionaries mad about gadgets and Communists and driven by the obsession to make everyone else in the world mad about them also.

The task, therefore, is to reveal to other people their spectacles so that they can take them off and see the culture of the United States and the spirit of its people for what it is in its own unique terms. The outward facts of any culture are the fruition of its spiritual roots. To understand the fruit without knowing the roots from within is impossible.

In removing the old spectacles, a false impression is likely to be created temporarily. Because the spiritual roots of the culture of the United States are what they are, certain ideologies are not prized as much in this country as they are in other countries of the world. As Dewey has noted of his fellow countrymen, "We are not in the habit of taking social and political philosophies very seriously." [1] This does not mean that these other ideologies are not respected. It means merely that the experience of the people of the United States is such that they have come upon spiritual factors in nature and man which inspire the conclusion that social philosophies taken elsewhere as absolute norms for the guidance of conduct are merely instrumental and secondary to spiritual norms and values of a different kind. As Dewey added, "We take them empirically and 'pragmatically.' " [2]

An example will make this clear. It can be exhibited best in the form of a question, What of Socialism and Socialist leadership as a basis for cultural unity and political leadership in the contemporary world?

The answer was given some years ago by the French Socialist leader Paul Ramadier when he failed after several attempts to form a Government and was forced to turn back his mandate to the President of France. Then M. Ramadier said, "There is no use for a Socialist to attempt to form a Government until the Socialists can agree upon a doctrine." The correctness of this judgment is confirmed by the similar failure of every French Socialist leader since then.

But why is agreement upon a doctrine so necessary? The theoretical reason is that there is no cultural, economic or political system except as men agree upon common norms for meeting their common problems and for ordering their cultural and social life. The practical reason is that when a Government made up of leaders and followers without a common doctrine face a crisis, such as the saving of the franc, they spread themselves out over the entire spectrum of political and economic possibilities. Then no agreement can be reached upon what to do. Consequently, that Government falls. The paradoxical situation, therefore, occurs in which the Socialists in France continuously receive the largest number of votes, yet cannot in practice run a Government. Being devoid of a common doctrine, they are in fact a discordant collection of microscopic minority parties.

The same impotence tends also to undermine their foreign policy. Possessing no common doctrine on foreign policy, a Socialist Government or Party sooner or later breaks into factions. With the coming into prominence of Mr. Aneurin Bevan, this fatal weakness of Socialist leadership in foreign affairs has finally caught up with British Socialism.

The precise steps in which it occurs are easy to trace. Being weak with respect to their economic and political doctrine and ideologies generally, only a few read their Marx, Lenin and Stalin with sufficient care, paying attention to the foreign policy specifications for practice, strategy and tactics, as well as the doctrine concerning the way to improve domestic economic conditions. Hence when Premier Stalin's French and British vanguard tell Mr. Bevan and other Socialists that they are all fellow Socialists and that the "capitalistic, fascist, imperialistic" United States is the real devil in the world, it seems very plausible to enough of the Socialists to prevent a Socialist Party or Government from agreeing on a foreign policy. In the contemporary world, this is fatal.

The same phenomenon occurs today in Australia in the former President of the United Nations, Mr. Herbert V. Evatt. It shows also among India's Socialists. The two top leaders of India's Socialist Party are among the most doctrinally specific and informed men on both domestic and foreign policy in the world today. There is far less wishful thinking about the nature of Soviet Russia and President Mao's China in their case than in the case of Prime Minister Nehru. They know every ideology in the West thoroughly. Their knowledge includes Marxist Communism. Hence, they realize its utter incompatibility with the parliamentary Socialism for which they stand. In addition they understand the spiritual roots of both Hindu and Muslim Indian culture. In fact their Socialism is better described as pluralistic Indian culturalism focusing on democratic political and economic initiative at the village level, than as faith in the nationalization and direction of everything from the federal level which characterizes so many Western Socialists. Unfortunately, however, many other Indian Socialists lack this exact knowledge of Marxist theory and practice and do not possess Jaiprakash Narayan and Asoka Mehta's other doctrinal convictions. Consequently many of them are outside the Socialist Party either in, or collaborating with, the Communist Party. The result is that India's Socialist Party failed to get the support in the recent Indian elections which it merits.

The impotence of Socialists on foreign policy shows in another way. Even when temporarily they achieve unity on domestic policy, their emphasis on nationalization tends to make domestic policy their main concern. The inclination then is to refuse to vote the funds necessary for an adequate defense of either themselves or their fellow countrymen.

This we see now in Mr. Bevan.[3] This also was the exact position in which the Italian and French Socialists found themselves immediately following the Communist coup in Prague. Men who wanted to vote the Socialist, rather than the Communist, ticket in the impending Italian and French elections found themselves afraid to do so, in the face of Communist observers at the polls, because of the likelihood that even if they won they would suffer the same liquidation at Communist hands as did their Czech brethren.

It remained consequently for the leadership of the non-Socialist United States to save and protect Socialism in Italy and France. This was done by a Republican majority in Congress led by the Democratic President Harry Truman voting the funds for a universal military draft a few hours after Masaryk's fatal "fall" from the window of the Foreign Office in Prague. This made it clear to all Europeans on both sides of the Iron Curtain that if those Socialists and others who do not want to be Communists vote as they prefer, they and the Governments in Italy and France which they elect will not be liquidated after the pattern of Rumania, Hungary and Czechoslovakia.

Incidentally in doing this, President Truman and the Republican Congress backed by the people of the United States saved the peace of the world. Certainly no one can doubt that if the pattern established up to and including Prague had spread through the rest of Europe, World War III would already be a matter of history. They and their countrymen can be as proud of the foreign policy of the United States since the Prague coup as they can be of its aid through the United Nations in preventing a successful aggression in Korea. To have been the major instrument in the saving of the peace of the world twice within a few years in an atomic age is no mean achievement for the foreign policy of any government. All statesmen can and do talk peace. Very few have succeeded twice in preventing a world war.

If there be any historians on this planet two centuries hence, they will not overlook the incisive, courageous man from Missouri and his Republican and Democratic supporters who, when almost everyone else had lost his nerve or was talking peace but doing nothing about it, dared to believe that free men acting under law can and will police free governments, and who in implementing this belief always knew what the score was. When President Truman, Secretary of State Acheson and the Congressmen in Washington drop their power politics and their eclecticism and act on principle, they are superb. They also win the cooperation of the majority of nations in the rest of the world.

This is part of the spirit of the people of the United States and of their foreign policy as seen at its best from within. Whatever may be their spiritual weaknesses, their spirit is not one that falls into helpless fragments in a domestic or international crisis.

Other people are quite right, therefore, when looking through their conceptual spectacles they see that the spirit of the people of the United States is not that of Socialism. They are quite wrong, however, when their conceptual spectacles leave them no other cubbyhole in which to put the American spirit than that of Tory imperialism or reactionary imperialistic right-wing Capitalism obsessed with gadgets and Communists.

The American people have no more objection to Communism, providing it restricts itself to those who want it, than they have to Socialism or to Conservatism or to Capitalism. The fact that their culture is not correctly described by any of these isms does not mean that they object when any other people believe in any of them. The United States has given its Marshall Plan aid to foreign governments irrespective of their social ideology. There have been recent rumors that it worked more smoothly with Mr. Attlee's Socialist Labour Government than has been the case with Mr. Churchill's recent Conservative one. Even if true, the difference, however, is a trivial one. The attitude toward a Communism which avoids aggression is no different. When the Marshall aid program was launched, it was taken for granted that it would go to the Communist satellites of Soviet Russia exactly as it goes to Communist Yugoslavia now. This was as true for the Republicans voting for Marshall Plan aid as it was for the Democrats. In fact the satellite Communist governments voted to accept this Marshall Plan aid and actually appointed their official representatives to attend the first meeting in Paris where the apportionment of the aid between different nations was to be decided.

It was not the American people or their leaders but the Soviet Russian Government which prevented this aid from going to Communist and non-Communist nations alike. When, therefore, Mr. Vishinsky tearfully laments the fact that there is not the cooperation between the United States and his country that existed during the war, he should also point out that the reason is because he and his General Staff told their Russian satellites and the United States that they do not want this cooperation. Otherwise the satellites would have been enjoying Marshall Plan aid for the past several years and the Cold War would have been quite unnecessary.

From this Russian rejection of cooperation, the people of the United States draw one inescapable conclusion. The fact that Communist nations, other than Soviet Russia, accepted Marshall Plan aid and appointed official representatives to receive it and then were prevented by Soviet Russia from doing so is objective proof of the fact that they are not independent Socialist Republics but are instead the helpless pawns of a Moscow directed and Stalinist dictated imperialism. "Satellites" is an understatement of their status.

It is the spirit of the people of the United States that if another people want to build their institutions on a particular ideology in their own independent way, that is their business and not the business of any other people. If the American people have recently become not quite as ready to recognize recent Communist nations, such as President Mao's China, it is because the foregoing objective evidence, that the European Communist nations are not free, causes one to wonder whether mainland China is free either.

Even so, the American people would have undoubtedly taken Communist China's position as a fact just as they have taken the position of the European Communist satellites as a fact, and just as Sir Gladwyn Jebb, after that sober reflection which we have come to associate with the British Foreign Office, has finally decided that the existence of the moon is a fact, had not China's Communists supported the North Korean Communists in their flouting of the law and morality of the world community and thereby demonstrated their present unfitness for membership in that community. When they or any other Communist people who apply for membership in the world community demonstrate their willingness and capacity to respect its rules, the people of the United States will welcome them as members just as they will welcome a people with any other ideology.

But to what ideological category are other people to assign the culture of the United States if it cannot be assigned to that of Socialism, Tory imperialism or reactionary imperialistic right wing Capitalism?

One must go to Philadelphia to answer this question. For at Philadelphia the spiritual values at the basis of the culture of the United States were first revealed. On May 10, 1775, following upon difficulties with the British, the Second Continental Congress of the American colonies met in this city set upon revolution. But even in revolution they felt it necessary to appeal to law and its spiritual norms. They found this law and its norms not in the behavior of George III but in the spiritual natural rights of all men from which law which is effective derives. They appointed, therefore, a committee of five to draw up the legal and spiritual principles under which they proposed to declare their independence from Great Britain.

This was a revolution, therefore, quite different from those of the present moment which are carried on underground and surreptitiously in defiance of a reasoned appeal to legal rules and objective principles. This first American revolution was launched in the open, aboveboard, in the name of law and of universally valid spiritual principles.

The committee of five who articulated these principles were Thomas Jefferson, John Adams, Benjamin Franklin, Roger Sherman and Robert R. Livingston. The final Declaration of Independence was practically in its entirety the work of Jefferson. The key to the spiritual values of the people of the United States ever since then appears in its first sentence. The basis for any law or government is not in any social theory of the relations of men to one another in society, but in the equal status of all men before "the Laws of Nature and of Nature's God." [4] In other words, according to the spirit of the people of the United States it is not the relation of men to one another in society but their relation to nature and to nature's universal laws before which all men are equal that is the criterion of the just, the good and the divine.

According to this concept of the spiritual, nature with its scientifically known laws, rather than any of the social theories of traditional or contemporary society, is man's spiritual tutor. This is why its spirit and its cultural fruits are always misunderstood by foreigners who attempt to assign it, because of their culturally conditioned spectacles, to any one of the conventional social philosophies.

The key to the people of the United States is that unlike their contemporaries born in the older cultures of the world, they were confronted in the Western hemisphere with virgin nature. Thus nature made by God, rather than the social isms at which traditional cultures have arrived, became their guide and mentor. As Longfellow said, instead of being taught merely by the books of men, they

> . . . read what is still unread
> In the manuscripts of God.[5]

It is primarily from nature and only secondarily from culture that the spirit of the people of the United States drinks its living waters. In his Phi Beta Kappa address, delivered at Harvard in 1837, Emerson said, "The first in time and the first in importance in the influences upon the mind is that of nature." [6] With Jefferson this was equally conscious and true. His father, Peter Jefferson, lacked a formal education but was a surveyor, landowner and a member of the Virginia House of Burgesses. In both agriculture and surveying he embodied this pristine relation to a virgin nature. The relation is not that, however, of Chiang Monlin's Confucian "naive observation." Surveying as practiced by Peter Jefferson involved the use of geometrical and optical laws and principles. Thus even with him it is man related to nature by means of the universal laws of nature as determined by sophisticated, rationally or theoretically formulated natural science that is of the essence of the spirit of his people.

With the son, Thomas, this became explicit. His father insisted that he study the Greek and Roman classics. Then he attended the College of William and Mary. From the classics Thomas acquired his knowledge of the Greek and Roman Stoics and their concept of just man as universal man. They teach us, he said, the "laws for governing ourselves," just as Jesus supplements this teaching with "the duties and charities we owe to others." [7] Jefferson emphasized, however, that it was his studies under Dr. William Small, the professor of mathematics at William and Mary, "a man profound in most of the useful branches of science," who "probably fixed the destinies of my life." [8] This occurred when Dr. Small made Jefferson aware that the facts of nature are fully known only when the experimentally verified, mathematically expressed, universal laws that they exemplify are specified, as illustrated by Newton's mathematical physics. This gave the lawful universalism of Greco-Roman Stoicism new empirically determinable changing content. It also required a new political philosophy of legal constitutionalism defined in terms of modern rather than of Greek or Roman philosophy. Jefferson found this new political philosophy in the empiricism of Bacon and in Newton's friend Locke. This is undoubtedly the reason why Jefferson wrote in a letter to Dr. Benjamin Rusk that, "Bacon, Newton and Locke . . . were my trinity of the three greatest men the world had ever produced." [9]

On the previous page of the same letter to Dr. Rusk, Jefferson added that both John Adams and he agreed upon "rational republicanism" as the principle for the new Republic. Here the mathematical deductive formulation of Newton's physics in terms of universal propositions had its influence. Chiang Monlin was quite right when, in his first visit to the United States, he saw that this country and the West are rooted in rationalism. It is in the theoretically constructed constitutional law entered into by a contract modeled on the universal laws of Newton's natural science and grounded in man's equality before such laws of nature that Jefferson, Adams, Franklin and their fellow authors of the Declaration of Independence and the Constitution of the United States found the spiritual source of the equality and freedom of their countrymen under law. It is not status in patriarchal family, ethnic tribe or man-made society as given inductively by natural history descriptive science, but contractually constructed universal law before which all ethnic, tribal and cultural distinctions become defined in terms of more fundamental common concepts, that gives the just and the good.

Through every stage of his life, this conception of nature and its empirically determined, theoretically constructed mathematical natural science dominated Jefferson's political and social thought and action. Following his return to private life after two terms as President, he founded the University of Virginia. When deciding upon what was to be studied and taught there, he wrote to Peter Carr saying that the "object" of the institution must be determined "with precision" by "taking a survey of the general field of science." [10] At every level of education from the elementary schools through the general schools to the university and to its professional schools, science occupies the center of emphasis and interest even though languages are important and the entire process culminates in philosophy. Nor is Jefferson's understanding of science superficial. It comprises Pure Mathematics, Mathematical Physics and "Physics, or Natural Philosophy." [11] He specifies that pure mathematics must include measure in the abstract, arithmetic, algebra and the calculus together with trigonometry, plain and spherical geometry, conic sections and transcendental curves. "Physico-

Mathematics" included similarly all of the present natural sciences.

Mathematical natural science and its philosophy is to be studied both for its own sake because of its liberating influence upon the mind and for its practical efficacy in relating men to nature more harmoniously so that nature's bounties are received. Social relations become secondary to this. He realized, however, that if applied natural science is to be effective in satisfying the social needs of men, it must derive from the rationalistic laws and theoretical principles of logically and mathematically formulated scientific theory. Mere inductive, naive observation or mere immersion in nature's continuum of immediacy will not be enough. Fully to become one with nature is to accept its laws and embody them in one's conduct. To the end of his life this interest and conviction persisted. In 1812 he wrote to John Adams saying, "I have given up newspapers in exchange for Tacitus and Thucydides, for Newton and Euclid, and I find myself much the happier." [12]

John Adams found this congenial reading. His son, John Quincy, with his interest in Tycho Brahe, Kepler and Newton and in the establishment of "lighthouses of the sky," would have found it even more so.[13] Franklin's similar concern with the laws and abstract theory of electrical phenomena and their importance in relating men to nature, if men are to be guided wisely by nature's wisdom rather than by "the fighting creeds of war-torn Europe," is well known.

In Emerson perhaps, this spiritual, experimental naturalistic universalism which is the soul of the people of the United States came to its richest and fullest initial expression. "Nature is loved by what is best in us," [14] he says. Nature also is known only experimentally, never with absolute finality, and always in terms of universal laws. Moreover, these laws are not read directly from the face of nature. Instead, they can be found only by the creative, speculative, imaginative, mathematical constructions of men. Thus he adds, "we bring with us to every experiment the innate universal laws." [15] Consequently, "only [those] who build on Ideas, build for eternity." [16] In other words, without mind and the freely inquiring imaginative spirit, with its theoretically proposed universal propositions, nature and the laws of its phenomena are unknowable.

Although the mind and spirit of man "proceeds on the faith that a law determines all phenomena," [17] man's poetic imaginative construction of a specific law of nature becomes experimentally confirmed at a given time only again to require a fresh construction. Inexhaustible nature continuously presents new facts which man's previously confirmed laws of nature fail to satisfy. Thus nature is as much an emancipator of the freely inquiring spirit from the rule of old and outmoded laws as it is the guarantee of freedom and justice under new and more adequate universal laws. For, writes Emerson, "the quality of the imagination is to flow, and not to freeze." [18] Thereby, "Nature is made to conspire with spirit to emancipate us." [19] This is why he adds,

. . . we love the poet, the inventor, who in any form, whether in an ode or in an action or in looks and behavior, has yielded us a new thought. He unlocks our chains and admits us to a new scene.[20]

The poet, however, who does this most effectively is the mathematical natural scientist with his imaginatively proposed and experimentally confirmed universal laws rather than the traditional poets of the old cultures who, because of the deposit of dead or dying social forms between themselves and nature, have lost connection with the spiritual roots in God-made nature that are the true inspiration of both societies and men. "Let us have a little algebra," he writes, "instead of this trite rhetoric,—universal signs, instead of these village symbols,— and we shall both be gainers." [21] "Our action should rest mathematically on our substance . . . [since] all things work exactly according to their quality and according to their quantity." [22]

Jefferson's father, surveying his Virginia farm by the use of instruments designed and operated in accordance with the laws of geometrical optics, illustrates what Emerson means. So does the Truman Point Four program in Asia.

This is a new conception of the moral and spiritual life as the harmony of man with nature. Whereas the Chinese attain this harmony with nature by an intuitive savoring of its flavors, the acceptance of its cyclical rhythms and the immersion of the self in its all-embracing vastness, the people of these United States harmonize themselves with nature, its divine law and its God by free, poetic imaginative "self-union" with its universal laws. Thereby they allow the divine spirit and its natural law to flow spontaneously in its creative inventiveness through the deeds of men to the relating of them more effectively and harmoniously to nature. What other people term gadgets become, when truly understood, the expression of this spontaneous divine creativity. To the people of these United States, the colleges of agriculture, the institutions of technology, the research laboratories of universities, of labor unions and of industry are but the contemporary illustration of St. Augustine's dictum, "Love, and do what thou wilt. . . . " [23] Emerson described it as "the theory of . . . self-union and freedom." [24] We are, he adds, "begirt with laws which," if we will but discover them and embody them in our actions, will "execute themselves." [25]

To the people of these United States this is the solution of the economic problem. It does not center, as the peoples of the traditional cultures suppose, in the belief in one or another of the traditional social isms taken as an arbitrarily assumed norm for the relating of men to one another in society. Its locus instead is in natural science.

This is why, if one wants to understand the culture of the United States, one must look not at its departments of economics, sociology or politics, important as they are, but at its universal education in the natural sciences and their skills, its agricultural colleges, technological institutes and research laboratories operated by government, university, industry and labor union. Only in nature, not in culture, does the intuitive and intellectual love of God speak directly to the spirit of man. Only

by embodying God's poetically discovered, experimentally verified universal laws of nature in one's life and then adjusting
the social relations of men to what results is the good life for
society to be obtained or the root meaning of the religious
and other classics of culture to be found.

From this point of view to take, as do the old cultures of
Europe and Asia and as do the New Zealanders and Australians
who copy economically outmoded and inefficient Britain, one
or another of the rival social philosophies for relating men to
one another in society as the criterion of the good society, is
merely to transfer an economically inefficient relation of men
to nature from one set of ineffective hands to another. Unless
men guide their social relations by the more effective relation
of themselves to nature which an ever increasing knowledge
of the laws of nature can alone provide there is no hope whatever, regardless of what social theories are introduced, for im-
proving the economic well-being of a particular people or of
mankind.

As Dewey has recently written, "Science through its physical
technological consequences is now determining the relations
which human beings, severally and in groups, sustain to one
another." [26] In other words, social relations are not first causes.
Instead, when correctly understood they are effects which flow
out of the theories used by men to relate themselves to nature.

Nor is this a phenomenon peculiar to the contemporary culture of the United States. Its Founding Fathers and its poets
were governed by this idea. All the great sages of the world,
Asian and Western, were also governed by it. It is only their
modern descendants, caught in cultural and social relations that
are the frozen and often dead deposits of the ancient Asian and
European sages' knowledge of nature, who have mistaken social
and cultural relations and theories for first causes.

The tragic consequences of this error show everywhere in the
contemporary world. The framers of Australia's economic policy were very proud, when they informed the writer in Sydney
in early August of 1949 that over the previous twenty years

they had been governing themselves by the principles of British neo-classical economic science supplemented with Keynes' postulate of full employment and with a Labor Court. Here was a government run by a Labor Party which had a doctrine. The writer was duly impressed.

But two days later in Melbourne the bubble burst. After having this doctrine and policy described to him, an informed Australian said, "Did my fellow countrymen who spoke to you with such pride of this economic doctrine tell you that during every year the total production of goods and services decreases?" Nor has the shift since then from a Labor to a Liberal Party Government helped matters, for a dispatch from Melbourne to *The New York Times* of July 15, 1952, speaks of the continuation of "the disastrous decline in primary production that began during the Labor regime."

Such is the fallacy of taking a particular social theory of the relations between men in society rather than the relation of men to nature as guided by nature's laws and their embodiment in human conduct the criterion of economic and social reform. Unless men follow God's laws as discovered in nature and embody them in their conduct to bring themselves more efficiently into harmony with nature, thereby releasing nature's tremendous bounties in the form of a greater total production of goods and services, all shifts from a government run with one social theory to a government guided by a different social ism will be in vain. It is not man-made social relations, but God's natural laws which are the key both to the spiritual foundations of the culture of the United States and to the meeting of the economic needs of mankind.

The Englishman, Sir Norman Angell, has recently reminded his countrymen that they or anyone else is completely mistaken if he thinks that the relatively high economic well-being of the people of the United States is due solely to the happy circumstance that they live in a large geographical area with rich natural resources. South America, he pointed out, has a greater area and greater resources relative to its population. Similarly, the British Commonwealth has far greater area and natural resources relative to its population, including the fifty million in Great Britain, than is the case with the United States. The truth of the matter is that South America, the British Commonwealth, Europe and Asia generally have fallen into the error of taking man-made custom and speculative man-made social theories rather than nature and its natural laws as their primary guide.[27]

Social relations derive from man's relation to nature. When this law is violated, peoples increasingly tighten their belts and move en masse toward starvation. The only good and effective way to put men together in society is the one which flows from the most efficient way of relating them to nature as determined by the laws of nature.

This naturalistic concept of the spiritual shows in John Dewey, Justice Holmes, Roscoe Pound and the American legal realists' conception of law, not as an absolute norm assumed hypothetically and *a priori* as a first cause, but as an instrument for social control and change. There is, moreover, no single social theory to be used instrumentally. Each social and problematic situation has to be resolved in its own particular way with its own particular social relations between men.

Unless this point is grasped, the falsity and impossibility of assigning the culture of the United States to one or another of the conventional social theories, such as Socialism, Capitalism, Tory Conservatism or Communism, will not be appreciated. Insofar as Capitalistic ways permit men to be related to nature more harmoniously and efficiently in the light of true knowledge of nature, such ways are chosen. Private industry with its prodigious investment in research concerning the laws of natural science and their application illustrates this choice. Insofar as government owned and operated power dams, forestry programs and river valley projects offer the opportunity to take greater advantage of the laws and instruments of natural science, this way the people of the United States freely and spontaneously choose. The Hoover Dam, ordered by a Republican President, the Grand Coulee and the Tennessee Valley Authority, ordered by Democratic administrations, illustrate this method. Another example is labor's rejection of a Labor Party and its use instead of unions with prodigious capital investments, supporting research and often recommending to management the scrapping of old for more efficient new equipment and the shifting of laborers from inefficient to more efficient skills. Always the criterion for judging which equipment and which skill is the most efficient and best is that of knowledge as given by natural science. Economic or social theory has little or nothing to do with the matter. American labor knows that the legislating of higher wages, longer hours, class or no class distinctions is as "a sounding brass or a tinkling cymbal" unless the efficiency of man's relation to nature, as determined by scientific knowledge of the laws of nature and their application, is increased.

Moreover, the education of the laborer and everyone else in the importance of the naturalistic scientific mentality and in its ever newly prescribed skills becomes as necessary as the new equipment and the new factories themselves. Jefferson, Adams, Franklin, Longfellow and Emerson, and many other Founding Fathers and spiritually minded poets also, expressed this same conception of the spiritual, as the scientifically natural which is universal, when they prescribed that education must be for everyone and not merely for the select few.

It would be a mistake to suppose, however, that the spiritual values in the foundation of the culture of the United States show only in its technology. This technology presupposes the experimentally verified, poetically and imaginatively discovered universal laws of theoretical natural science. These laws in turn presuppose the freely inquiring human spirit nurtured, fed and stimulated by the universal spirit of nature. Thus this spiritual naturalism is a naturalism of the human spirit in the very process of being a naturalism of nature and of nature's art of technology coming to free and creative expression through human beings. From the very beginning, the spiritual founders of these people saw that the distinction of the old cultures between the fine arts and the applied arts was an artificial one. The Greek word for art is τέκγη. Thus technology expresses the root meaning of the word "art" better than does the word "painting," and technology is as much the art of nature expressing itself through men as is painting.

Law is similar. Like technology it is an instrument; it is not an *a priori* absolute or first cause. For this reason it is as much judge-made as judge-declared. As the lawyer and public servant, David Lilienthal, has put the matter:

Diversity and flexibility, rather than a stereotyped hard-and-fast system, is an essential part of such a noble concept of society as is ours. We get our economic services in the way that at the time seems to work best, that will in a particular situation best advance our underlying purposes. We do not start with all the answers, the economic answers or political answers. We make the answers up as we go along. Thus, American industry is owned and operated, by and large, by competitive private enterprise; yet . . . the Senate of the United States voted unanimously to establish public ownership and management in one of our largest industries, and make it a government monopoly—I refer of course to the atomic materials industry. That appeared to be the thing to do at the time, for reasons related to the facts of atomic energy, not for ideological reasons taken out of some book of economic dogma. The most rock-ribbed mid-Western town I know has for many years owned and operated its own electric power and light plant. Is this then a "socialist" town? Hardly! Its water service has been privately owned for the same period. There is a privately owned university; a public junior college. No one considers that these things are inconsistent; and of course they are not, except to the dogmatist who thinks we have a fixed "system." In the same town there is a farmers' feed co-operative that is not quite private or quite public, operating side by side with a big privately owned feed company. There are private banks, there are non-profit insurance companies, there are state-owned liquor stores. We would never consider adopting government ownership or control of newspapers partly because of their educational character; but our school system, the cornerstone of American education, is almost entirely publicly owned and managed. This is all part of the familiar picture of American diversity, of American flexibility.[28]

It would be a mistake, however, to assume that this relativity of social legal norms is completely footloose, controlled by no norms which are absolute. There is judge-declared law as well as judge-made law in the United States. This showed most recently in the declaration by a court of lower jurisdiction that President Truman's seizure of the steel industry is unconstitutional. It shows also in the Bill of Rights and in the separation of powers.

How is this paradoxical and apparently contradictory relation between law conceived as a social instrument and law conceived as a norm for judging social instruments to be reconciled? For reconciled it must be if decision makers and judge-made law are not to underwrite dictatorship. On certain basic normative principles even judges and even a president elected by the people must operate within the law and under its absolute and unqualified control.

The resolution of this paradox is already at hand. Insofar as legal norms are merely social norms, they are instrumental and relative. Insofar as legal norms are absolute, binding judge and statesman and even the passions of the people themselves, they find their basis in nature and in the theories of natural science. Social laws are not, as many instrumentalists in the United States have supposed, merely relative to social interests. Nor are they judged merely by their social consequences. To reach this conclusion would be to lift social goals of a certain kind again to the status of first causes. Social relations and goals are instrumental with respect to their natural law antecedents; not with respect to their social consequences. If putting men in certain social relations permits the more efficient relation of men to nature as specified by the laws of natural science, that social and legal instrumentation of the prescription of natural science is chosen. Thus the Government of the United States is a government by instrumental social norms judged as to their validity by objectively determined and verified laws of nature. Law is at once instrumentally and socially relative and judge-made and naturalistically absolute and judge-declared.

But even in its absoluteness, law is a changing thing. For as the poet Emerson has made clear to us and as the sequence of universal laws and theories of Western natural science demonstrate, the universal laws of nature are discovered only by the poetic, algebraic imagination of free spirits; and the poetic imagination flows, it is not fixed. Even so, through the flow there are certain constancies. Always law is universal and always lawful universalism presupposes and protects freedom. Hence the absoluteness of the separation of powers and the Bill of Rights. This is why Dewey today quotes with approval Jefferson's statement made long ago, "Nothing is unchangeable but inherent and inalienable rights of man." [29]

Because all cultural and social relations go back thus to nature and the tutelage of the human spirit by nature and because the culture of the people of the United States is the only one in the world today which most freshly and vitally expresses this basic spiritual insight, it is likely to be the major influence determining the final step which mankind makes along the path from a few cultural political units to a single cultural world community that effectively and universally meets the economic needs of all mankind.

It appears to have but one rival—Marxist Communism. Nor is this an accident. For Marxist materialistic Communism, like the spiritual experimental naturalistic universalism of the United States affirms the primacy of man's relation to nature over the relation of men to one another in society. This is why something more than the transferring of an inefficient relation of men to nature from one set of ineffective hands to another takes place when either the people of the United States or the Communists touch a society.

There is, however, a vast difference between the Communistic and the American conception of this primary relation of man to nature. The Communists, following Marxist materialism, make the material tools of production the basic factor. From this come all social relations, cultural ideals and even marching orders for the leaders of society and the human spirit. The people of the United States had the good fortune to have virgin nature and her universal laws of natural science rather than Karl Marx as their spiritual mentor. Their tutor taught them that the freedom required for and revealed in the knowing of nature comes first. Then come imaginatively suggested universal laws, found only by the freely inquiring poetic human spirit using "algebraic" or universal mathematical symbols rather than what Emerson termed "village" or tribal symbols. Third, comes the testing of the truth or falsity of these imaginatively suggested universal laws by recourse to careful quantitative experiments. And finally from these laws, when verified and used to suggest new ways in which matter can be put together, come novel material tools and the more harmonious and hence efficient relation of men to nature.

Thus, according to this concept of the spiritual, instead of materialistic doctrine deterministically and dialectically ordering free spirits about, there is no doctrine in any field except as free spirits, nurtured by nature rather than by books, find it and verify it. Also, instead of the material tools of production determining what men and their ideas must be and do, free spirits and their freely discovered and tested ideas or theories determine what material tools can be made. In short, in relating men to nature, freely inquiring spirits and the laws of nature which free spirits find come first and material tools and the "physical production forces" come afterward.

In knowing nature man comes also upon a new knowledge of himself. He finds first that he is a freely inquiring spirit. He learns also that without this there would be nothing else, no theories about "materialism," scientific laws of nature known by men, or the efficient material tools which derive from them. If to be good, therefore, is to act and build a society in accord with true, complete knowledge of oneself, then the basic principle of any society must be freedom for the freely inquiring spirit. In fact if this is not put first, increasingly efficient tools will not be discovered and "the physical production forces" will be self-defeating. This is why Communism will fail to meet the economic needs of men and success will crown the way of the United States.

By free inquiry, man finds also that any individual thing in nature is truly known only when the universal laws which it exemplifies are known. Expressed in terms of human individuals, this means that man's full knowledge of himself requires that he think of himself not merely as a freely inquiring spirit but also as an instance of universal law. Man is no exception to nature's rules. Therefore, he also must freely accept universal law before which all men are treated alike. For law which holds only for some men is not a universal law. Thus arise the two basic values of individual freedom under law the same for all men. In short, freedom and justice are reconciled and shown to entail one another. If, therefore, as Socrates said, to be virtuous is to "know thyself" and if knowledge of oneself involves these two things, then it follows that only that society is the virtuous one which is governed by a constitutional universalism that presupposes and protects free inquiry.

There is, however, nothing novel about this spiritual conception of the basis of liberty and justice. We found the same concept of the spiritual to be at the basis of Greco-Roman Christian Western civilization. Only its content, as Jefferson learned from his trinity, Bacon, Newton and Locke, has changed since then.

It would be a mistake, however, to conclude that the next step from the cultural political units noted in a previous chapter to an even larger single cultural political unit must restrict itself to the Greco-Roman, Hebrew-Christian West. Islam stems also from a synthesis of the same Greek and Hebrew Christian elements. Its contemporary resurgence and reformation, as envisaged by Iqbal of Lahore, Maulana Abul Kalam Azad of New Delhi and others, rest on the conception of spiritual man as a man under universal laws which presuppose and protect the freedom of the individual spirit.

Even in Aryan Hinduism, with its emphasis on *ṛita* and *dharma,* we find the same thing.[30] Unfortunately, however,

Aryan Hinduism constructed its Laws of Manu and its subsequent commentaries thereon not upon the universal theoretically constructed universal laws of nature before which all men are equal, but upon men as given inductively in society as members of tribes and castes. Providing *dharma* is given in practice a truly universal content, as is the case in the new Constitution of India, Aryan Hindu India as well as Islam can become ideologically one with the Greco-Roman Hebrew-Christian modern liberal West.

Only in the solidarity of non-Aryan Far Eastern Asia do we find a cultural political unit rooted in a concept of the spiritual other than that of determinate universal law. There we find intuitive, warmly felt man-to-manness and the art of mediation, rather than an appeal to legal codes and constitutional principles, to be the primary and preferred way to the peaceful relating of men. But even there moral man is universal man. This non-Aryan Asian moral universalism, which is emotive and existential [31] rather than theoretical and lawful in character, is to be found, however, by softening down the transitory, perishing differentiations between men to bring out the warmly felt, immediate, all-embracing vastness which is the same in all men and is, therefore, universal man. It is this which comes to expression in the Confucian Chinese thesis that moral man is always a peace-maker in the sense of a mediator and which has been exhibited in all its spiritual and political power in Gandhiji's pacifism.

Here also the attempt to bring all the nations of the world under the rule of law with effective police action the automatic responsibility of all, will probably meet its greatest obstacle. For insofar as traditional non-Aryan Asian values operate in the masses of the non-Islamic Asian people and in their leaders, there will be the tendency on their part to assume no responsibility for the policing of the law, because of the Gandhian teaching that it is always evil to use force and the Buddha's suggestion that the peace-maker always pursues "the middle path." Instead they will be inclined to a neutral role of non-attachment pursuing the middle way between the aggressor and the policeman, thereby in the name of morality and peace putting both the aggrieved party and the policeman in the bad light of being as much if not more of a disturber of the peace than the aggressor.

Obviously there is nothing that will encourage a political aggressor to satisfy his hunger more than the existence of such peace-making neutrals in the world community. For their presence assures him that if he grabs enough quickly and then puts himself immediately on the defensive, the policeman and the aggrieved party will have to use more force in preventing his aggression from succeeding than he used in making the aggressive grab in the first place. He can then be reasonably sure that the mediator who does not believe in force will affirm to the world that the policeman and the aggrieved nation are worse war-makers than he. Thereby he can have considerable hope that the morale of both the community and the police force will be weakened or broken so that his venture will succeed. Even if this does not occur and he finds himself forced to give up his loot, he knows that by continuing his fighting he can count on the neutral peace-maker to be available to urge a compromise in the name of peace which will save his face and probably give him something more than he had before he started.

It is not necessary, however, that this difficulty arise. It can be avoided if the non-Aryan Asian and the Aryan Hindu, the Muslim and the Greco-Roman Christian Westerner alike realize that man, when truly and fully known, is both the Gandhijian, non-Aryan Asian existential spiritual universal and an instance of the universal spirit which is the divine λόγος. In short, there is both the intuitively felt emotive love of God revealed in existential intuition and the theoretically known, lawfully expressed intellectual love of God revealed through the definite Word.

Then it will be seen that man truly and fully expresses the complex nature of the divinity, which is in him only when he judges other men or groups of men acting as nations, by the universal law before which all men are equal, and assumes along with other men his full share of the responsibility for enforcing that judgment, while at the same time keeping as warm as possible the all-embracing existential component of the Divine Self which is common to the law-breaker, the judge and the policeman. It will become evident also that the proper time for the intensive application of the Gandhijian mediational pacific spirit is before a dispute erupts into a violation of the universal law and after the aggressor has returned to law-abiding ways.

What this amounts to basically is that some uses of force are not evil. Even the Lord Krishna of Gandhiji's beloved Gita tells Arjuna that after he has given himself completely to Brahman, he is then to engage in battle. Jesus drove the money changers out of the temple. Only that use of force which completely denies the intuitive oneness of oneself with one's other and which violates the universal λόγος is evil. When, however, force is used only in the name of the universal law before which all men and nations are equal and then solely defensively, after the manner of the policeman, in order to prevent violators of that law from making evil triumph over virtue, it is good. Perhaps this distinction between the sword used defensively in the name of and in defense of the law, and the sword used aggressively in violation of that law is what Jesus meant when he made the seemingly incomprehensible statement that He, the Prince of Peace, "came not to send peace, but a sword." [89]

When, moreover, every person and nation accepts the responsibility not merely to judge by the law but also to assume a full share of the duty for the enforcement of that judgment, the morale of the community becomes so strong and the triumph of the policeman over any violator becomes so evident ahead of time to any potential aggressor that peace is likely without the use of force. It works its beneficent influence because of the moral and spiritual unity and firmness of the community merely by being there in reserve. This is why the creation of a world law based on the principle of living law pluralism, described in

Chapter XII, in which there can be no veto of either the judicial verdict or everyone's responsibility for policing that verdict, is so important. Only in this way can we achieve effective peace with the minimum possible use of force.

It appears, so far as the foreign policy of the United States is concerned, that its course from Philadelphia through Pearl Harbor and Hiroshima is to Cosmopolis, that single earthly polity whose model is the unity of the Asians' intuition and the Occidentals' constitutional image of the universal City of God. Neither power politics nor eclecticism but spiritual naturalistically grounded universalism is the scientific, realistic and only practical way to relate ourselves to other peoples and nations.

The same is true for the United Nations and the International Court of Justice. The cultural values and moral and spiritual principles of the world in all their living law diversity and also in their unity, rather than precedent, power politics jockeying or momentary isolationistic expediency, constitute the realistic basis for resolving the ideological conflicts and disturbances of our world by peaceful means rather than the suicidal resort to war in an atomic age.

The spiritual resources necessary to give peace to this troubled world are at hand provided that the leaders of the United Nations and of each nation within the United Nations will but make use of them. The time is here to drink of the life-giving waters. If the corns of wheat which are the respective faiths of men will but fall into the ground and die, thereby receiving the spiritual food necessary for their nurture, they and this war-torn and war-weary old world can bloom again. For each of the faiths in the gardens of men has its spiritual Philadelphia and the way from Philadelphia to Cosmopolis is clear.

NOTES

CHAPTER I

1. Ehrlich, Eugen, *Fundamental Principles of the Sociology of Law*, Walter L. Moll, translator, Harvard Studies in Jurisprudence, Vol. V, Harvard Univ. Press, Cambridge, 1936.
2. Sorokin, Pitirim A., "Lasting and Dying Factors in the World's Cultures," in *Ideological Differences and World Order*, F. S. C. Northrop, editor, Yale Univ. Press, 1949 (hereafter referred to as *ID & WO*), pp. 429–441. See also, Kluckholn, Clyde, "The Philosophy of the Navaho Indians," *ID & WO*, pp. 356–384.

CHAPTER II

1. Vandenberg, Jr., Arthur H., *The Private Papers of Senator Vandenberg*, Houghton Mifflin Co., Boston, 1952, p. 1.
2. Chakravarti, Tripurai and N. C. Bhattacharyya, "The New China As I Have Seen It," *Monthly Bulletin*, The Ramakrishna Mission Institute of Culture, Vol. III, No. 1, Jan. 1952, pp. 7–12.

CHAPTER III

1. *The Statesman*, Delhi, Oct. 14, 1949, p. 7.
2. *Ibid.*
3. *The Modern Review*, Calcutta, Vol. LXXXX, No. 6, Dec. 1951, pp. 427–428.

CHAPTER IV

1. Gandhi, M. K., *Gandhi's Autobiography, The Story of My Experiments with Truth*, Public Affairs Press, Washington, 1948, p. 4.
2. *Ibid.*, p. 6.
3. *Ibid.*, p. 90.
4. *Ibid.*, p. 91.
5. *Ibid.*, p. 154.
6. *Ibid.*, p. 328.
7. Wofford, Jr., Clare and Harris, *India Afire*, John Day Co., New York, 1951, p. 168.
8. Okakura, Kakasu, *The Ideals of the East*, John Murray, London, 1903, p. 1.
9. Wofford, *op. cit.*, pp. 211–212.
10. Gandhi, *op. cit.*, p. 234.

11. *Ibid.*, p. 197.
12. *Ibid.*, p. 235.
13. *Ibid.*, pp. 167–168.
14. Northrop, F. S. C., "Philosophical Anthropology and World Law," *Transactions of The New York Academy of Sciences,* Ser. II, Vol. 14, Dec. 1951, No. 2, pp. 109–112.
15. Wofford, *op. cit.,* p. 147.
16. Gandhi, *op. cit.,* p. 308.
17. Müller, F. Max, ed., *The Sacred Books of the East* (hereafter *SBE*), Oxford, 1882, Vol. VIII, *The Bhagavadgita with the Sanatsugatiya and the Anugita,* pp. 51–52.
18. *Ibid.*, pp. 59, 60.
19. *Ibid.*, p. 106.
20. Müller, *SBE,* Vol. XV, *The Brihadâranyaka-Upanishad,* Pt. II, 1884, pp. 10, 14, 311.
21. *Ibid.*, p. 171.
22. Wofford, *op. cit.,* p. 171.
23. Chaudhuri, Nirad C., *The Autobiography of an Unknown Indian,* Macmillan, New York, 1951, p. 429.

CHAPTER V

1. Rama Rau, Santha, *East of Home,* Harper's, New York, 1950, p. 30.
2. Madariaga, Salvador de, *Englishmen, Frenchmen, Spaniards,* Oxford Univ. Press, London, 1931.
3. Müller, *SBE,* Vol. VI, *The Quran,* Pt. I, 1880, p. 95.
4. Gandhi, *op. cit.,* p. 194.
5. *Ibid.*, p. 296 ff.
6. *Ibid.*, p. 481.
7. *Ibid.*, p. 365.
8. Müller, *SBE,* Vol. VIII, *op. cit.,* p. 80.
9. Woodroffe, Sir John, *Shakti and Shâkta,* Luzac, London, 1929, pp. 240–271.
10. Northrop, F. S. C., *The Meeting of East and West* (hereafter *TMEW*), Macmillan, New York, 1946, pp. 436–478.
11. *Ibid.*
12. Chiang Monlin, *Tides from the West,* Yale Univ. Press, 1947, pp. 9, 19.
13. *Ibid.*, p. 258.
14. *Ibid.*, p. 258.
15. Northrop, *TMEW, op. cit.,* Plates XIII–XVI and Chapters IX and X.

16. Chiang Monlin, *op. cit.*, p. 249.
17. Lin Yutang, *The Wisdom of Confucius*, Modern Library, New York, 1938, p. 106.
18. Gandhi, *op. cit.*, p. 308.
19. *Ibid.*, pp. 427–428.

CHAPTER VI

1. Joardar, N. G. D., opinion expressed in a lecture at the Yale Law School, February 1952. See also, Chaudhuri, *op. cit.*, and Chatterji, Suniti Kumar, "Krishna Dvaipāyana Vyāsa and Krishna Vāsudeva" in the *Journal of the Royal Asiatic Society of Bengal,* Letters, Vol. XVI, No. 1, 1950, pp. 73–87.
2. Ramaswami Aiyar, Sir C. P., in a lecture at the Yale Law School, March 1952.
3. Müller, *SBE*, Vol. XXV, 1886, *The Laws of Manu*, pp. 230–233 *passim*.
4. *Ibid.*, pp. 241, 243–245, 248.
5. *Ibid.*, pp. 251, 252.
6. *Ibid.*, pp. 228–229.
7. Karaka, D. F., *Betrayal in India,* Gollancz, London, 1950, and Wofford, *op. cit.*
8. Cullen, Tom A., "Spirit of Subhas Bose, . . ." *New Haven Evening Register,* New Haven, Conn., April 16, 1952.
9. Maine, Sir Henry S., *Ancient Law, Its Connection with the Early History of Society and Its Relation to Modern Ideas,* John Murray, London, 1908, p. 151.
10. As quoted by Wofford, *op. cit.*, p. 168.
11. *The Constitution of India,* India Press, New Delhi, 1949, p. 9.
12. *Ibid.*, p. 14.
13. Russell, Richard J., and Fred B. Kniffen, *Culture Worlds,* Macmillan, New York, 1951, p. 414.
14. Alexander, Horace, *New Citizens of India,* Oxford Univ. Press, 1952, p. 118.
15. *The Five Year Plan, A Short Introduction,* Government of India, Delhi, 1951, p. 4.
16. *Ibid.*, pp. 18–19.
17. *Ibid.*, p. 4.
18. Karve, D. G., *Indian Population,* Economic Handbooks, No. 3, National Information and Publications, Bombay, 1948, p. 15.
19. *Ibid.*, p. 16.
20. *Ibid.*, p. 32.
21. *The Five Year Plan, op. cit.*, p. 24.

22. *Ibid.*, pp. 6–7, 9.
23. As quoted in Wofford, *op. cit.*, p. 267.
24. *The Five Year Plan, op. cit.*, pp. 10–11.
25. *Ibid.*, p. 27.
26. *Ibid.*, p. 11.
27. Karve, *op. cit.*, p. 17.
28. *Ibid.*, p. 45.
29. As quoted by Alexander, *op. cit.*, p. 117.
30. *The Five Year Plan, op. cit.*, p. 20.
31. Alexander, *op. cit.*, p. 112.
32. I am indebted to the expert on the Asian economy of Japan, Professor Jerome B. Cohen, for the suggestion, made to me in a conversation, of putting the matter in this way.

CHAPTER VII

1. *The Times of India*, Bombay, Jan. 16, 1951.
2. Chiang Monlin, *op. cit.*, p. 251.
3. *Ibid.*, p. 114.
4. *Ibid.*, pp. 257–258 and p. 251.
5. *Ibid.*, p. 258.
6. *Ibid.*, p. 74.
7. *Ibid.*, p. 114.
8. *Ibid.*, p. 112.
9. Needham, Joseph, *Human Law and the Laws of Nature in China and the West*, Oxford Univ. Press, 1951. See also Northrop, *TMEW, op. cit.*
10. Chiang Monlin, *op. cit.*, p. 252.
11. *Ibid.*, pp. 137, 139–140.
12. *Ibid.*, p. 140.
13. Lin Yutang, *My Country and My People*, John Day, New York, 1939, pp. 172–213.
14. Chiang Monlin, *op. cit.*, p. 139.
15. The Gospel According to St. Matthew, 10:35.
16. Hsien Chin Hu, *The Common Descent Group in China and Its Functions*, Viking Fund Publications in Anthropology, No. 10, New York, 1948, p. 95.
17. *Ibid.*, p. 95.
18. *Ibid.*, pp. 95–96.
19. *Ibid.*, p. 96.
20. Chiang Monlin, *op. cit.*, p. 7.
21. *Ibid.*, p. 12.

22. Liu Shih-Fang, "Westernized Administration of Justice and Chinese Racial Characteristics," as translated by Alfred Wang, Yale Law Library, p. 1.
23. *Ibid.,* p. 1.
24. *Ibid.,* pp. 1, 2.
25. *Ibid.,* p. 2.
26. *Ibid.,* p. 2.
27. *Ibid.,* pp. 2–3.
28. *Ibid.,* pp. 3–4.
29. *Ibid.,* p. 4.
30. *Ibid.,* p. 4.
31. Chiang Monlin, *op. cit.,* pp. 255–256.
32. *Ibid.,* p. 256.
33. Northrop, F. S. C., "Asian Mentality and United States Foreign Policy," *The Annals of the American Academy of Political and Social Science,* July 1951, pp. 118–127.
34. Einstein, Albert, *The World As I See It,* Covici Friede, New York, 1934, pp. 31–32.
35. Chiang Monlin, *op. cit.,* p. 245.
36. "Kishan," "Mechanisation of Agriculture," *The Modern Review,* Calcutta, January 1952, p. 44.
37. Chiang Monlin, *op. cit.,* p. 112.
38. *Ibid.,* pp. 245–246.
39. *Ibid.,* pp. 248, 245.
40. I am indebted to Mr. Harold G. Wren, formerly Junior Naval Intelligence Officer in Japan, for these observations.
41. Cohen, Jerome B., *Japan's Economy in War and Reconstruction,* Univ. of Minnesota Press, Minneapolis, 1949, p. 427.
42. I am indebted to my Japanese student, Mr. Yoshiro Kashihara, for making me aware of this fact and to him, Mr. Hidenori Kitagawa and the aforementioned Mr. Wren for calling my attention to the importance of this linguistic factor.

CHAPTER VIII

1. Iqbal, Allama Sir Muhammad, *The Complaint and the Answer,* translated by Altaf Husain, Muhammad Ashraf, Lahore, 1948, p. ix.
2. *Ibid.,* p. ix.
3. *Ibid.,* pp. ix–x.
4. Iqbal, Sir Mohammad, *The Reconstruction of Religious Thought in Islam,* Oxford Univ. Press, London, 1934, p. 170.
5. *Ibid.,* pp. 155, 177.

6. Iqbal, *The Complaint and the Answer, op. cit.,* pp. 2, 3, 5, 7, 9.
7. *Ibid.,* pp. 20–22.
8. *Ibid.,* pp. 23, 24, 25, 26, 28, 29, 30.
9. *Ibid.,* pp. 30, 31.
10. *Ibid.,* pp. 33–34.
11. Iqbal, Sir Muhammad, *The Tulip of Sinai,* translated by A. J. Arberry, The Royal India Society, London, 1947, p. vii.
12. *Speeches and Statements of Iqbal,* compiled by "Shamloo," Al-Manar Academy, Lahore, 1948, p. 7.
13. *Ibid.,* p. 3.
14. *Ibid.,* p. 5.
15. *Ibid.,* pp. 8–9.
16. *Ibid.,* p. 9.
17. *Ibid.,* pp. 9–10.
18. *Ibid.,* p. 10.
19. *Ibid.,* pp. 10, 11.
20. *Ibid.,* pp. 10–11.
21. *Ibid.,* pp. 39–40.
22. Syed, Dr. M. Hafiz, "Liaquat Ali Khan," *The Modern Review,* Calcutta, Vol. LXXXX, No. 6, Dec. 1951, p. 462.
23. Iqbal, *Speeches,* etc., *op. cit.,* p. 12.
24. *Ibid.,* pp. 12, 18.
25. *Ibid.,* p. 25.
26. Gandhi's *Letters to a Disciple,* Harper's, New York, 1950, p. 135.
27. Iqbal, *Persian Psalms,* Pts. I and II, translated by Arthur J. Arberry, Muhammad Ashraf, Lahore, 1948, Poem 51, p. 45, and Poem 41, p. 36.
28. Tagore, Radindranath, "Gitanjali" in *Collected Poems and Plays of Rabindranath Tagore,* Macmillan, New York, 1937, Verse LXXI, pp. 33–34.
29. *Ibid.,* Verse C, p. 46.
30. Iqbal, *The Tulip of Sinai, op. cit.,* Verses 16, 22, 38 and 46, pp. 4, 5, 8 and 10.
31. Iqbal, Dr. Sir Muhammad, *The Secrets of the Self,* translated from the original Persian with an introduction and notes by Reynold A. Nicholson, Macmillan, 1920, revised edition 1940, reprinted by Muhammad Ashraf, Lahore, 1944, p. xxx.
32. *Ibid.,* pp. xvii–xviii.
33. Kramrisch, Stella, *The Hindu Temple,* Univ. of Calcutta, Vol. I, 1946, p. 12.
34. Iqbal, *Secrets of the Self, op. cit.,* p. xviii.
35. *Ibid.,* pp. xviii–xix.
36. *Ibid.,* pp. xxvi–xxvii.

37. *Ibid.*, pp. xxvii, xxix.
38. *Ibid.*, p. xxix.
39. Iqbal, *Letters of Iqbal to Jinnah,* Shaikh Muhammad Ashraf, Lahore, 1944, pp. 15, 16.
40. *Ibid.*, p. 16.
41. Iqbal, *Speeches and Statements, op. cit.,* pp. 55–56.

CHAPTER X

1. The Book of Job, 22:22.
2. Deuteronomy 6:1, 2.
3. Psalm 19:7.
4. The Gospel According to Saint Luke, 12:53.
5. Inge, Dean W. R., "Conclusion," *Science, Religion and Reality,* Joseph Needham, ed., Macmillan, New York, 1925, pp. 345–389; see also "Religion," *The Legacy of Greece,* R. W. Livingstone, ed., Oxford Univ. Press, London, 1921, pp. 25–56.
6. Chaudhuri, *op. cit.*
7. Maine, *op. cit.*, p. 151.
8. Waddy, Lawrence, *Pax Romana and World Peace,* Norton, New York, 1950, p. 3.
9. Nussbaum, Arthur, *A Concise History of the Law of Nations,* Macmillan, New York, 1947, p. 17.
10. Radhakrishnan, Sir Sarvapalli, *East and West in Religion,* Allen and Unwin, London, 1933; and *Eastern Religions and Western Thought,* Oxford Univ. Press, London, 1940. See also my article, "Radhakrishnan's Conception of the Relation Between Eastern and Western Cultural Values," in *The Philosophy of Sarvapalli Radhakrishnan,* Paul A. Schilpp, Ed., The Library of Living Philosophers, Tudor Publishing Company, New York, 1952, pp. 633–658.
11. Reyes, Alfonso, *Ultima Tule,* Imprenta Universitaria, Mexico, D.F., 1942, pp. 93, 115, 123, as translated from the Spanish by Northrop in *TMEW, op. cit.,* p. 66. See also Edmundo O'Gorman, *Fundamentos de la Historia de America,* Imprenta Universitaria, Mexico, D.F., 1942.
12. The Gospel According to Saint John, 1:1.
13. Waddy, *op. cit.*, p. 5.
14. *Ibid.*, p. 22.
15. Arnold, E. Vernon, *Roman Stoicism,* Cambridge Univ. Press, 1911, pp. 101, 104.
16. *Ibid.*, p. 101.
17. *Ibid.*, p. 179.
18. *Ibid.*, p. 104.

19. *Ibid.,* p. 105.
20. *Ibid.,* p. 127.
21. Waddy, *op. cit.,* p. 36.
22. *Ibid.,* p. 37.
23. *Ibid.,* p. 37.
24. As paraphrased from *The Republic of Plato,* Book VII, line 533, B. Jowett translation, Oxford Univ. Press, 1888, p. 236.
25. Cicero, M. T., *De Officiis,* Book II, "Expediency," translated by Walter Miller, Loeb Classical Library, Putnam, New York, 1928, p. 175.
26. *Ibid.,* p. 175.
27. Waddy, *op. cit.,* p. 22.
28. *Ibid.,* p. 26.
29. *Ibid.,* p. 26.
30. Arnold, *op. cit.,* p. 382.
31. Dorsey, Gray L., "Two Objective Bases for a World-wide Legal Order," in *ID & WO, op. cit.,* p. 462.
32. Arnold, *op. cit.,* p. 318.
33. *Ibid.,* p. 406.
34. *Ibid.,* pp. 406–407.
35. *Ibid.,* p. 127.

CHAPTER XI

1. McIlwain, Charles H., *Constitutionalism: Ancient and Modern,* Cornell Univ. Press, Ithaca, 1947, p. 57.
2. *Ibid.,* p. 62.
3. *Ibid.,* p. 60.
4. *Ibid.,* p. 62.
5. Radcliffe, Lord, "Power and the Problem of Its Control," The Reith Lectures, *The Listener,* Dec. 20, 1951, p. 1061.
6. Radcliffe, Lord, "Makers of the American Constitution," *The Listener,* Nov. 29, 1951, p. 923.
7. Arnold, *op. cit.,* p. 271.
8. Nasmith, David, *Outline of Roman History,* Butterworths, London, 1890, p. 200, sec. 1.

CHAPTER XII

1. *A Handbook of Marxism* (hereafter *Handbook*), International Publishers, New York, 1935, p. 1042.
2. Stalin, Joseph, *Dialectical and Historical Materialism* (hereafter *D & HM*), Little Lenin Library, Vol. 25, International Publishers, New York, 1940.

3. Stalin, J., *Foundations of Leninism* (hereafter *F of L*), Little Stalin Library, No. 1, Laurence & Wishart, London, 1942.
4. *Ibid.*, p. 84.
5. Kennan, George F., *American Diplomacy, 1900–1950*, Univ. of Chicago Press, Chicago, 1951, Appendix.
6. Reston, James, "Our Ways in Diplomacy," *The New York Times*, Sept. 30, 1951, Book Review Section, p. 3.
7. Kennan, *op. cit.*
8. Stalin, *D & HM, op. cit.*, pp. 5, 6–7.
9. *Ibid.*, p. 14.
10. *Handbook, op. cit.*, pp. 1031–1032.
11. *Ibid.*, pp. 1009–1010.
12. Stalin, *D & HM, op. cit.*, p. 11.
13. *Ibid.*, p. 15.
14. *Ibid.*, p. 17.
15. *Ibid.*, p. 17.
16. *Ibid.*, p. 19.
17. *Ibid.*, p. 27.
18. *Ibid.*, p. 30.
19. *Ibid.*, p. 31.
20. *Ibid.*, p. 28.
21. *Ibid.*, p. 29.
22. *Ibid.*, p. 31.
23. *Ibid.*, p. 45.
24. *Ibid.*, p. 45.
25. *Ibid.*, p. 34.
26. Stalin, *F of L, op. cit.*, p. 21.
27. *Ibid.*, p. 23.
28. *Ibid.*, pp. 47, 48.
29. *Ibid.*, p. 52.
30. *Ibid.*, p. 108.
31. *Ibid.*, p. 96.
32. *Ibid.*, p. 109.
33. Troeltsch, Ernst, "The Ideas of Natural Law and Humanity," in Otto Gierke, *Natural Law and the Theory of Society*, translated and with an introduction by Ernest Barker, Cambridge Univ. Press, 1934, Vol. I, Appendix I, pp. 201–222.
34. Stalin, *F of L, op. cit.*, p. 17.
35. *Ibid.*, p. 17.
36. *Ibid.*, p. 20.
37. *Ibid.*, p. 31.
38. *Ibid.*, p. 80.

39. *Ibid.*, p. 77.
40. *Handbook, op. cit.*, p. 984.
41. Stalin, *F of L, op. cit.*, p. 96.
42. *Ibid.*, p. 97.
43. *Ibid.*, pp. 97, 96.
44. *Ibid.*, p. 96.
45. *Ibid.*, p. 90.
46. *Handbook, op. cit.*, p. 885.
47. Stalin, *F of L, op. cit.*, p. 98.
48. *Ibid.*, p. 98.
49. *Ibid.*, p. 98.
50. *Ibid.*, p. 100.
51. *Ibid.*, p. 100.
52. *Ibid.*, p. 100.
53. *Ibid.*, p. 106.
54. *Ibid.*, p. 106.
55. *Ibid.*, p. 106.
56. *Ibid.*, p. 106.
57. *Ibid.*, p. 107.
58. *Ibid.*, p. 109.
59. *Ibid.*, p. 110.
60. *Ibid.*, p. 110.
61. *Ibid.*, p. 110.
62. *Ibid.*, pp. 110, 111.
63. *Ibid.*, p. 111.
64. *Handbook, op. cit.*, pp. 756–757.
65. As quoted by Mintauts Chakste in "Soviet Concepts of the State, International Law and Sovereignty," *The American Journal of International Law*, Vol. 43, 1949, p. 36.
66. Chakste, *op. cit.*, p. 27.
67. *Ibid.*, p. 27.
68. *Ibid.*, p. 34.
69. Stalin, *F of L, op. cit.*, pp. 51, 53.
70. *Ibid.*, p. 85.
71. *Ibid.*, p. 86.

CHAPTER XIII

1. U.S. Atomic Energy Commission, *The Effects of Atomic Weapons*, June 1950, Appendix E-11, p. 437.
2. Pound, Roscoe, "Toward a New Jus Gentium," *ID & WO, op. cit.*, pp. 1–17.

3. Muggeridge, Malcolm, "Notes on the Way," *Time and Tide,* London, Vol. 26, No. 33, Oct. 6, 1945, p. 829.
4. I am indebted for this information to India's former Ambassador to Egypt, the distinguished scholar of Muhammadan law and present director of India's Civil Service Commission, Dr. Asaf A. A. Fyzee, of Bombay and New Delhi.
5. Ehrlich, *op. cit.* See also the author's "Contemporary Jurisprudence and International Law," *Yale Law Journal,* 1952.

CHAPTER XIV

1. Fyzee, A. A. A., *Islamic Culture,* The International Book House, Bombay, 1944; *Outlines of Muhammadan Law,* Oxford Univ. Press, 1949.
2. As quoted by Anne O'Hare McCormick in *The New York Times,* April 9, 1952.
3. Northrop, *TMEW, op. cit.,* Chapter II.
4. Troeltsch, *op. cit.*
5. Franck, Herman A. W., "East German Protestantism," *Yale Divinity News,* Vol. XLVII, Jan. 1952, p. 4.

CHAPTER XV

1. Kennan, *op. cit.*
2. Compare the practice of his Appendix with the theory of the chapters of his book.
3. Corbett, P. E., *Law and Society in the Relations of States,* Harcourt, Brace, New York, 1951.
4. Dewey, John, *Freedom and Culture,* Putnam's, New York, 1939, p. 116.
5. Acheson, Dean, "What Is the Present? What of the Future?" *New York Times,* Magazine Sec., Aug. 5, 1951, pp 7 ff.
6. Political Union debate, "The United States As a New World Leader—In What Direction?" Dec. 1, 1951.

CHAPTER XVI

1. Dewey, *op. cit.,* p. 93.
2. *Ibid.,* p. 93.
3. Bevan, Aneurin, *In Place of Fear,* Simon & Schuster, New York, 1952.
4. The Declaration of Independence.
5. Longfellow, Henry Wadsworth, "The Fiftieth Birthday of Agassiz," *The Oxford Book of American Verse,* Bliss Carman, editor, Oxford Univ. Press, New York, 1927, p. 91.

6. Emerson, Ralph Waldo, *Nature, Addresses, and Lectures,* Riverside Edition, Vol. I, Riverside Press, Cambridge, 1883, p. 86.
7. Jefferson, Thomas, *The Writings of Thomas Jefferson,* edited by H. A. Washington, Taylor and Maury, Washington, D.C., 1854, Vol. VII, p. 139.
8. *Ibid.,* Vol. I, 1853, p. 2.
9. *Ibid.,* Vol. V, 1853, p. 559.
10. *Ibid.,* p. 643.
11. *Ibid.,* pp. 645–646.
12. *Ibid.,* Vol. VI, 1854, p. 37.
13. Koch, Adrienne, and William Peden, *The Selected Writings of John and John Quincy Adams,* Alfred A. Knopf, New York, 1946, p. xxxvii.
14. Emerson, Ralph Waldo, *Essays,* Second Series (hereafter, Emerson, Second Series), Houghton, Mifflin, New York, 1893, p. 171.
15. *Ibid.,* p. 187.
16. *Ibid.,* p. 192.
17. Emerson, *Nature,* etc., *op. cit.,* p. 59.
18. Emerson, Second Series, *op. cit.,* p. 37.
19. Emerson, *Nature,* etc., *op. cit.,* p. 55.
20. Emerson, Second Series, *op. cit.,* p. 37.
21. *Ibid.,* p. 38.
22. *Ibid.,* p. 100.
23. St. Augustine, "Homilies on the First Epistle of John," translated by the Rev. H. Browne, *A Select Library of the Nicene and Post-Nicene Church Fathers of the Christian Church,* Paul Schaff, ed., Christian Literature Co., New York, 1888, Vol. VII, Homily VII, Sec. 8, p. 504.
24. Emerson, *Essays,* First Series, Houghton, Mifflin, New York, 1892, p. 126.
25. *Ibid.,* p. 129.
26. Dewey, *op. cit.,* p. 154.
27. Angell, Sir Norman, "Imperialism Re-interpreted," *The Listener,* Vol. XLVII, No. 1200, Feb. 28, 1952, pp. 327–328.
28. As quoted by T. V. Smith, "The New Deal as a Cultural Phenomenon," *ID & WO, op. cit.,* pp. 224–225. Professor Smith's entire essay should be read in conjunction with this Chapter.
29. Dewey, *op. cit.,* p. 156.
30. Kane, P. V., *History of Dharmaśāstra,* Bandarkar Oriental Research Institute, Poona; 1930. See also Northrop, F. S. C., "Naturalistic and Cultural Foundations for a More Effective

International Law," *Yale Law Journal,* Vol. 59, Dec. 1950, pp. 1430–1450.

31. Datta, D., and S. Chatterjee, *An Introduction to Indian Philosophy,* Univ. of Calcutta, 3rd ed., 1948, p. 431.
32. The Gospel According to St. Matthew, 10:34.

INDEX

Abdulla, Dada, 61
Abyssinia, 12, 16, 28, 29, 30
Acheson, Dean, 47, 302, 315
Adams, John, 317, 319–321, 326
Adams, John Quincy, 321
Adenauer, Konrad, 279–282, 293
Africa, 68, 148, 183, 279, 287, 308
Ahimsa, 81
Akbar, 162
Alexander the Great, ix
All-India Muslim League, 88, 158, 160, 165
Allah, 149, 154–155
Allahabad, 158
Alsace, 294
Alsace-Lorraine, 281
Ambedkar, Bhimrao Ramji, 52
American Revolution (1775–1781), 317
Angell, Sir Norman, 325
Anglo-American world, 31, 58, 308
Anthropology, 3, 5
Arabia, 57, 68, 171
Architecture, 154; in Agra, 152; in Alhambra, 155; in Bengal, 152; in Delhi, 152, 155; in Hyderabad, 152
Aristotle, 161, 202, 206, 214, 223
Arjuna, 78–79, 86, 335
Arnold, Vernon E., 202, 210–211
Art: Buddhist, 79–80; Chinese, 77, 79–80; French impressionistic, 79; Hindu, 79; Western, 79
Asia, 11, 12, 16, 31–33, 37, 38, 43, 52, 66–69, 71–78, 81–85, 119, 121–122, 144, 146, 148, 163, 166, 173, 179–180, 183–185, 196, 263–264, 301, 303, 323–324,

326; mediation in, 57, 59; neutrality of, 174, 333–334; solidarity of, 58–60, 68, 150, 181, 277–278, 286, 308, 333; Westernization of, 108–110, 113–114, 117–136, 144–148, 173
Asia Minor, 201
Asian attitude toward the U.S.A. and the West, 173–185
Assyria, 57
Athens, 153, 202
Atlantic Pact Council, 38
Atomic bomb, 2, 11, 34, 129, 259, 303
Attlee, Clement, 43, 303, 315
Augustus (Octavianus Caesar), 193, 201–203, 209, 214
Aurobindo, Shri, 52
Australia, 20, 40–42, 104, 186, 195, 285, 313, 324–325; Labor party in, 325; Liberal party in, 325
Austria, 281, 284, 290
Azad, Maulana Abul Kalam, 172, 278, 332

Bacon, Francis, 319, 332
Bagchee, Moni, 37
Bali, 68, 277
Baluchistan, 165
Banerji, J. K. 39
Bangkok, 12, 115, 148
Barker, Sir Ernest, 246
Bavaria, 281, 290
Bay of Bengal, 154
Belgium, 279, 281, 293
Benares, 73
Bengal, 150

351

356